EUROPE AT THE CROSSROADS

Europe at the Crossroads

Confronting Populist, Nationalist, and Global Challenges

Edited by
Pieter Bevelander & Ruth Wodak

NORDIC ACADEMIC PRESS

FSC
www.fsc.org

MIX
Paper from
responsible sources
FSC® C007584

Nordic Academic Press
P.O. Box 148
SE-221 00 Lund
Sweden
www.nordicacademicpress.com

© Nordic Academic Press and the authors 2019

Typesetting: Stilbildarna i Mölle, Frederic Täckström
Cover design: Lönegård & Co
Cover images: Upper left: NMR, Nordic Resistance Movement,
at a rally in central Stockholm, 12 December 2016. Mynttorget, Gamla stan.
Photo: Frankie Fouganthin/Wikimedia Commons.
Upper right: iStock/BrasilNut1.
Beneath: iStock/KatarzynaBialasiewicz. EU flag: iStock/Zedelle.
Print: ScandBook, Falun 2019
ISBN 978-91-88909-18-3

Contents

Europe at the crossroads
An introduction

Pieter Bevelander & Ruth Wodak

Pressing issues

When we started to discuss the outline and organization of the symposium 'Contesting the Populist Challenge: Beyond "Orbánism" and "Trumpism" and the Normalization of Exclusion', which took place at Malmö Institute for Studies of Migration, Diversity and Welfare (MIM), Malmö University, on 16 and 17 November 2017, we had no idea that such a general title, 'Europe at the Crossroads', would prove to be as timely and relevant as it has become at the time of writing this introduction, now 18 months later and only weeks before the European Parliament election of 2019. Indeed, the election has now been labelled as fateful by many leading politicians, who argue that the results might determine the future of the EU in unpredictable and possibly dangerous ways—ways which might see the implosion of the union and its liberal democracies, and could well trigger greater tension and conflict. The 'crossroads', as frequently mentioned by the likes of the French President, Emmanuel Macron, imply a choice between an integrated Europe consisting of liberal democracies and a Europe of sovereign nation-states united by only economic concerns and regulations.[1]

The European Union (EU), Europe, and many other parts of the world are experiencing the rise of the radical right, and a growing accommodation with the programmes of such parties.[2] Migration, climate change, 'national' nostalgia for the past, and the destabilization of liberal democracies are dominating public debate in all EU member states and beyond.

This volume is an urgent response to the challenges posed by the radical right and populist far-right parties to the idea of a 'social Europe' and a more egalitarian world.[3] Its aim is to offer a scholarly, political interdisciplinary critique of the continuing rise and dynamic of the populist far right and radical right in Europe. We have therefore brought together political scientists, sociologists, historians, demographers, policymakers, and discourse analysts to investigate the rise of the far right from multiple perspectives. The first section of the book addresses the general considerations of identity politics and the politics of the past, everyday performances, and the micropolitics of the far right, together with an assessment of the various theoretical approaches that can explain the rise of these parties and programmes, and a close look at the tension between EU institutions, regulations and rules, and far-right populist government coalitions. In the second part of the book, we focus on specific topics such as global warming, migration, gender politics, racism, and challenges to liberal-democratic institutions, drawing on in-depth case studies of several European countries (Austria, Germany, Greece, Hungary, Poland, Sweden, Switzerland, and the UK).

Apart from the impact of the so-called refugee crisis of 2015, the Brexit referendum in 2016, Trump's election to the presidency of America in 2016, and the changing global balance of power between China, Russia and the US ever since, the rise of far-right populist parties in the wake of such developments has been a cause of great concern to the EU establishment and many national mainstream parties (Mudde & Kaltwasser 2017; Rydgren 2017; Wodak & Krzyżanowski 2017). Interestingly, however, the apparent chaos in UK politics while Britain negotiates its exit from the EU has led to much greater cohesion and unity amongst the remaining 27 member states than anybody would have expected. When studying the latest opinion poll for the EU election conducted by European Election Stats, it becomes obvious that both the European People's Party and the Progressive Alliance of Socialists and Democrats (S&D) would lose seats in the upcoming election when compared to the 2014 election. The far right, however, looks to make gains, and, together, these parties would see their share increase to around 18.4 per cent of the electorate and come close to the socialist block—which is predicted to receive 19.6 per cent of the vote (europeanelectionsstats.eu). Eurosceptic voices are loud, but are no longer campaigning to leave the EU; they would like to strengthen national sovereignty without cutting all their ties to the EU.

The Bulgarian political scientist Ivan Krastev maintains in his widely acclaimed book *After Europe (Europadämmerung)* (2017) that migration is the single most important factor behind the discontent in Eastern and Western European countries and the significant cleavage between them. It is not the *numbers* of refugees and migrants that are of such importance, he continues; it is the brain drain from Eastern European countries, with millions of Poles, Czechs, Bulgarians, Slovaks, Hungarians, and Romanians who have left and are continuing to leave their homes, leaving many people afraid that 'their' culture, language, and traditions might die out. This is why, Krastev argues, they close their borders to migrants and refugees coming from elsewhere, especially if the latter are Muslim. The sociologist Zygmunt Bauman (2003) also emphasizes the many problematic issues arising in our globalized cities (and societies) when the host population necessarily confronts 'strangers' who come from elsewhere. Of course, Bauman argues, migration has always existed, and fear of strangers has always been a widely shared sentiment. Strangers are defined as 'agents moved by intentions that one can at best guess but would never know for sure' (2003: 26). Furthermore, while focusing on the effect of migrants on everyday life in Europe's cities, Bauman states that,

> Whatever happens to cities in their history and however drastically their spatial structure, look, and style may transform over years and centuries, one feature remains constant: cities are spaces where strangers stay and move in close proximity to each other. Being a permanent component of city life, the ubiquitous presence of strangers within sight and reach adds measure of perpetual uncertainty to all city dwellers' life pursuits; that presence, impossible to avoid for more than a brief moment, is a never drying source of anxiety and of the usually dormant, yet time and again erupting, aggressiveness. (Bauman 2003: 27)

Obviously, Krastev and Bauman point to a fear many people have of 'others'; the fear that is then used to political ends by far-right populist parties. However, as will be elaborated on in Section 2 below, there exist many different forms of mobility and a range of categories of migrants. Moreover, significant differences exist between 'strangers': for example, between asylum seekers, refugees, various types of migrants, and tourists. Specific—Muslim—migrants and asylum seekers are easily instrumentalized as scapegoats for all common woes, a very simplistic explanation for complex social, economic, and political challenges.

In this way, the populist far-right politics of fear is fuelling such arguments: a fear of foreigners, a fear of losing out, a fear of being 'invaded'—which is substantiated by threat scenarios proclaiming an apocalyptic catastrophe if the imaginary of a pluralistic, multilingual, cosmopolitan and diverse EU were to win over a nativist body—and border politics that suggests the closing of even more borders in order to protect the 'true' Austrians, Finns, Hungarians, or French (see the chapters by Eger, by Bentsen & Bevelander, and by Wodak in this volume). In such a perspective, images of old enemies are evoked, related inter alia to traditional antisemitic stereotypes of world conspiracy, and metonymically condensed in the many posters and slogans directed by the Hungarian Prime Minister, Viktor Orbán, against the American Jewish philanthropist George Soros, who is allegedly masterminding the immigration of refugees both to Europe and to the US (see chapters by Grabbe & Lehner and Balcer in this volume). 'Taking back control' has thus become the slogan of choice for the far right, drawing on the pro-Brexit campaign (Goodwin & Milazzo 2017).

In this introduction, we will not elaborate on all the factors that contribute to 'Europe at the crossroads'; instead, we focus specifically on some relevant facts about migration and their interdependence with political changes and developments, and then briefly introduce each chapter in turn, setting out how their interdisciplinary perspectives contribute to our understanding of the complexities with which Europe and the EU are currently confronted.

Migration, mobility, and refugees

In today's migration research, there is an ongoing debate about how to look at the movement of people. One is the classic way—migration—which has traditionally been associated with humans crossing political borders to settle in countries with relatively stable borders. The other is simply defined as physical relocation, geographically and temporally—mobility—and is fuelled by the increasing diversity in migration patterns and forms (Faist 2013; Malmberg 1997).

In line with Bauböck (2018), a number of developments have influenced ongoing discussions on migration and mobility. Since the mid-1970s, international migration has grown substantially from about 100 million (Hammar & Tamas 1997) to 258 million people globally. Globalization, economic restructuring, political change, and development have all been identified as being behind this rise. Still, this is not more than about 3.5 per cent of the total world population, and has remained quite stable over time, since the world population has increased at the same rate.

However, these figures tend to be underestimates because of the crude migration measurement systems that are in place, which do not include temporary and circular migrants who remain abroad for less than a year. Likewise, asylum seekers, foreign students, and intra-corporate transfers are categories of migrants who are less well accounted for in the population statistics. And then there is international tourism, which has increased sharply in the last 50 years. International tourists cross borders but are not defined as migrants, since they do not take up residence or work and do not change the demographic composition of the sending and receiving countries. Nevertheless, as Bauböck (2018: 2; also Schuck 2008) points out, tourism has an indirect effect on states' ability to control migration:

> Building walls and mobilizing armies at the border in order to deter irregular migrants does not help to curb the increasing numbers of people who enter states at airports, harbours and border crossing points with tourist visas and who subsequently overstay.

Further to the general distinction between migration and mobility, other sociopolitical developments have also blurred the two concepts. One is the growing number of multiple citizens—citizens who enjoy the right to enter several countries as internal migrants and who have become mobile. According to Bauböck et al. (2018), emigrants are now allowed to retain their original nationality while also adopting that of their host countries in 58 per cent of 175 states. In addition, 64 per cent of these 175 states have dropped the so-called renouncement requirement—that applicants for host-country citizenship have to renounce their previous citizenship. At the same time, in recent decades many European states have increased their requirements for immigrants wishing to obtain both permanent residency and subsequent citizenship (Bauböck & Tripkovic 2017; Wallace Goodman 2011). These contradictory developments in citizenship legislation have created both more mobile citizens and more mobile denizens—immigrants who have resided in host countries for a long period without becoming naturalized citizens, but who have a substantial set of rights (Hammar 1990), and who now want to meet the requirements for citizenship of the receiving country.

Finally, the establishment of the EU's free movement regime, in which individuals with citizenship of a member state have free access to other EU territories in order to work and settle, has resulted in increased and diverse forms of mobility. A number of enlargements of the EU (in 2004, 2007, and 2013) overnight opened up the EU to free mobility for citizens of these states.[4] Internal EU migration has since then grown substantially and now accounts for about 12 million people, with the UK and Germany as the largest receiving countries, and Poland and Romania as the largest sending countries (European Union 2017). In addition, the Schengen Agreement of 1995 allows free movement in the Schengen area for third-country nationals with a Schengen visa; thus, these individuals have the right to internal mobility for 90 days. This system reached a critical point in 2015 when large numbers of asylum seekers from various countries torn by war or long-term political instability arrived on the southern shores of Europe in Greece, Italy, and Malta. These people had entered not just a country, but the actual territory of the EU, and many headed north towards Austria, Germany, and Sweden (Eurostat 2016; Triandafyllidou et al. 2018).

In connecting immigration and mobility with anti-immigrant attitudes, one hypothesis holds that the opposition to immigration is guided by 'identity' and identity politics. The majority of the population seek to preserve a traditional way of life, restoring the country to what it—possibly—looked like when they and their parents grew up. When the demographic composition alters due to a higher proportion of migrants, previously more homogenous nation-states become more heterogeneous, and this can give rise to negative attitudes towards immigration in the domestic population. In this perspective, immigration is seen as culturally threatening. From this it follows that the migrants are not necessarily perceived as inferior to 'us', but as different (Bauman 2003, 2016).

However, it is unclear whether the gradual growth in the number of either migrants or mobile people is a major factor in the increase in anti-immigrant attitudes, political campaigns, and even strongly anti-immigrant political parties and governments (Bohman & Hjerm 2014; Strömbäck & Theorin 2018). Given the context—for example, the migration history of the country, the immigration policies in place, and its colonial past—there are different degrees of 'unwelcomeness' in attitudes towards the different religious, ethnic, and racial groups. However, for individuals who take an anti-immigrant stance, the difference between an EU mobile citizen and a third-country national seems to be fuzzy; they are all perceived as foreigners who are unwelcome. The outcome of the Swiss federal popular initiative 'against mass immigration', the Brexit referendum, and the attacks on Roma in many European countries are examples of such attitudes. Another factor that fuels the anti-migrant discourse is the fallacious argument that immigrants are not paying their way or their taxes, are unemployed or taking jobs away, and are a burden on the welfare state. In fact, the empirical evidence is mixed, and depends on a variety of factors (Rowthorn 2008; Borjas 1999; Razin et al. 2011). The hypothesis here consists of the assumption that the opposition to immigration is guided by economic self-interest. The majority population seeks to avoid greater competition for scarce resources. Explanations that emphasize economic threats commonly fall into the category of 'ethnic competition'.

This argument grew in importance in the 1980s and 1990s, when the integration problems of recent non-European migrants in Western European countries became visible, with high unemployment levels for immigrants relative to the native population, and emerging ethnic segregation in cities. However, the actual integration of migrant groups in, say, the labour market varies considerably by group and by context. The migrants' educational background and admission status, together with policies in place to overcome initial barriers such as language proficiency, and structural factors such as the level of discrimination faced by the group or the individual, are all key factors for understanding the position of immigrants or immigrant groups in host societies (Bevelander & Pendakur 2014; Dustman et al. 2017).

Even if studies (for example, Oxford Economics 2018 for the UK; Ruist 2013 for Sweden) show that labour migrants from the EU have employment levels similar to those of natives and that they pay into the welfare system as much as natives do, they are still perceived as undesirable foreign migrants by many right-wingers. Refugees, who have substantial barriers to overcome and take longer to find gainful employment and are able to contribute to the welfare system, are even seen as 'non-integrable'. It is worth noticing that, in the case of refugees from third countries, it is often other attributes—such as their religion and other 'cultural' differences—that are simply unwanted (Otterbeck & Bevelander 2006). The current discourse in Europe is one of 'integration pessimism', predicting the end of multiculturalism, all of which is decisively exploited by the far right. The histories of millions of Europeans—who migrated to other parts of the world, thereby proving that integration was not achieved over a couple of years, but, rather, took generations—seem to be forgotten. Current research in Europe generally shows that, since the 1960s, the intergenerational settlement process of immigrants and their descendants has moved and continues to move steadily ahead (Alba & Foner 2015; Bade et al. 2011). Yet in today's Europe, fear of 'the stranger' and worries about a potential loss of control over immigration continue to dominate the political debate (for example, Simmel 1950).

Outline of this volume

In the first chapter, Matthew Feldman stresses three important longer-term trends across Europe (and, to a lesser extent, the US) that have converged in recent years. The first is for a European far right to substantially gain in vote share this century, and which, for the first time since 1945, is represented in several (coalition) governments. This success draws on the manifold ways in which far-right movements reframed their political message for the mainstream—for example, from ethno-centrism and biological racism to one of nativism and cultural identity. Another trend, Feldman argues, should be called that of the 'near right'—the trend that brackets traditional conservatives with the more familiar far right. This so-called 'illiberal democracy' bridges the gap between the centre ground and the far right. Here, Feldman also maintains that drawing parallels to the interwar period in Europe could be dangerous, misleading, and even fallacious. However, he emphasizes that liberal self-confidence is often seen to be faltering, raising a third, distinct theme: irresolute norms, institutions, and ideological self-confidence. The undermining of liberal-democratic institutions might have strong effects because of social media and communication silos. In this way, Feldman concludes, the traditional cordon sanitaire—an invisible boundary that traditionally separates the far right from mainstream politics by means of civic, if not always civil, engagement—is under greater pressure now than at any time since 1945.

Heather Grabbe and Stefan Lehne take these new and emerging sociopolitical developments and use them to investigate the authoritarian trends that they claim are a far greater threat to the EU's future than Brexit is. They elaborate on the ways in which not only is democracy at stake in Hungary and Poland, but also, more generally, the EU's community of law. The EU's rules-based regional order, they argue, benefits businesses and citizens alike. Since 2015, however, its foundations have been under attack from within by far-right populist parties in government, who are defying EU laws and court decisions. The authors are adamant that, if these institutions are to survive, the rule of law and fundamental values must be defended by national political leaders, and not only EU institutions. However, as Grabbe and Lehne maintain, political leaders in other member governments have been reluctant to become actively involved; although most have little sympathy with the parties in power in these countries, they remain wary of taking EU-level action. This chapter examines the reasons for their reluctance and discusses the implications, for the whole of the EU, of the continued erosion of democratic standards and the rule of law.

In the third chapter, Ruth Wodak argues that a huge frame shift in political communication has taken place—a shift from post-war conventions of political debate to a 'post-shame' era. She first defines the key concepts, used by so many scholars but in vague ways. Populism, neo-authoritarianism, illiberalism: all are frequently used to describe or explain the rise of the far right in Europe and beyond, but with little sense of what they actually mean. Wodak then presents a discourse-historical approach to the micropolitics of the far right—the manifold ways in which the specific far-right ideology is produced and reproduced in many contexts and genres. She illustrates the principal discursive strategies used by far-right populist politicians in their front- and backstage performances, with a focus on Austrian, Italian, and Hungarian data. She concludes with a summary of what constitutes 'normalization', or the acceptance of far-right views in both content and form, prominently supported by the tabloid press and catering to rich and powerful elites. These ingredients form an integral part of the post-shame era, she argues.

Floris Biskamp discusses six different theoretical perspectives on right-wing populism in the fourth chapter. Following a trajectory from the political, through the psychological, social, and cultural, back to the political and ultimately to the economic, the six perspectives comprise, inter alia, a model of democratic representation and its gaps, and a theory of authoritarian resentment—an approach that points to racializing power and hegemony, and the hypothesis of a new cultural cleavage. Biskamp illustrates that each of these perspectives highlights not only specific aspects of right-wing populism, but also the blind spots and weaknesses of other perspectives.

In the fifth chapter, Maureen Eger and Sarah Valdez investigate the changes in far-right ideology over time. After describing recent electoral gains on the national and European levels, the authors claim that neo-nationalism—a form of nationalism seen when nation-state boundaries are settled, but thought to be under threat—is the underlying ideology of contemporary radical-right parties. A detailed analysis of the Manifesto Project data shows that contemporary parties are increasingly making nationalist claims. In framing their opposition to globalization, supra-national organizations, and multiculturalism, the parties cite negative economic, sociocultural, and political consequences for the nation-state, thus resorting to the politics of fear. Their investigation also shows that the radical-right parties are increasingly characterized by nationalism, thus distinguishing them from the other major party families.

Salomi Boukala deals with the mainstreaming of far-right discourse, the normalization of political enmity, and the resurgence of historical divisions in the Greek political scene. In the sixth chapter, she first provides the key elements in recent Greek history and the Greek debt crisis (2010–2017). She then explores the means by which far-right rhetoric has been legitimized by the main opposition party, conservative New Democracy, and has led to the rediscovery of a 'communist threat'. In so doing, she applies argumentation theory integrated with a discourse-historical approach. More specifically, drawing on Hannah Arendt's work on totalitarianism, Boukala shows how the 'ideology of terror' as a mode of persuasion was used by New Democracy's leadership to stigmatize Syriza (Coalition of the Radical Left) as the 'red enemy' of the Greek nation. In addition, by analysing the pre-election campaigns (2012 and 2015) of New Democracy's former leader, Antonis Samaras, and statements on security by the party's current leader, Kyriakos Mitsotakis, she charts the attempts to juxtapose Europe and Greece while emphasizing the 'politics of hate' against the left wing.

In Chapter 7, Bernhard Forchtner analyses the far-right discourse about climate change in general and the case of Austria in particular. He sheds light on the heterogeneous Austrian case by analysing paradigmatic 'satellite actors'—the monthly extreme-right magazine *Die Aula*, the Internet blog *unzensuriert.at*, and the weekly *Zur Zeit*—which do not officially belong to the far-right party FPÖ, but which are, nevertheless, closely connected to it. Forchtner also traces their dominant strategies—the arguments used to justify and legitimize far-right stances on manmade climate change—and, to a degree, the semantic features of nomination and predication, in order to illustrate the role which climate change communication plays for the far right.

In Chapter 8, Markus Rheindorf and Sabine Lehner focus on the constructions of national identity and identities, the 'body of the nation' or the 'national body' from a far-right perspective. They argue that the electoral successes of far-right movements across Europe, and particularly of far-right parties such as Austria's FPÖ, Germany's AfD, or Hungary's Fidesz, indicate an acceptance of such positions in mainstream politics and society at large, and thus they elaborate on Eger's assumptions. As part of this, the particular combination of nativist, heteronormative, and sexist positions that characterizes the body and gender politics of the extreme right has been normalized. For example, since 2005, the controversial but immensely popular artist, Andreas Gabalier, has successfully infused this sector of popular culture with a body and gender politics that is shared with the extreme right. Gabalier has used interviews and other public occasions as well as social media to propagate his outspoken views on gender-related issues such as family life, marriage, homosexuality, and gender roles. Rheindorf and Lehner illustrate that his stage persona, performances, and other contributions to the discourse have to be viewed alongside those of the FPÖ and its members, insofar as they share key ideologemes with respect to gender and body politics. The analysis focuses on the recontextualization of contemporary extreme-right gender and body politics both in the FPÖ's programme and in Gabalier's lyrics and public statements.

Adam Balcer discusses, in Chapter 9, significant developments in anti-Muslim and anti-immigrant sentiment in Poland. Here Islamo-phobia has become the distinctive feature of right-wing populism. Analyses of the results of various elections in Europe have shown that right-wing populists playing the anti-Muslim card are paradoxically the most popular in regions characterized by a low share of Muslim communities, and Poland is a particularly interesting case in point: Muslims are an extremely small and well-integrated minority in Polish society, yet, although the country has no conflicts with Muslim countries and is not faced with a massive inflow of Muslim refugees, anti-Muslim feeling has risen dramatically in recent years. Islamophobia in Poland distinguishes itself for the scale of its religious, antisemitic, and historical references and its strong link to the rejection of modern, European, secular and liberal paradigms, mixed with a soft Euroscepticism in the name of traditional and conservative values. Its attractiveness to a degree derives from the ethnic shape of the nationalism that is highly popular in Polish society, and the persistence of old antisemitic clichés and stereotypes. In this way, Islamophobia is now one of the few elem-ents that unites what is a deeply divided Polish society. It is a fact that neither the liberal, moderately conservative, and left-wing parties nor the Roman Catholic Church have reacted decisively to the anti-Muslim identity narrative promoted by the ruling far-right populists.

In the tenth chapter, Beint Bentsen and Pieter Bevelander focus on the Swedish case. In three consecutive elections, the Sweden Democrats (SD) grew from 5.7 per cent of the vote in 2010 and 12.9 per cent in 2014 to 17.5 per cent in 2018. Many studies have tried to explain this political phenomenon. Bentsen and Bevelander search for a more differentiated set of explanations by asking to what extent the future electorate—adolescents—resembles the current political situation in Sweden. They use unique representative information from the 2013 High School Attitude survey of Swedes aged 15–19 to assess the correlation of a wide variety of potential factors, including individual demographics, family, school, and society, as well as attitudes on the propensity to have right-wing populist-party (RWPP) preferences. It is apparent that potential SD voters are largely male adolescents from lower socio-economic backgrounds, living in small- and medium-sized towns where the SD is already an established party. These individuals feel threatened by future immigration, are dissatisfied with democracy, and have little interest in politics. Surprisingly, the data are congruent with the existing adult surveys.

Finally, Gianni D'Amato rounds off the volume in Chapter 11, in which he analyses recent developments in the far-right populist Swiss People's Party (SVP/UDC, Schweizer Volkspartei). In Switzerland, anti-immigrant populism has been a winning strategy since the late 1990s. The SVP transformed itself over the course of 30 years from a party with an 11 per cent share of the vote in 1987 to the strongest party, with 29 per cent support, at the last parliamentary election in 2015. D'Amato claims that the new cleavage between cosmopolitanism and communitarianism favours the rise of this populist political organization. The importance of this cleavage is analysed by looking at the SVP-led 'initiative on self-determination'. This constitutional amendment seeks to address the privileging of domestic law over international law, and in particular the European Convention on Human Rights. The sovereignists have worked to limit fundamental rights in a pluralist society and to affirm the unlimited reign of the popular will against an institutional division of powers, arguing for the sovereignty's totalitarian connotations. D'Amato goes into the pros and cons of the initiative in detail, and concludes with a political-theoretical assessment of the populist strategy, which, in this case, did not win the vote.

Notes

1 https://www.theguardian.com/commentisfree/2019/mar/07/macron-europeans-french-president.
2 See Wodak 2015 for an extensive account of the terminological debate about the far right. In this volume, rather than dwell at length on the issue, the contributors use terms of their own choosing and definition—right-wing populism, the radical right, the far right, the populist far right, and so on.
3 Egalitarian under the Human Rights Charter (as part of the European Treaty since 1 December 2009, http://www.europarl.europa.eu/charter/pdf/text_en.pdf) and the UN Sustainable Development Goals (to end poverty etc., https://www.un.org/sustainabledevelopment/poverty/).
4 The new member states of the EU in 2004 were Poland, Malta, Slovakia, Slovenia, Lithuania, Hungary, the Czech Republic, Cyprus, Estonia, and Latvia; in 2007, Romania and Bulgaria; and in 2013, Croatia.

References

Alba, R. & N. Foner. (2015), *Strangers No More: Immigration and the Challenges of Integration in North America and Western Europe* (Princeton).

Bade, K., P. C. Emmer, L. Lucassen & J. Oltmer (2011), *The Encyclopedia of European Migration and Minorities* (Cambridge).

Bauböck, R. & M. Tripkovic (eds.) (2017), *The Integration of Migrants and Refugees: An EUI Forum on Migration, Citizenship, and Demography* (Florence) [e-book].

— (2018), 'Migration and mobility: European dilemmas' (Knowledge for Change Lecture Series 6; Malmö).

— I. Honohan & M. Vink (2018), *Medborgarskapslagar: En Global Jämförelse* (DELMI Policy Brief 2018:9).

Bauman, Z. (2003), *City of Fears, City of Hopes* (London).

— (2016), *Strangers at our Doors* (London).

Bevelander, P. & R. Pendakur (2014), 'The labor market integration of refugee and family reunion immigrants: a comparison of outcomes in Canada and Sweden', *Journal of Ethnic and Migration Studies*, 40/5: 689–709.

Bohman, A. & M. Hjerm (2014), *Radikala Högerpartier och Attityder till Invandring i Europa* (DELMI rapport 2014:1), www.delmi.se/demokrati#!/radikala-hogerpartier-och-attityder-till-invandring-i-europa-rapport–20141.

Borjas, G. (1999), 'Immigration and welfare magnets', *Journal of Labor Economics*, 17/4: 607–37.

Dustmann, C., F. Fasani, T. Frattini, L. Minale & U. Schönberg (2017), 'On the economics and politics of refugee migration', *Economic Policy*, 32/91: 497–550.

Eurostat (2016), ec.europa.eu/eurostat/statistics-explained/index.php/Asylum_ statistics.

Faist, T. (2013), 'The mobility turn: A new paradigm for the social sciences?' *Ethnic & Racial Studies*, 36/11: 1637–46.

Goodwin, M. & C. Milazzo (2017), 'Taking back control? Investigating the role of immigration in the 2016 vote for Brexit', *Journal of Politics & International Relations* 19/3: 450–64.

Hammar, T. (1990), *Democracy and the Nation State: Aliens, Denizens, and Citizens in a World of International Migration* (Aldershot).

— & K. Tamas (1997), 'Why do people go or stay?', in T. Hammar, G. Brochmann, K. Tamas & T. Faist (eds.), *International Migration, Immobility and Development: Multidisciplinary Perspectives* (Oxford).

Krastev, I. (2017), *Europadämmerung: Ein Essay* (Frankfurt).

Malmberg, G. (1997), 'Time and space in international migration', in T. Hammar, G. Brochmann, K. Tamas & T. Faist (eds.), *International Migration, Immobility and Development: Multidisciplinary Perspectives* (Oxford).

Mudde, C. & C. R. Kaltwasser (2017), *Populism* (Oxford).

Otterbeck, J. & P. Bevelander (2006), *Islamofobi: En Studie av Begreppet, Unga domars Attityder och Unga Muslimers Utsatthet* (Stockholm).

Oxford Economics (2018), *The Fiscal Impact of Immigration on the UK: A Report for the Migration Advisory Committee*, assets.publishing.service. gov.uk/government/uploads/system/uploads/attachment_data/file/759376/ The_Fiscal_Impact_of_Immigration_on_the_UK.pdf.

Razin, A., E. Sadka & B. Suwankiri (2011), *Migration and the Welfare State: Political-Economy Policy Information* (Boston).

Rowthorn, R. (2008) 'The fiscal impact of immigration on the advanced economies', *Oxford Review of Economic Policy*, 24/3: 560–80.

Ruist, J. (2013), 'Östeuropéers rörlighet är lönsam för de rikare EU-länderna', *Ekonomisk Debatt*, 41/8: 19–25.

Rydgren, J. (ed.) (2017), *The Oxford Handbook of the Radical Right* (Oxford).

Schuck, P. H. (2008), 'Law and the study of Migration', in C. B. Brettell & J. F. Hollifield (eds.), *Migration Theory: Talking across Disciplines* (New York).

Simmel, G. (1950), *The Sociology of Georg Simmel* (New York).

Strömbäck, J. & N. Theorin (2018), *Attityder till Invandring: En Analys av Förändringar och Medieeffekter i Sverige 2004–2016* (DELMI rapport 2018:4), www.delmi.se/samhalle#!/attityder-till-invandring-en-analys-av-forandring-ar-och-medieeffekter-i-sverige-2014-2016-rapport-1.

Triandafyllidou, A., M. Krzyżanowski & R. Wodak (eds.) (2018), 'Mediatization and politicisation of the refugee crisis in Europe', special issue, *Journal of Immigrant & Refugee Studies*, 16/1–2.

Wallace Goodman, S. (2011), *Naturalisation Policies in Europe: Exploring*

Patterns of Inclusion and Exclusion (EUDO Citizenship Observatory 2010/07 Comparative Report), hdl.handle.net/1814/19577.

Wodak, R. (2015), *The Politics of Fear: What Right-Wing Populist Discourses Mean* (London).

— & M. Krzyżanowski (eds.) (2017), 'Right-wing populism in Europe and USA: contesting politics and discourse beyond "Orbánism" and "Trumpism"', special issue, *Journal of Language and Politics*, 16/4.

Acknowledgements

This book is the result of a symposium held in Malmö in 2017 on the initiative of Ruth Wodak, the Malmö University 2017 Willy Brandt Guest Professor. Wodak's and Pieter Bevelander's shared interest in the discourse of the new far right, right-wing populism, and attitudes towards immigrants, ethnic, and religious groups encouraged them to bring scholars together to discuss the complex challenges facing 'social Europe' posed by the rise of the far right.

We would like to thank the participants at the Malmö symposium, and especially the authors and reviewers for their individual input into this volume. We would also like to thank Merja Skaffari Multala, Angela Bruno Andersen, Hedvig Obenius, and Louis Tregert for their invaluable help in organizing the symposium.

We are grateful to Nordic Academic Press, Annika Olsson, and Charlotte Merton for their hard work in getting the book to press so quickly, and to Karin Magnusson for checking the references.

We would also like to thank the Institute for Human Sciences, Vienna, for Wodak's senior fellowship in 2018/19, which allowed her to work on this volume in a wonderful, supportive environment.

The publication of this book would not have been possible without the generous financial support of the City of Malmö through the Willy Brandt Guest Professorship in collaboration with the Malmö Institute for Studies of Migration, Diversity and Welfare—thank you!

The editors
May 2019

CHAPTER 1

On radical right mainstreaming in Europe and the US

Matthew Feldman

This chapter focuses on three longer-term trends across Europe (and to a lesser extent, the US) that have converged in recent years.[1] The first is a European far right that has substantially gained in vote share this century and, for the first time since 1945, is in several coalition governments. In practice, this success was born of an ideological trade-off, whereby far right movements reframed their political message for the mainstream, from ethno-centrism and biological racism to one of nativism and cultural identity. Another trend is the emergence of what will be called here the 'near right', straddling traditional conservatives and the more familiar far right. This 'illiberal democracy', or 'right-wing populism', has gained enormous force across the continent of late, bridging the gap between the centre ground and far right in a way that demands new approaches—and critically interrogating older ones. Importantly, drawing parallels to the interwar period in Europe is full of pitfalls that can mislead as much as instruct. Yet like then, just when it is needed most, liberal self-confidence is faltering, raising a third, distinct theme: a faltering of norms, institutions, and ideological self-confidence. This has had the two-pronged effect, in turn, of making reliable sources hard to distinguish from 'fake news', on the one hand; while on the other, further entrenching communication silos—online echo chambers that promote political discord, insults and worse. Together, these system stressors have put the traditional cordon sanitaire—an invisible boundary traditionally separating the far right from mainstream politics via civic, if not always civil, engagement—under greater pressure than at any time since 1945.

The far right's challenge to liberal democracy

Liberal democracies are facing an increasingly clear challenge today: the development and effects of a congealing 'far right' in Europe. At the time of writing, what have been called 'post-fascist' parties have entered coalition government in Austria (the Austrian Freedom Party) and Italy (La Lega Nord, now shorthanded as 'Lega'), on the one hand; while on the other, once centre-right and now increasingly 'illiberal democracies' in Poland, Hungary and the US erode fundamental democratic norms by embracing far-right positions on nativism and authoritarianism. This pincer movement towards what can be called a near-right politics is, in turn, the long-term result of the mainstreaming of previously radical right policies—above all 'Fortress Europe' and 'Fortress US' for non-white migration—which are posing acute challenges to the post-war Euro-American settlement. In taking the long view of some of these converging developments, this chapter returns to a pressing interwar question, so long dormant, that is emerging once again: 'Could it happen here?'

Recognizing and then defining the 'it' of far-right politics, and its connection to historical fascism, remains a vexatious issue (for example, Camus & Lebourg 2017: 53 ff.). Protestors and left-wing activists see fascism in the politics of Trump, Orbán, and Salvini, to name but three political elites. Conservatives tend to be less sure, even if they see a clear divide between themselves and nativist, often explicitly racist, campaigns by insurgent parties such as Alternative for Germany (Alternative für Deutschland, AfD) or the Sweden Democrats (Sverigedemokraterna, SD)—parties that entered national parliaments in 2017 with 13 per cent, and 17 per cent of the vote in 2018, respectively. To this challenge, historians and political scientists bring forth small libraries of commentary and analysis, with often sharp disagreement over terminology (on the debate over the definition of the radical right, see, for example, Eatwell 2000; and Mudde 1996, 2017). To avoid getting too bogged down in an article

24

concerned with different issues, it nevertheless remains the case that what is variously called the (neo-)fascist, radical right, far right, or, most opaquely, national populist usually boils down to a handful of commonly identified features. These Wittgensteinian family resemblances, or 'faces' of the far right, have been usefully summarized in a book whose title identifies one of the principle challenges to liberal democracies at present, *Trouble on the Far Right*:

> far-right activism should be understood as tactically oriented in the short run; at the same time, it may also target gradual changes in mindset, discourse, values, loyalties and legitimacy in the long run. One aspect of the long-term strategy is the professionalised political appearance of many right-wing organizations, which has contributed to the gradual disappearance of a cordon sanitaire: a figurative firewall that the political mainstream would previously use to block far-right influences. (Actors base their ideology and action on the notion of inequality among human beings, combining the supremacy of a particular nation, 'race' or 'civilization' with ambitions for an authoritarian transformation of values and styles of government.) (Fielitz & Laloire 2016: 16)

Rather than perpetuating 'the academic "war of words" on far-right definitions' or 'simplistic schemes of plug and play designs' (Fielitz & Laloire 2016: 18), the editors helpfully

> use *far right* as an umbrella term to subsume actors, attitudes and behaviours, spanning from those which articulate dissent within the framework of representative democracy but are not geared toward the entire system (radical right) to those which deny the values, rules and arenas of democracy, impelling a revolutionary overthrow ('extremist right'). [As a distinct ideological world view] actors base their ideology and action on the notion of inequality among human beings, combining the supremacy of a particular nation, 'race' or 'civilization' with ambitions for an authoritarian transformation of values and styles of government (actors base their ideology and action on the notion of inequality among human beings, combining the supremacy of a particular nation, 'race' or 'civilization' with

ambitions for an authoritarian transformation of values and styles of government. (Fielitz & Laloire 2016: 17–18)

Seen in this way, the far right is a praxis of revanchist ethnonationalism, hostile to the many of the fundamental principles of liberal democracy.

Fully twenty-five years ago, a pioneer in this area of study, Hans-Georg Betz (1993: 413), defined 'radical, right-wing populist parties' in definitive terms, setting out their key platforms and ideas:

> Radical right-wing populist parties are radical in their rejection of the established sociocultural and sociopolitical system and their advocacy of individual achievement, a free marketplace, and a drastic reduction of the role of the state. They are right-wing in their rejection of individual and social equality, in their opposition to the social integration of marginalized groups, and in their appeal to xenophobia, if not overt racism. They are populist in their instrumentalization of sentiments of anxiety and disenchantment and their appeal to the common man and his allegedly superior common sense.

A generation on, it is remarkable how far this scholarly convergence on the ideological tenets of populist radical right parties has advanced. To take just two recent examples, Elise Saint-Martin (2013: 4) offered a sophisticated template for European radical right parties in the twenty-first century:

> radical right parties rely on appeals to national sentiments defined in ethnic terms; reject cosmopolitan conceptions of society; react to rising non-European immigration; oppose globalization and reject European integration which they see as undermining national sovereignty and identity; and brand themselves as anti-parties, criticizing domestic political elites as corrupt and removed from the 'common people' ... I have chosen to categorize the radical right according to three (3) defining features: nativism, socio-authoritarianism, and populism.

And as Ov Cristian Norocel rightly argued in a recent doctoral thesis, these and similar features (most recently antisemitism and anti-Muslim prejudice) form the core of radical right ideology, which extends from parties to less formal movements and groups:

> The ineliminable components of radical right populist ideology are the identification of a Manichean opposition between a 'corrupt elite' and a 'pure people'. The said people of radical right populist ideology is not only pure, but also constitutes an indivisible whole, whose sovereign will finds its most appropriate manifestation in the figure of a respected leader. What is worth underlining here is that the aforementioned purity of people, and the intrinsically interrelated fear of pollution, rests on exclusivist definitions of the 'rightful' inhabitants of a certain nation–state, in a decidedly nativist nationalist manner This has a key economic aspect—namely, welfare chauvinism—which delineates the 'pure' people and their birthright to the nation–state's welfare infrastructure from those underserving Others: a dynamic category that may include allegedly parasitical social groups, resented ethnic/'racial', religious, and/or sexual minorities, along a logic of nationalist solidarity. (Norocel 2013: 18)

From Betz and Mudde to early career researchers today, the radical right has become a well-understood phenomenon amongst scholars of political science, history, sociology, gender studies, and psephology. As this suggests, the varying organizational faces of the far right—street marches, populist politicians, even political violence and terrorism—have been the subject of commentary that dwarfs the coverage of other ideological groupings.

Put another way, everyone seems to be talking about the far right. So what is all the buzz about? Is the far right 'back', and if so, how can liberal democracy best respond?

Historical parallels as a double-edged sword

While historical parallels have their place, the far right poses different challenges than the interwar fascism before it did. Indeed, perspectives from the interwar history of fascism can cloud as much as illuminate views of the far right today. History does not repeat itself—can never simply replicate itself—but it does sometimes echo, point, or even

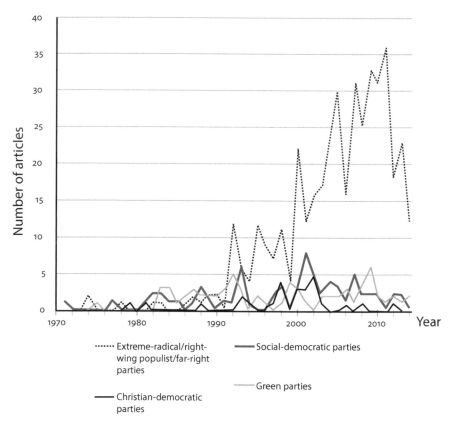

Figure 1.1. Scholarly articles about the far right (adapted from Mudde 2017: 2).

nudge. For the far right, the historical experience of transnational fascism (Bauerkämper 2010) after the Great War often boils down to the wartime Axis, the stigma of which the far right, in its various guises since 1945, has consistently tried to negate, excuse, or otherwise overcome (Feldman 2015: 9). For several decades after the Second World War, the results of what should be properly called neo-fascist distancing tactics were mixed at best (Bastow 2002). Indeed, the early twentieth-century context is so different to that of 1930s Europe that political, mobilizational, and even intellectual responses are just as likely to provide counterproductive historical examples for our current milieu.

It bears repeating that historical analogies are a double-edged sword, which, at least when it comes to the far right today, can be used as much for defence—such as drawing lessons from the interwar rise and consolidation of fascism in Europe—as it can be used for attack, whether in terms of Antifa street confrontations, or in rhetorically tarring far-right groups as Nazis and fascists (as can be seen in countless placards at any counterdemonstration against the far right today) (see Wodak & Forchtner 2014, which includes an example from Vienna). Equally, history provides more nuanced explanations than slogans such as 'No pasaran!' allow (from the Spanish Civil War)—a blunderbuss that risks making the issue of far-right legitimization worse rather than better. Care should be taken in drawing the historical parallels between fascism and the contemporary far right.

It scarcely needs be said, however, that most journalism and non-specialist literature compound these problems. In terms of historical fiction, for example, consider the October 1935 publication of *It Can't Happen Here*, Sinclair Lewis's novel republished in 2017—which sold like hot cakes following Donald Trump's inauguration in January 2017. Offering a standard Marxist view of fascism long ago discarded by most scholars (Griffin 2008), Lewis imagines big business as the reactionary hand behind a semi-legal dictatorial regime—a mix of Nazi racism and Fascist economic corporatism, sprinkled with heavy doses of paramilitary violence:

> Pushing in among this mob of camp followers who identified political virtue with money for their rent came a flying squad who suffered not from hunger but from congested idealism: Intellectuals and Reformers and even Rugged Individualists, who saw in Windrip, for his clownish swindlerism, a free vigor which promised a rejuvenation of the crippled and senile capitalistic system. (Lewis 2017: 79)

By this account, American liberalism had become 'cramped by a certain respect for facts which never enfeebled the press-agents for Corporism' (Lewis 2017: 283) which oversees concentration camps and summary executions, arrests much of Congress and later invades Mexico 'as a protection against the notorious treachery of Mexico and the Jewish plots there hatched'. The regime ultimately brings about another American civil war. Opposing the aggressive tyrants, Buzz Windrip and his henchmen, who whip up extremes of nationalist hysteria, is the journalist-cum-protagonist, Doremus Jessup, a sort of prototype 'Liberal American Humanitarian' (58). Revealingly, he is hampered by 'a certain respect for facts' (283); troubled by bad educational standards, he is only too aware that all utopias 'end in scandal, feuds, poverty, griminess, disillusion' (114). Watching with horror as a 'program for revitalizing the national American pride' turns swiftly into a bloody dictatorship, Jessup concludes, 'It can happen here' (243).

At the point in which Lewis's warning was written, of course, fascist movements were very much on the march in Depression-era Europe. It was concern at the rise of fascism in Europe that led Lewis to write the novel in the summer of 1935—even though events were to swiftly overtake his fiction. Ahead of a 1-million-strong rally in September 1935, the Third Reich hurried to introduce the so-called Nuremberg Laws, that quintessence of administrative inequality, making Jews legal aliens in Germany (Knox 2000: 145). Less than three weeks later, Fascist Italy invaded Abyssinia, with a trail of chemical weapons in their expansionist wake. These events markedly changed the picture of interwar Europe, generating the classic, indeed rightly indelible, picture of fascist aggression and legalized persecution. *It Can't Happen Here*'s seductive warning of imminent fascist dictatorship fit the roiling times of crumpling democracies and militaristic nationalism in Europe, but less so the US in the 1930s, with its puny Silver Shirt movement (Steigmann-Gall 2017: 108), and far less so in our day—save for those crying wolf by denouncing Trump as some kind of fascist dictator.

'If Trump as fascist dictator' does not warrant analytical scrutiny in terms of historical parallels (Matthews 2016), surely more helpful is the view that many fascist tropes were dangerously mainstreamed in interwar Europe. Extreme ideas, as the historian Aristotle Kallis (2013: 55–6) rightly reminds us, 'begin their life-cycle as politically and socially marginal and radical counter-propositions to established, "mainstream" cognition. By transgressing widely accepted boundaries between "acceptable" and "unacceptable" premises or prescriptions, they are essentially attempting to remap these established cognitions and subvert the mainstream "frames" that support them.' In the context of the 1930s, what Kallis elsewhere calls the 'fascist effect' became a kind of 'brand' that even non-fascists wished to emulate. To take just one historical instance, consider the impact of the Nazi race laws:

When one looks at the diffusion of the 'racial' anti-Jewish paradigm in 1930s Europe, it becomes obvious that the model pioneered by the Nazi regime with the 1935 'Nuremberg Laws' broke taboos and, in so doing, activated and/or empowered pre-existing, yet latent or partly suppressed anti-Jewish demand in other countries. This contributed critically to its reproduction—in a 'domino effect' style—across other European countries in 1936–39. It also served as both a legitimizing (and viewed as 'successful') precedent and a 'successful' bold model for shaping similar 'solutions' to the so-called 'Jewish problem' outside Nazi Germany. (Kallis 2013: 56)

From this perspective, in several European states between the wars, the danger was in fascism becoming normalized or domesticated, or rather of the mainstream becoming fascistized. A paradigmatic instance was the conservative elite, like the Junkers and civil servants in early 1930s Germany who were disdainful of democracy and willing to co-opt Nazism as a bulwark to smash what they broadly understood to be 'the left'—or so they thought. As it turned out, fascism's political opportunism and mobilizational appeal, first in Italy and then in Germany, soon overwhelmed the reactionary elites once it had its hands on the machinery of state power (Knox 2000). It should be remembered that Nazism rested on widespread popular appeal—including 40 per cent of the working-class vote—and most of the Gestapo's later arrests came from ordinary informants (Gellately 2001: 136 ff.). These were as much 'consensus dictatorships' as autocratic tyrannies. Right across Europe, new democracies established after the Great War fell one after another to right-wing authoritarianism, like shakily placed dominoes, until fewer than a dozen democracies remained in the west and north on the eve of the Second World War. In much of the former Russian, German, and Austro-Hungarian empires, democracy failed to put down solid roots or galvanize widespread popular support, such that the UK, France, Switzerland, Belgium, the Netherlands, Ireland, Denmark, Sweden, Norway, and Finland were the only remaining democracies in Europe by the outbreak of the Second World War (Linz 2003: 226).

From the margins to the mainstream revisited

Perhaps the last time the mainstream felt such a sense of acute alarm was in the years following the fall of the Berlin Wall. Speaking for many, exactly sixty years after Sinclair Lewis's warning, the celebrated novelist and intellectual Umberto Eco penned 'Ur-Fascism' (1995) for the *New York Review of Books*, widely disseminated then, and since taken as a popular guide for gauging whether a particular country is 'going fascist'. His concern had been triggered by what Martin Lee and others have called an 'ideological facelift' by the far right (2000: 388)—one starting to pay dividends following the demise of the once great enemy, the Soviet Union.

Perhaps the best example came from Eco's native Italy, where, in 1994, a relaunched, explicitly 'post-fascist' Alleanza Nazionale (AN), tracing its now-rejected heritage to ex-Fascist militants who established the Movimento Sociale Italiano in 1946, joined the first Silvio Berlusconi government alongside the more extreme La Lega Nord, together comprising 33 of 64 members of the government (ironically enough, a rebranded La Lega joined a right-wing coalition Italian government in early 2018). In January 1995, the AN restyled itself as a mainstream party at the pivotal Fiuggi Conference (Carioti 1996), which positioned the movement alongside the Belgian Vlaams Blok, the French Front National, and the Austrian Freedom Party as allegedly mere populists vying for national office. Even though the *New York Times* reported on 31 March 1994 that 'several hundred young skinheads gave straight-arm neo-Fascist salutes while mingling with a crowd of National Alliance supporters at a victory rally' (Cowell 1994), this did not stop polls from finding AN leader Gianfranco Fini to be the most popular politician in Italy by early 1995. That same year, in 'Ur-Fascism', Eco grudgingly admitted, 'I have no difficulty in acknowledging that today the Italian Alleanza Nazionale ... has by now very little to do with the old fascism' (Eco 1995: 407).

Next door in Austria, more troublingly, the FPÖ, a party initially founded by ex-Nazi activists in 1955, had sufficiently distanced itself from its past, under the charismatic Jörg Haider's march to the mainstream, that it received more than 1 million votes—22.5 per cent of the national vote and 43 seats in 1994 (Fallend 2004). In part, it was these kinds of electoral breakthroughs that moved Eco to declare:

Ur-Fascism is still around us, sometimes in plainclothes. It would be so much easier for us if there appeared on the world scene somebody saying, 'I want to reopen Auschwitz, I want the Blackshirts to parade again in the Italian squares.' Life is not that simple. Ur-Fascism can come back under the most innocent of disguises. (Eco 1995: 415)

Eco's sentiments are still apposite today. Yet just as importantly, although more neglected, there is a key difference between fascism and the far right implied by Ur-Fascism: that the latter is more than just a disguise for the former.

Specialists—let alone those unfamiliar with the extensive literature—are likely then to misdiagnose the dangers to liberal democracy of approaching the far right today principally through the lens of historical fascism. If we are going to historicize, we may do it better by departing from the sociologist Juan Linz's contention (as summarized by Kallis 2015: 9) that interwar fascism's ascendency was due mostly to 'a profound institutional crisis that deprived the liberal-democratic systems of their much-needed legitimacy in the eyes of elites and public opinion alike'. Linz has rightly been lauded for showing the way in which Axis regimes influenced other authoritarian practices in interwar Europe. Yet perhaps more timely is his identification of unsuccessful liberal hegemony across continental Europe in the years following the Great War—so starkly at variance with its history after 1945. For Linz, the 'crisis and breakdown of democracy' between the wars was as much a product of liberal-democratic failure as radical right success:

Failure of the liberal-democratic political class and governmental instability or inefficacy were even more important; these allowed small groups of conspirators to end democracy or democratization with the passive acquiescence of kings, non-conspiratorial militaries and populations that were unwilling to support the regime and even welcomed the dictatorships with a sense of relief and even hope. (Linz 2003: 248)

The parallels between historical fascism and the far right can distract as much as instruct, for at least two reasons. On this point, Pierre-Andre Taguieff has argued that

Neither 'fascism' or 'racism' will do us the favour of returning in such a way that we can recognise them easily. If vigilance was only a game of recognizing something already well-known [*sic*], then it would only be a question of remembering. Vigilance would be reduced to a social game using reminiscence and identification by recognition, a consoling illusion of an immobile history peopled with events which accord to our expectations or our fears. (Taguieff 1993: 54)

This assessment was made in reference to the Nouvelle Droite (ND), and it introduces, if indirectly, one of two essential changes that took place among neo-fascists in the Cold War era. The first of these is ethno-pluralism, which Taguieff denounces as 'differentialist racism': 'the tactical dressing of inegalitarian racism, as an *acceptable reformulation* making an appeal to an ideological keyword (*difference*)' (2001: 212, original emphasis).

After May 1968, faced with the despised 'cultural hegemony' of a liberal-left France, the ND brought together neo-fascist activists for pivotal ideological revisions. The movement and its many publications were avowedly 'metapolitical', since the ND claimed not to seek political influence, but rather an assault on the so-called 'laboratories of thinking' in the media, universities, and government. According to the group's main interpreter today, Tamir Bar-On, 'De Benoist's logic was that if he explicitly recognized other cultures according to cultural elements rather than biological ones and rejected the notion of cultural superiority, then how could he be labelled a "racist"?' (2013: 14). This differentialism undertook a long march, over decades, in rejecting a key tenet of historic fascism: white—or national—supremacy. In its place was the 'right to difference' and the countercharge it was the multicultural 'race-mixers' who were the real racists. Instead, the ND alleged it valued all cultures equally—but it was the integrity of the ethnos that mattered above all.

Given the well-established radical-right pedigree of its chief ideologues across Europe (Aleksandr Dugin, Guillmaume Faye, Dominique Venner, Pierre Krebs, and Michael Walker), it appears this was simply white separatism through the back door: fascist 'blood and soil' in politically correct language. [2] Yet its cumulative effect over more than two generations has been staggering—and perhaps successful in its aims. Indeed, according to Camus and Lebourg, the ND has 'taken root in a lasting matter as an intellectual project' (2017: 151). Crucially, it has provided intellectual cover for far-right groups to publicly move away from claims of racial superiority in favour of protecting national–cultural identities. In this view, all ethnies are purportedly equal so long as they are not weakened by immigration, multiculturalism, or intermixing.

By replacing race with identity, a populist doorway could be opened by once-toxic movements and political parties, with a new message aimed at mainstream audiences. Differentialism has been adopted lock, stock, and barrel by far-right groups aiming for mainstream, populist appeal—presenting anti-immigration, anti-multiculturalism and racial nationalism as merely the defence of indigenous cultures globally and no more than a 'first amongst equals' preference. Shorn of its neo fascist trappings, 'the foreign' can once more be directly and allegedly 'unprejudicially' against 'the native'—an attempted end-run around conventions against inciting prejudice and discrimination. The baleful achievements of this idea can be seen insomuch that the recent refugee crisis seems to have led to a greater mobilization in far-right support than the earlier financial crisis (with the exception of Golden Dawn in the special case of post-bailout Greece, see Pirro & van Kessel 2017).

Alongside this slow change was the second, more practical calculation noted above: far-right parties, in attempting to influence public policy in Europe, jettisoned the revolutionary and totalitarian dynamics of interwar fascism. This, incidentally, is also what separates them from more minor, extreme-right groups of neo-fascists and neo-Nazis. The calculus was a straightforward one: anti-establishment populism within an entrenched liberal framework. Parenthetically, populism is not a core feature of either fascism or the far right, it is a mobilizational and communications strategy used by right and left alike (think of Podemos in Spain or Syriza in Greece, for example—usually distinguished between populist radical right and populist radical left, as in Roodujin et al. 2017), and it is absent in many smaller, elitist fascist and far-right movements—not least the Nouvelle Droite. In order for far-right parties to be 'de-demonized', in the words of Marine Le Pen (Lichfield 2015), there could be no reminder of the infamous fascist style: no paramilitarism, no semi-divine leader, no fascist chants or salutes, and certainly no parading blackshirts.

Accordingly, the revolutionary-right challenge of yesteryear is not that faced today. There will be no replay of coloured shirts from the past, nor the totalitarian dynamic of historical fascism before 1945. Today, the descendants of this ideology wear suits, are often hostile to their parentage, and, above all, have accepted, at least for now, the hegemony of liberal democracy in Europe. To date, no country that became a liberal democracy in post-war Europe has succumbed to dictatorship, even if some, like Hungary, Poland, and perhaps the US, have become 'illiberal democracies'—that is, retaining the majoritarian trappings of democracy, while curtailing civil and political rights for opponents and minorities. In this way, the spectre of fascist war and racial tyranny may not be a useful historical lesson for the present; by contrast, populist appeal and a crisis of legitimacy in the mainstream raise awkward questions.

Do leopards change their spots?

True, many of the recognisable far-right characteristics Eco so perceptively noted are still discernible, such as conspiracy theorizing, authoritarian governance and anti-liberalism/socialism. Yet broadly speaking, these movements have truly learnt to speak the language of reform rather than revolution. In Gianfranco Fini's populist transition of the Alleanza Nazionale from neo-fascism to post-fascism, for instance, the previous leader, Pino Rauti, maintained a hardline stance that brought about a party split and the formation of the neo-fascist (and unashamedly pro-Republic of Salò) Movement Tricolour Flame. Variations on this discordant Italian theme were repeated by France's Front National in the west, by the Sweden Democrats in the north and the Slovak National Party in the east (which took 8.6 per cent of the 2016 national vote and 15 parliamentary seats). All of these parties purged their more extreme activists in the bid for greater legitimacy. Even Marine Le Pen's father, Jean-Marie, was dismissed from the Front National for his antisemitism—a new taboo for far-right parties so keen to swap historical Judeo-prejudice for Islamo-prejudice today (see, for example, Camus & Lebourg 2017; Richardson 2018).

Alongside shedding the most militant, unbending, or outspoken neo-fascists, a second path to legitimacy while keeping committed activists aboard is to develop a kind of coded language that can be termed doublespeak (Feldman & Jackson 2014; Richardson 2018). Of course, all political parties triangulate in order to 'manage their message', but this is far closer to deception for far-right parties. Scholars talk about a 'front stage' of moderation and reform presented to the outside world against a persisting 'backstage' of committed extreme-right activists largely kept out of public sight (Feldman & Jackson 2014: 10). Bridging the two are dog-whistle terms (such as 'international financiers' to mean Jews) and populist themes such as immigration or law and order.

A perfect example of this front-stage–backstage dynamic could be seen in the now nearly defunct British National Party (BNP), which in its heyday had scores of local and parish councillors in Britain, and, from May 2009, two MEPs. Only a decade earlier, photographs had showed then leader John Tyndall dressed in Nazi regalia and depicted him with David Copeland, who killed several and maimed dozens more in an April 1999 attacks on gay and ethnic minority areas in London. With 'modernization' pledges patterned on the examples of the far right in France, Austria and Italy, Nick Griffin took over later that year, attempting to balance a front-stage stress on identity and monoculturalism with backstage activism by neo-fascist militants. Again and again, Griffin insisted that a desire to 'teach the truth to the hardcore' needed to be subordinated to the populist moderation that he believed would spell electoral breakthrough (cited in Feldman & Jackson 2014: 7). In fact, only a month before the European elections in 2009, which took Griffin and Andrew Brons into the European Parliament with nearly one million votes (6.3 per cent), the BNP released an astonishing 'Language and Concepts Discipline Manual' for use by 'backstage' activists (for instance, Rule 1 fancifully states: 'We are *not* a "racist" or "racial" party'; cited in Feldman 2015: 8). If to a less stark degree, this front-stage–backstage dynamic was replayed all over Europe as part of the legitimizing march by far-right parties. It also should be remembered, moreover, that neo-fascists and the far right know their history as well as anyone (for an excellent analysis of radical right doublespeak in contemporary Britain, see Richardson 2018).

So, if history can be as much a blessing as a curse in approaching the far right, and with the latter being a swiftly moving target, altering key elements of its core praxis in order to reach the mainstream (for example, swapping racism for identity, or illiberal populism for revolutionary ultranationalism), the question may then be asked 'Where are we now?' For one, things are speeding up. This entails more than just the effects of social media, where 280-character slogans and patchy digital literacy in Europe and the US means that far-right outpourings seemingly receive publicly polarized responses, ranging from 'fascist' to 'common sense'. The far right is neither of these—unless we let it be—but instead represents a well-co-ordinated revamp that has allowed far-right parties to be mainstreamed. This has had two significant political effects that are only now being felt.

The first point is that far-right parties continue to go from strength to strength. In 2016, the FPÖ's Norbert Hofer came within 350,000 votes of winning the Austrian presidency with 46 per cent of the vote— the highest result ever for either a fascist or a far-right candidate in Europe (for further discussion of the 'Austrian case', see Wodak 2018). There can be scarcely a blunter warning. Marginally less stark, since 1994—depending on how the term 'far-right party' is defined—as many as 24 government coalitions in 12 European countries have included far-right parties (Mudde 2017: 8). Still, others point to longer-term trends in Western and Central Europe, going as far back as the idiosyncratic Danish People's Party in 1973, but more specifically to the 1980s political breakthroughs for the Front National in France and the Vlaams Blok in Belgium.

Although the term, and political practice, of cordon sanitaire had first been applied to the Vlaams Block following its 1988 result in Antwerp, when it garnered 17.7 per cent of the vote in the city, only three years later, on 'Black Sunday', Filip Dewinter's VB claimed nearly 7 per cent of the national vote, winning 5 Belgian senators and 12 delegates in the Chamber of Representatives. This familiar story in Europe was not just national, but regional and transnational as well. In 2004, the Vlaams Blok took 32 seats in the Flemish parliament, with nearly a quarter of the electorate's vote. That year, with nearly one million votes, it also took three seats in the European Parliament (Van Holsteyn 2018). Only a Belgian judicial ruling against Vlaams Blok for 'incitement to discrimination' stopped its rise in November 2004, when a new party emerged, Vlaams Belang (Erk 2005). The latter formed part of the short-lived European political party Identity, Sovereignty, Tradition between January and November 2007. Although I would not share Martin Schulz's definition of this group as 'fascist', his 2011 warning about the mainstreaming potential of far-right parties mirrors, in its way, the historian Aristotle Kallis's argument about the mainstream of the interwar 'fascist effect':

> The new fascist parliamentary grouping perpetrated permanent breaches of convention in a way that has become systematic. When no sanctions were imposed for racist, xenophobic or antisemitic statements, they were presented as permissible and therefore no longer subject to prosecution or sanction in the future. By deliberate breach of taboos, racist, xenophobic and antisemitic remarks were thrust into normal daily parliamentary affairs. In our opinion, this is an extremely dangerous development. (Schulz 2011: 28)

It is precisely these breaches of convention by what might be called the 'far-right effect' that a leading political scientist on the subject, Cas Mudde, understands as 'pathological normalcy'—a breach of the civic cordon sanitaire as much as the political one:

> Establishing boundaries between populist radical right parties and mainstream right-wing parties has been significantly complicated by the rise of populist radical right *politics* in Europe, i.e. nativist, authoritarian, and populist discourses and policies from mostly mainstream parties. (Mudde 2016: 16)

Nor is Mudde alone in this concern. In fact, several books on the far right this decade alone employ the term 'mainstream' in the subtitle. In terms of voter appeal, Tjitske Akkerman summarizes this mainstream appeal effectively: 'Negative attitudes toward asylum seekers, legal and illegal immigration and multiculturalism prevail among radical-right voters and are the main reason why voters support these parties' (2012: 511).

To the question 'Where is the far right now?' the answer then must be 'Virtually mainstreamed'. That in itself is surely a challenge to liberal stability and legitimacy, and perhaps even a long-term threat to democratic security. This may be due to any number of factors: what has been dubbed a 'right turn' in Europe, away from inclusion and assimilation; the skilful use of pro-identity and nativist populism; or, again, propitious conditions in Europe (for example, historically low levels of political trust, shocking acts of jihadi Islamist terrorism and what is usually termed the refugee crisis). Nevertheless, a key concern should *also* be the new political terrain that the far right has opened this century. Like a vortex, anti-Muslim and broader nativist sentiment is sucking in new political players to the far right's (notionally) left and right. In terms of the latter, consider the development of the alt-right in the US, championed by no less than President Trump's sometime chief strategist Steve Bannon, ex-editor of 'the platform for the alt-right', Breitbart News (SPLC 2017). While there are many spokes to the alt-right wheel, its hub is the overt white supremacism pushed by the man who coined the term alt-right, Richard Spencer (Hawley 2017). Following Trump's election on 8 November 2016, footage appeared of celebrations at the National Policy Institute that Spencer heads, in which he urged supporters to 'party like it was 1933', followed by fascist salutes and chants of 'Heil Trump!'[3]

Aided by a sophisticated use of social media and guaranteed funding from the conservative American publisher William Regnery, Spencer is now a familiar voice in the mainstream American media calling for, in his words, 'a racially based state'. That quotation was given to *Rolling Stone*, and its publication perhaps exacerbated the problem by giving Spencer high-profile media exposure in the same month as Trump won the election, without fundamentally challenging his racist views:

> 'We've been legitimized by this election,' he says. While the campaign itself was a huge boost to the movement, Trump's election, he says, has brought the Alt-Right to 'a new level.' 'Legitimacy is ... an unmeasurable, intangible thing that is everything.' ... 'We want to be radically mainstream—that is, we really want to enter the world, we want our ideas to be at the table, and people to listen to them,' says Spencer. (Posner 2016)

There is little that is backstage about what Spencer claims would be merely a case of 'peaceful ethnic cleansing', and his aim to rehabilitate historical fascism is unmistakeable (Kentish 2017). This is revolutionary right-wing neo-fascism masquerading as a vision of reform. It is white paint over asbestos. Yet, in place of far-right parties that at one time were firmly beyond the cordon sanitaire, this is the new fringe, trying to find meme-friendly ways to advance biological racism back into the mainstream. From CasaPound in Italy to the transnational British Blood and Honour music scene, these would-be fashionable white supremacists are, of course, not the only neo-fascist game in town (Fielitz & Laloire 2016; Feldman & Jackson 2014). Yet what the alt-right and overt fascists share is the attempt to force neo-fascism back onto the public agenda. No doubt, this attempted rebranding owes much to the political space vacated by a far right that is moving towards the mainstream.

Conclusion

Finally, and perhaps most troublingly, in terms of the political tectonic plates moved by the mainstreaming of the far right, there is what I term the 'near right', sometimes also called 'right-wing populism'. One example of this trend is the Law and Justice Party in Poland (Prawo i Sprawiedliwość, PiS), described by Jean Yves-Camus and Nicolas Lebourg in cognate terms as an example of a 'radicalized conservative right' (2017: 241). Another instance is the 'illiberal democracy' now proudly touted by Victor Orbán's Fidesz Party in Hungary, exemplified above all by its disgraceful attack on the CEU, on gender studies programmes generally, and on liberal scholarship everywhere. It now holds a parliamentary supermajority and can change laws and liberal norms nearly at will.

Yet perhaps the exemplar of this near-right populism is Brexit. Few will forget the xenophobic fever leading up to the 23 June 2016 referendum, resulting in a 41 per cent increase in hate crimes in what might be termed a form of celebratory racism at the outcome. Indeed, of the nearly 6,000 reported hate crimes reported in the four weeks following the vote to leave the EU, more than half 'specifically referred to the referendum in the abuse' (Virdee & McGeever 2018: 1808). Needless to say, not all leave voters were xenophobic; however, it seems clear that all racist voters chose Brexit. Yet for this well-established spike in xenophobia, what responsibility might UKIP—the emboldened

Figure 1.2. The leave.eu 'Breaking Point' poster (https://www.theguardian. com/politics/2016/jun/16/nigel-farage-defends-ukip-breaking-point-poster-queue-of-migrants, accessed 7 May 2019).

near-right Eurosceptic party—have for trafficking in rhetoric and images like the infamous 'Breaking Point' poster, unveiled a week before the vote? That the notorious image was actually of refugees in Slovenia trying to enter Croatia was surely of less import than that those depicted had dark skin.

More recently, and once more in territory more redolent of the far right, both the one-time leader of UKIP, Nigel Farage, and the Prime Minister of Poland, Beata Szydło, quickly weighed in on the Westminster attack of 22 March 2017, which left four dead in a self-directed terrorist act by the 52-year-old Islamist convert, Khalid Masood, born and raised as Adrian Elms in southern England. They blamed 'immigration', but were presumably not talking about Britain in the 1960s—when Masood was born in Britain's Home Counties. On 23 March 2017, they were trying to stigmatize rather more recent arrivals:

> We've made some terrible mistakes in this country, and it really started with the election of Tony Blair back in 1997, who said he wanted to build a multicultural Britain ... I'm sorry to say that we have now a fifth column living inside these European countries. (Nigel Farage, quoted in Warren 2017)

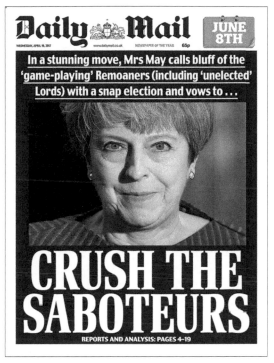

Figure 1.3. The *Daily Mail* front page on 10 April 2017.

I hear in Europe very often: 'Do not connect the migration policy with terrorism', but it is impossible not to connect them. (Beata Szydło, quoted in Montgomery 2017)

Fanning the populist flames is an emboldened near-right media, from the Dutch *Geenstijl* ('No Style') blog to Breitbart News in the US. Nor have print newspapers been immune. For example, what is one to think of the cover of Britain's best-selling newspaper, the *Daily Mail*, declaring 'Crush the Saboteurs' (that is, 'Remainers' opposed to Brexit) the day after Theresa May's call for a snap election in Britain in 2017?

'Immune' is a word worth closing with, in the sense of Kenan Malik's apt phrase, 'Democracy is in rude health. It is liberalism that is in trouble' (2017). By eating away at the foundations of liberal democracy—tolerance, human rights, individual conscience—the risks to liberal democracy by the far right may, in years to come, be

43

most palpably felt in the weakening of immunological defences, both political and civic. As this chapter argues, the risks are not posed by an assault on power like between the wars, nor even by a fundamental rupture with democracy, as the cases of Hungary and now Poland may suggest. But it is an ideological assault on the liberal status quo in Europe nonetheless. Xenophobia acts like arsenic on the European body politic, administered not only by far-right parties, but increasingly by a populist near right, and by newly emboldened neo-fascists. That means extra susceptibility in a major crisis. And it also means the germs of a collective madness are again in the air, as in Albert Camus's novel of wartime occupation, *La Peste*: 'When you see the misery it brings, you'd need to be a madman, or a coward, or stone blind, to give in tamely to the plague' (1948: 115).

We need 'political immunologists' desperately today. For if liberalism fails over the next generation, it will be because we, its guardians, failed it. Let us demonstrate that liberal values include the protection of minority groups, equality of rights, and freedom from fear. This is the kernel of liberalism. Perhaps not of liberal democracy as such, the actual mechanics of governance in Europe, but certainly of liberal moderation, the petrol that makes it all work. It is that tank which in the end needs refilling with a bit more liberal horsepower: an evidence-based, even passionate, restatement of fundamental democratic values in the face of potential attacks from without and, especially in the years to come, from foreseeable attacks by what may be described as a fifth column (Feldman 2015) within liberal praxis.

Notes

1   I am grateful to Ruth Wodak and to Charlotte Merton for her helpful comments on earlier drafts of this article. I would also like to offer my thanks to Pieter Bevelander and Ruth Wodak for welcoming me to the symposium from which this timely special issue derives. I am also grateful to Dr Archie Henderson for his acumen and assistance with the materials referenced in the bibliography.

2   Aleksandr Dugin is a Russian 'neo-Eurasianist' with ties to the Kremlin; Dominique Venner was a long-time French radical right activist, who committed suicide at the altar of Notre-Dame in 2013; Guillmaume Faye is a journalist and leading ideologue of the 'metapolitical' French New Right; and

the writings of Pierre Krebs and Michael Walker were ideological offshoots in Belgium and Britain, respectively.

3 For a video recording of this speech, with commentary on cited quotations, see *New Zealand Herald*'s 'The Big Read: Insight the alt-right world of Richard Spencer' (23 November 2016), www.nzherald.co.nz/world/news/article.cfm?c_id=2&objectid=11753791 (all websites last accessed 7 April 2019).

References

Akkerman, T. (2012), 'Comparing radical right parties in government: Immigration and integration policies in nine countries (1996–2010)', *West European Politics*, 35/3: 511–29.

Bar-On, T. (2013), *Rethinking the French New Right: Alternatives to Modernity* (London).

Bastow, S. (2002), 'A neo-fascist third way: the discourse of ethno-differentialist revolutionary nationalism', *Journal of Political Ideologies*, 7/3: 69–88, reprinted in R. Griffin & M. Feldman, *Fascism, Critical Concepts*, v: *Postwar Fascism* (London, 2004).

Betz, H. (1993), 'The new politics of resentment: Radical right-wing populist parties in Western Europe', *Comparative Politics*, 25/4: 413–27.

Bauerkämper, A. (2010), 'Transnational fascism: Cross-border relations between regimes and movements in Europe 1922–1939', *East Central Europe*, 37: 214–46.

Camus, A. 1948, *The Plague*, trans. Stuart Gilbert (London).

Camus, J.-Y. & N. Lebourg (2017), *Far-right politics in Europe*, trans. Jane Marie Todd (London).

Carioti, A. (1996), 'From the ghetto to the Palazzo Chigi: The ascent of the National Alliance', *Italian Politics*, x. 91–110, reprinted in R. Griffin & M. Feldman *Fascism, Critical Concepts*, v: *Postwar Fascism* (London: 2004).

Cowell, A. (1994), 'Italy's neo-fascists: Have they shed their past?' *New York Times*, www.nytimes.com/1994/03/31/world/italy-s-neo-fascists-have-they-shed-their-past.html.

Eatwell, R. (2000), 'The rebirth of the "Extreme right" in Western Europe', *Parliamentary Affairs*, 53/3: 410–14.

Eco, U. (1995), 'Ur-Fascism', *New York Review of Books*, 405–416, reprinted in R. Griffin & M. Feldman, *Fascism, Critical Concepts*, v: *Postwar Fascism* (London: 2004)

Erk, J. 2005, 'From Vlaams Blok to Vlaams Belang: The Belgian far right renames itself', *West European Politics*, 28/3: 493–502.

Fallend, F. (2004), 'Are right-wing populism and government participation incompatible? The case of the freedom party of Austria', *Representation: Journal of Representative Democracy*, 40/2: 115–30.

Feldman, M. & P. Jackson (eds.) (2014), *'Introduction' Doublespeak: The Framing of the Far-Right since 1945* (Stuttgart).

— (2015), 'Hate-baiting: The radical-right and "fifth column discourse" in European and American democracies today', *Journal of Political Criminology*, 1/1: 7–19.

Fielitz, M. & N. Laloire (eds.) (2016), *Introduction: Trouble on the Far Right* (Dusseldorf).

Gellately, R. (2001), *Backing Hitler: Consent and Coercion in Nazi Germany* (Oxford).

Griffin, R. (2008), 'Exploding the continuum of history: A non-Marxist's Marxist model of fascism's revolutionary dynamics', in M. Feldman (ed.), *A Fascist Century: Essays by Roger Griffin* (Basingstoke).

Hawley, G. (2017), *Making sense of the alt-right* (London).

Kallis, A. (2013), 'Breaking taboos and 'Mainstreaming the extreme': the debates on restricting Islamic symbols in contemporary Europe', in R. Wodak, M. KhosraviNik & B. Mral (eds.), *Right-Wing Populism in Europe: Politics and Discourse* (London).

— (2015), 'When fascism became mainstream: The challenge of extremism in times of crisis', *Fascism*, 4: 1–24.

Kentish, B. (2017), 'White supremacist leader Richard Spencer forced to hold press conference in flat as hotels refuse to take him', *The Independent*, www.independent.co.uk/news/world/americas/richard-spencer-charlottesville-protests-white-supremacist-press-conference-flat-hotels-refuse-a7894236.html.

Knox, M. (2000), *Common destiny: Dictatorship, foreign policy and war in fascist Italy and Nazi Germany* (Cambridge) ((first pub. 1997).

Lee, M. (2000), *The beast reawakens* (London).

Lewis, S. (2017), *It can't happen here* (London) (first pub. 1935).

Lichfield, J. (2015), 'Front national family feud? Marine Le Pen and her relatives clash over French far-right party's response to Paris terror attacks', *The Independent*: www.independent.co.uk/news/world/europe/front-national-family-feud-marine-le-pen-and-her-relatives-clash-over-french-far-right-partys-10006562.html.

Linz, J. (2003), 'Fascism and non-democratic regimes', in H. Maier (ed.), *Totalitarianism and political religions: Concepts for the comparison of dictatorships*, iii: *Theory and History of Interpretation*, trans. Jodi Bruhn (London).

Malik, K. (2017), 'Liberalism is suffering but democracy is doing just fine', *The Guardian*: www.theguardian.com/commentisfree/2017/jan/01/liberalism-suffering-democracy-doing-just-fine.

Matthews, D. (2016), 'I asked 5 fascism experts whether Donald Trump is a fascist. Here's what they said', *Vox*, www.vox.com/policy-and-politics/2015/12/10/9886152/donald-trump-fascism.

Montgomery, J. (2017), 'Polish prime minister: 'Impossible not to connect terrorism with migration policy'', *Breitbart News*, www.breitbart.com/london/2017/03/23/polish-prime-minister-impossible-not-connect-terrorism-migration-policy/#bbvb.

Mudde, C. (1996), 'The war of words: Defining the extreme right party family', *West European Politics*, 19/2: 225–48.

— (2016), 'The study of populist radical right parties: Towards a fourth wave', C-Rex working paper 1, Centre for Research on Extremism, September, www.sv.uio.no/c-rex/english/publications/c-rex-working-paper-series/Cas%20Mudde:%20The%20Study%20of%20Populist%20Radical%20Right%20Parties.pdf.

— (2017), *The populist radical right: A reader* (London).

Norocel, O. C. (2013), 'Our people—A tight-knit family under the same protective roof: A critical study of gendered conceptual metaphors at work in radical right populism' (PhD diss., Helsinki), helda.helsinki.fi/bitstream/handle/10138/42162/ourpeopl.pdf?sequence=1.

Pirro, A. & S. van Kessel (2017), 'United in opposition? The populist radical right's EU-pessimism in times of crisis', *Journal of European Integration*, 39/4: 405–20.

Posner, S. (2016), ''Radically Mainstream': Why the Alt-Right Is Celebrating Trump's Win', *Rolling Stone*, www.rollingstone.com/politics/politics-features/radically-mainstream-why-the-alt-right-is-celebrating-trumps-win-110791/.

Richardson, J. (2018), *British Fascism: A Discourse-Historical Analogy* (Stuttgart).

Roodujin, M., B. Burgoon, E. J. van Elsas & H. G. van de Werfhorst (2017), 'Radical distinction: Support for radical left and radical right parties in Europe', *European Union Politics*, 18/4: 536–59.

Saint-Martin, Elise (2013), 'The front national: Model for the radical right?' *University of Ottawa*, ruor.uottawa.ca/bitstream/10393/26189/1/St-Martin_Élise_2013_mémoire.pdf.

Schulz, M. (2011), 'Combatting right-wing extremism as a task for European policy-making', in *Is Europe on the 'Right' Path? Right-wing extremism and right-wing populism in Europe* (Berlin).

SPLC (Southern Poverty Law Center) (2017), 'Breitbart exposé confirms: Far-right news site a platform for the "alt-right"', *Hatewatch Files*, www.splcenter.org/hatewatch/2017/10/06/breitbart-exposé-confirms-far-right-news-site-platform-white-nationalist-alt-right.

Steigmann-Gall, R. (2017), 'Star-spangled fascism: American interwar political extremism in comparative perspective', *Social History*, 42/1: 94–119.

Taguieff, P.-A. (1993), 'Discussion or inquisition? The case of Alain de Benoist', *Telos* 98/9: 34–54.

— (2001), *The Force of Prejudice: On Racism and Its Doubles*, trans. and ed. Hassan Melehy (London) (first pub. 1987).

van Holsteyn, J. J. M. (2018), 'The radical right in Belgium and the Netherlands', in J. Rydgren (ed.), *The Oxford Handbook of the Radical Right* (Oxford).

Virdee, S. & B. McGeever (2018), 'Racism, Crisis, Brexit', *Ethnic & Racial Studies*, 41/10: 1802–19.

Warren, J. (2017), '"Foul!" Labour MP accuses Farage of "whipping up hate" in wake of Westminster attack', *Daily Express*, www.express.co.uk/news/uk/783421/Nigel-Farage-Labour-MP-accuses-whipping-hate-multicultur-alism-comment.

Wodak, R. & B. Forchtner (2014), 'Embattled Vienna 1683/2010: Right-wing populism, collective memory and the fictionalisation of politics', *Visual Communication*, 13/2: 231–55.

— (2018), 'Driving on the right: The Austrian Case', Centre for Analysis of the Radical Right, *Insight blog*, www.radicalrightanalysis.com/2018/04/09/driving-on-the-right-the-austrian-case/.

CHAPTER 2

The EU's values crisis

Past and future responses to threats to the rule of law and democratic principles

Heather Grabbe & Stefan Lehne

Authoritarian trends threaten the EU more than Brexit does.[1] Not only is democracy in Hungary and Poland at stake, but so is the EU's community of law. The EU's rules-based regional order benefits business and citizens alike. Its legal framework proved remarkably resilient during recent crises over the euro and migration. But its foundations are under attack from the inside by populist parties in government who are defying EU laws and court decisions.

For nearly a decade, a political crisis over values and rule of law has been slowly building in Europe. The EU institutions have now taken a firm stance, but member governments are still hesitating about how to respond, with many taking steps and then pulling back. Since 2017, the Commission has taken legal action against the current governments in Warsaw and Budapest for violating specific EU laws, and has proposed going further on Poland owing to a systemic threat to the rule of law. The European Parliament voted to activate the first part of Article 7 of the Treaty on European Union against Hungary in September 2018 for the same reason. Other measures are under consideration to reinforce rule of law, particularly as part of the next Multiannual Financial Framework (the EU's seven-year budget).

If the foundations of the EU are to survive, however, the rule of law and fundamental values need to be defended by national political leaders as well as the EU institutions. However, political leaders in the other member governments have been reluctant to involve themselves actively; although most have little sympathy with the parties in power in Hungary and Poland, they are cautious about EU-level action. This chapter examines the reasons for their reluctance and discusses the implications for the whole EU of the continued erosion of democratic standards and the rule of law.

The politics of values at EU level

The EU's role in the protection of values and institutional matters within its member states has evolved significantly over the last two decades, but it still lacks a solid legal basis and political consensus. Initially, European integration was primarily about economic cooperation. The creation of a community of law was fundamental to providing a high degree of certainty and stability to citizens and business, and it remains the EU's great comparative advantage over rising powers and other investment destinations.

Until the end of the Cold War, respect for the rule of law, democracy and fundamental rights was little discussed, with members expected to keep their own houses in order. Values were first mentioned in the Maastricht Treaty of 1992, and the relevant commitments were strengthened in subsequent revisions. The most detailed elaboration is Article 2 of the current Lisbon Treaty: 'respect for human dignity, freedom, democracy, equality, the rule of law and respect for human rights, including the rights of persons belonging to minorities ... in a society in which pluralism, non-discrimination, tolerance, justice, solidarity and equality between women and men prevail' (EUR-Lex 2012a). However, while the EU's members prominently featured these values in their external policies, and made them conditions for future members, they remained reluctant to give the Union a role in supervising the practices of countries already inside. The legal framework on values is minimalist in comparison with the elaborate body of law on economic integration. The EU's treaties even commit the Union to 'respect the national identities of the member states, inherent in their fundamental structures, political and institutional, inclusive of regional and local self-government' (EUR-Lex 2012b).

The prospect of taking in post-communist countries prompted

the introduction of a safeguard in 1999 to prevent a reversion to authoritarian rule in unconsolidated democracies. It later became Article 7 of the current treaties, with three stages: under 7(1), four-fifths of the EU's members can determine in the Council that there is a 'clear risk of a serious breach by a Member State of the values referred to in Article 2', based on a reasoned proposal by one-third of the member states, the European Parliament, or the Commission (EUR-Lex 2012c). Under 7(2), the European Council (the heads of state and government) can decide by unanimity that there is a 'serious and persistent breach' after hearing from the offending state (EUR-Lex 2012c); 7(3) then allows the Council to decide by qualified majority to suspend certain of that country's rights, including its government's voting rights in the Council (EUR-Lex 2012c).

The threshold for activating Article 7(2) was set very high—at unanimity minus one—to make sure that it could only apply in extreme cases, such as a military coup. Despite the disrespect of values in several countries over the years and the recommendations of both the Commission and European Parliament to activate Article 7, the EU's governments have so far failed to take concerted action for four major reasons.

The sovereignty reflex

National governments' desire to protect themselves from outside interference remains a major constraint on the supranational oversight of values. Supporters of the original federalist vision of European integration, such as the Benelux countries, were more open, whereas the more sovereigntist France, Denmark, and UK insisted on keeping the EU out of national governance. When new members joined in 2004 and 2007, they were not keen on surrendering their newly regained sovereignty to the EU, and saw themselves as potential targets of Article 7. As a result, when the Charter of Fundamental Rights gained legal force under the Lisbon Treaty, it was hedged about with restrictions on judicial mechanisms to enforce its provisions. Notably, the EU's Court of Justice is only allowed to rule on violations of the Charter if they happen in the context of implementing EU law.

The sovereignty reflex grew stronger after 2008, when the financial and migration crises weakened the EU's appeal as a pole of stability and prosperity, and revealed the downsides of interdependence. Although they agreed to more EU powers to save the euro, national governments have reasserted their sovereignty on other matters.

The premium placed on cooperation

The daily work of the EU relies on its members trusting one another, with national ministers and officials negotiating in dozens of working groups and councils. Despite their diversity in terms of population size and economic power, officials treat one another with respect in a culture of equality and collegiality. This sense of common purpose is essential if a community of 28 countries is to work efficiently, find compromises, and move forward on complex policies. It is a vital characteristic of the EU that makes it much more effective than other multilateral forums. However, it creates a strong preference for reaching decisions by consensus, working on an issue until everyone agrees, and only rarely pushing it to a formal vote in the Council.

To preserve the collegiality that allows for day-to-day progress, the members prefer to overlook problematic behaviour on the part of individual governments, hoping that awkward partners will self-correct and come back to the social rules that allow the EU to work. To accuse another member state of violations of fundamental values and to threaten it with isolation and sanctions would disrupt the culture of cooperation. Only under extreme circumstances would governments be willing to engage in open confrontation.

Within the club, there are sub-groups whose members are averse to criticizing one of their own. Some are regional, such as the Visegrad, Nordic, and Benelux groups. Others are based on shared interests, for example the net recipients, or Mediterranean agricultural producers. One of the most significant is the party families to which MEPs, Commissioners, and governments belong. The European People's Party, the largest and most powerful of the party families, is particularly prone to overlooking bad behaviour rather than punish or cast out misbehaving national parties.

The glasshouse syndrome

Heads of government are even more reluctant to criticize one of their peers because they worry about setting a precedent that could one day be turned against them. No EU country has a perfect record on values and principles. National leaders and EU institutions for too long turned a blind eye to problems like former Prime Minister Berlusconi's dominant position in the Italian media and Greece's massive institutional shortcomings until they threatened the survival of the euro. The same mindset among leaders also makes it hard for the EU to tackle corruption in members states.

Migration and terrorism have made governments even keener to maximize their margin of manoeuvre rather than enhancing EU-level supervision, especially those that wish to introduce restrictive measures in future. They know that giving EU institutions a significantly stronger role on values could expose many of them to criticism. Moreover, the need for unanimity to activate Article 7 sanctions means that two members can deadlock the mechanism by protecting each other. Hungarian Prime Minister Viktor Orbán declared in July 2017 that he would 'always bear solidarity with the Poles' against what he called an 'inquisition', making it impossible to achieve unanimity (Byrne 2017). It is hard to imagine that his Polish counterpart would refuse to return the favour.

Reverse deterrence

Article 7 is often called 'the nuclear option' because everyone is afraid of using it. Its potential damage deters potential users more than it disciplines potential targets. If activation fails because it does not muster sufficient support, the target government could interpret the outcome as an acquittal that legitimates its actions. If Article 7 does go ahead, it can trigger an escalation that fuels nationalist sentiment against the EU. Public opinion in that country might rally around the government, as happened in Austria in 2000 when the formation of the Schüssel-Haider coalition triggered bilateral diplomatic sanctions by the other members. Claims of 'unfair outside interference in our national sovereignty' can even reinforce authoritarian tendencies by delegitimizing domestic criticism.

A government that is committing a serious and persistent breach of EU values is unlikely to subject itself meekly to the censure of its peers and return to the path of virtue, particularly if the survival of the ruling elite is at stake. Moreover, that elite can damage the EU by turning to outside powers such as Russia or Turkey, or disrupt EU business by refusing to cooperate across the board. If a government is thoroughly antagonized and spirals away from the EU's values base, it can cause great damage to the Union's policies and interests. And there is no mechanism to force a member out of the EU.

As a result of these four inhibitions to action, EU governments have a strong default response. At first, they try to ignore offensive behaviour. Then they outsource monitoring and criticism to the Commission, Parliament, and the Council of Europe. If that fails to do the trick, some leaders are prepared to criticize the behaviour, but most just hope that the party will be voted out by its own electorate. However, when it comes to Poland and Hungary, all these procrastination strategies ran out of road in 2017 and the EU was forced to respond.

Dismantling the rule of law in Hungary and Poland

For too long, other governments viewed the Fidesz and PiS governments' behaviour as unpleasant domestic illiberalism. But what started as infractions of democratic practice when Fidesz returned to power in Hungary in 2010 and Law and Justice (PiS) took office in Poland in 2015 turned into state capture of formerly independent institutions in those countries—which undermines the implementation of EU law. The Commission and Parliament have now taken strong positions, but the member governments in the Council are still sitting on the fence.

The Commission concluded in 2016 that the PiS government's attempts to gain control of the Polish constitutional tribunal were a systemic threat to the rule of law. It launched a dialogue under the 'Rule of Law Framework', a new mechanism introduced in 2014 as a precursor to Article 7 (European Commission 2014). After that dialogue yielded no results and the Warsaw government tried to push through new laws to control the other courts, the Commission triggered the first part of Article 7 in 2018. Together the measures 'would abolish any remaining judicial independence ... judges will serve at the pleasure of the political leaders and be dependent upon them from their appointment to their pension,' according to Commission First Vice-President Frans Timmermans (Timmermans 2017). The European Parliament had already expressed concern about these measures 'endangering democracy, fundamental rights and the rule of law in Poland' (European Parliament 2016).

Meanwhile, the Commission also decided to take the Hungarian government to court over laws that would restrict the operations of universities and NGOs that receive foreign funding, followed by laws to criminalize any assistance to asylum seekers and would-be immigrants. It has already taken legal steps against Hungary for its harsh treatment of asylum seekers and its refusal (along with the Czech Republic and Poland) to take refugees relocated from Italy and Greece under a plan adopted by the Council, where Hungary was outvoted.

The measures on higher education, NGOs, and asylum seekers taken in 2017-18 followed others since 2010 that put the government in control of the Hungarian media and constitutional court. For many years, Fidesz has enjoyed the most powerful source of protection in the EU system: its membership of the European People's Party. This large group of centre-right parties for years shielded Orbán from EU criticism, whereas PiS enjoyed less protection from the much smaller and less disciplined group of European Conservatives and Reformists. The EPP has still kept Fidesz as a member, but many of its parliamentarians lost patience and voted for a European Parliament resolution in May 2017 that proposed to launch Article 7 because of the 'serious deterioration of the rule of law, democracy and fundamental rights' (European Parliament 2017).

In previous years, Orbán had backed down under EU pressure, and brought the measures to control the media and public institutions into line with the letter of EU law, if not its spirit. But in spring 2018 he made denigration of the EU and its institutions part of his re-election campaign, and introduced more measures afterwards. The European Parliament then approved a report in September 2018 that documented the problems in Hungary and recommended activation of the first part of Article 7. Many EPP members voted for this action, including the president of the group in the parliament, Manfred Weber, but he made no effort to eject Fidesz from the EPP.

Meanwhile, the ECJ judgement on the infringement proceedings about the Higher Education Law did not come in time to prevent the Central European University (CEU) from being forced to leave Budapest for Vienna at the end of 2018. Orbán had refused to sign the agreement his ministers negotiated with New York State, making it impossible for the university to comply with the new law and accept new students for its dual-accredited degrees. This was the first time since the Second World War that a university was closed down in an EU country because of political persecution.

Rising stakes for the whole EU

There is both a functional and normative case for the defence of values at EU level. Deep integration—especially with a single market and area of freedom, security, and justice—requires intensive daily cooperation between governments and societies at every level. On the functional side, they need a common basis of principles such as legal certainty, prohibition of arbitrariness, independent and impartial courts, and equality before the law. Countries, like individuals, can only trust one another if they also share values of democracy and rights, because these are what define acceptable behaviour between stakeholders. If that trust evaporates, cooperation stops and integration unravels.

The EU's functioning deteriorates when the rule of law does not work properly in all of its member states. Everything in the EU's single market and its justice and home affairs cooperation depends on well-functioning independent court systems in all the countries; without it, the EU would corrode from the inside. The body of EU law relies on decentralized implementation and enforcement. Deep integration requires deep trust. EU members recognize the decisions of one another's courts, and rely on one another's regulatory institutions to implement product and environmental standards.

If a country's justice minister can control every level of the court system, as PiS's proposed laws would allow in Poland, court decisions could be politicized, but judges in other countries would still be bound to abide by them under the principle of mutual recognition (European Commission 2008). This would create mistrust that undermines judicial cooperation, and also the overall quality of the business environment in Europe, as the single market would no longer be a level playing field.

Political influence over the judiciary would disrupt judicial and police cooperation, too, as many judicial councils in other countries have stated (European Network of Councils for the Judiciary 2017). It would make other members reluctant to send their citizens for trial in that country under the common arrest warrant, which they are supposed to do automatically. It also affects the Schengen area of passport-free travel, which has no border controls, so EU members rely on one another's police and customs authorities to enforce the law fairly and well. Deterioration in the rule of law can also make governments less disciplined about implementation of EU law. And if a government does not take its own constitution seriously, it is unlikely to apply EU law rigorously.

In Hungary and Poland, the problem is not just damage to the rule of law, but also open defiance of legally binding decisions. Both governments refused to take in any asylum seekers from Greece or Italy under the relocation scheme adopted in 2015 (the Czech Republic and Slovakia only took a tiny number). In 2017 the PiS government announced it would not abide by a ruling by the EU Court of Justice that it should stop logging in the ancient Białowieża forest. The risk of contagion is high: if you see your neighbour getting away with not obeying the law, your motivation to comply yourself diminishes. The EU loses cohesion when its members do not trust their peers to implement and enforce what they have agreed collectively. The European Court of Justice in 2018 confirmed to the Irish High Court that it could refuse to extradite a Polish citizen because of doubts about the independence of the Polish court system—a very significant indication of mistrust in the legal order of a member state. The EU faced a similar problem when Italy and Greece failed to fulfil their obligation to register refugees under the Dublin asylum system.

The normative case is that values listed in Article 2 are intrinsically linked, since violating rights usually involves violating the rule of law. The EU has long defined itself as a normative project, and its treaties contain many references to its aim to promote its values, such as in Article 3(1) and Article 13(1). Moreover, the Treaty on European Union has many references to the legal obligation of member states to promote these values. Would-be members have to 'respect and promote the values in Article 2' (Article 49), while members have to 'refrain from any measure which could jeopardize attainment of the Union's objectives' (Article 4(3)) and engage in 'mutual sincere cooperation' with the EU's institutions (Article 13 (2)).

There is also an external policy case to be made for member states to adhere to values and principles. The EU loses external clout if its members do not stick to their Treaty obligations and respect its values. In the Balkans and neighbours to the East and South, the EU promotes improving the functioning and independence of these countries' judiciaries and reducing corruption through better rule of law. It is much harder to convince their politicians to stop influencing the courts when the Union's own members are doing the same thing.

Governments on the fence

The Commission and Parliament have set out why the measures taken in Hungary and Poland contravene EU laws and values, and followed a consistent legal approach. But further action has to be taken by the Council following their launching of Article 7(1). All EU-level action must be well framed and communicated to avoid fuelling nationalism and a sense of East–West divide, which has also widened because of the debate about the future budget of the EU and potential 'variable geometry' through different kinds of membership. The Polish and Hungarian governments are using every opportunity to claim that they are being unfairly targeted by the members that joined before 2004. All EU actors must therefore communicate clearly that this is about protecting core standards, and that similar steps will be taken against any offending government. Strong statements from other Central European governments would be particularly helpful. The EU can also counter claims of double standards by getting tougher on bad behaviour by member states across the board, particularly on corruption and misuse of public funds (especially EU funds).

Meanwhile, there are new initiatives for EU institutional and policy reform to tackle the problems. There are plenty of options to consider (Bard et al. 2016). Most pertinent to the cases of Hungary and Poland are greater possibilities for judicial review by the Court of Justice, to capture the cumulative effect of a series of infringements that creates a systemic challenge (De Schutter 2017).

Money matters too. Member states are considering the Commission's proposals for the next Multiannual Financial Framework (the EU's budget), which includes new instruments to protect the EU's financial interest in the rule of law governing use of EU funds (European Commission 2017a). They look likely to agree new conditions to reduce access to EU funds if a country displays a general deficit in governance and rule of law. This will be complicated to introduce, legally and politically, but it would have a powerful deterrent effect. In the meantime, a more rigorous enforcement of existing rules on the misuse of funds would strengthen popular support for EU action against abuse of power in all its members (Šelih et al. 2017; Butler 2018).

The EU has to get more active in countering false claims. Two-thirds of Hungarians have a favourable view of the EU, as do three-quarters of Poles (Stokes et al. 2017). To try to reduce this level of support, the Hungarian government in 2017 funded a huge campaign of anti-EU slogans and false claims about the EU's role in deciding energy prices, taxes and migration, among other things. To counter this propaganda, EU actors need to communicate the facts about the Union's laws and policies, as the Commission did for the first time with a rebuttal fact-sheet (European Commission 2017b). This kind of engagement helps Hungarian and Polish civil society to hold their own governments to account and uphold their own constitutions, and shows that criticism of governments does not mean rejection of their citizens.

Conclusion

The EU institutions are running against the global trend by defending liberal values at a time of rising illiberalism and nationalism. But they have no choice because the EU's legal and normative framework, which is essential to its deep economic and political integration, is under major threat. If the other EU actors allow two members to get away with reneging on core commitments, the contagion effect will be huge, both in the EU and its wider region. More governments will be tempted to override constitutional checks and balances, to intimidate journalists, and to silence critical voices in universities and NGOs.

The EU's role is not to get involved in political fights within its member states. Members should remain free to decide their own constitutional arrangements through national democratic processes. But the EU's institutions have to defend common standards on the core obligations that allow members to trust one another to stick to commitments, and ensure citizens and businesses can operate across borders without discrimination. The rule of law is fundamental to this trust.

The priority now is a sustained, targeted, and coordinated campaign by national leaders at two levels. The first is for the heads of state and government to convince Orbán and Kaczyński to change course. They have to hear tough words from national capitals expressing full support to the actions of the Commission and Parliament. Both leaders need to know that if they do not backtrack, there will be a high price to pay.

At the same time, the EU's institutions and the other member governments have to communicate publicly why values are essential to the functioning of policies that deliver benefits for European citizens. The ultimate hope for remedy lies with the tens of thousands of Hungarians and Poles who have been protesting over the past few years against the attempts to capture their states. They need to hear the support of other Europeans for safeguarding democracy and the rule of law in their countries, because it matters for everyone.

Note

1   This draft is an updated and expanded version of Heather Grabbe & Stefan Lehne, *Defending EU Values in Poland and Hungary* (Brussels: Carnegie Europe, 2017).

References

Bard, P., S. Carrera, E. Guild & D. Kochenov (2016), 'An EU mechanism on democracy, the rule of law and fundamental rights', *CEPS Papers in Liberty and Security in Europe*, www.ceps.eu/system/files/LSE%20No%2091%20 EU%20Mechanism%20for%20Democracy.pdf.

Butler, I. (2018), *Two proposals to promote and protect European values through the Multiannual Financial Framework* (Brussels).

Byrne, A. (2017), 'Hungary's Orban vows to defend Poland from EU sanctions', *Financial Times*, www.ft.com/content/b1bd2424-6ed7-11e7-93ff-99f383b09ff9.

De Schutter, O. (2017), *Infringement proceedings as a tool for the enforcement of fundamental rights in the European Union* (Brussels).

EUR-Lex (2012a), Consolidated version of the Treaty on European Union, Article 2, eur-lex.europa.eu/legal-content/EN/TXT/?uri=celex:12012M002.

— (2012b), Consolidated version of the Treaty on European Union, Article 4, eur-lex.europa.eu/legal-content/EN/TXT/?uri=CELEX%3A12012M004.

— (2012c), Consolidated version of the Treaty on European Union, Article 7, eur-lex.europa.eu/legal-content/EN/TXT/?uri=celex:12012M007.

European Commission (2008), *Growth internal market, industry, entrepreneurship and SMEs*, www.europarl.europa.eu/sides/getDoc.do?pubRef=-//EP//TEXT+TA+P8-TA-2017-0216+0+DOC+XML+V0//EN.

— (2014), *Building a European area of justice*, ec.europa.eu/justice/effective-justice/rule-of-law/index_en.htm.

— (2017a), *EU budget*, ec.europa.eu/budget/mff/index_en.cfm.

— (2017b), '*Stop Brussels*': *European Commission responds to Hungarian national consultation*, ec.europa.eu/commission/publications/stop-brussels-european-commission-responds-hungarian-national-consultation_en.

European Network of Councils for the Judiciary (ENCJ) (2017), *Statement by the Executive Board of the ENCJ on Poland—17 July 2017*, www.encj.eu/index. php?option=com_content&view=article&id=243%3Astatementboardpoland-july2017&catid=22%3Anews&lang=en.

European Parliament (2016), *Recent developments in Poland and their impact on fundamental rights as laid down in the Charter of Fundamental Rights of the European Union 2016/2774(RSP)*, www.europarl.europa.eu/sides/getDoc. do?pubRef=-//EP//TEXT+TA+P8-TA-2016-0344+0+DOC+XML+V0//EN.

— (2017), *European Parliament resolution of 17 May 2017 on the situation in Hungary*, www.europarl.europa.eu/sides/getDoc.do?pubRef=-//EP//TEXT+TA+P8-TA-2017-0216+0+DOC+XML+V0//EN.

Šelih, J., I. Bond & C. Dolan (2017), *Can EU funds promote the rule of law in Europe?* (Brussels).

Stokes, B., R. Wike & D. Manevich (2017), *Post-Brexit, Europeans more favourable toward EU*, Pew Research Center, assets.pewresearch.org/wp-content/uploads/sites/2/2017/06/06160636/Pew-Research-Center-EU-Brexit-Report-UPDATED-June-15-2017.pdf.

Timmermans, F. (2017), *Opening remarks of First Vice-President Frans Timmermans: College readout on grave concerns about the clear risks for independence of the judiciary in Poland to the European Parliament* (European Commission), europa.eu/rapid/press-release_SPEECH-17-2084_en.htm?locale=EN.

CHAPTER 3

Analysing the micropolitics of the populist far right in the 'post-shame era'

Ruth Wodak

As of November 2018, a greater number of parliamentarians from far-right parties formed part of national European governments than did those hailing from the left of the political spectrum.[1] Simultaneously, opinion polls ahead of elections to the European Parliament on 26 May 2019 predict yet another upsurge for these parties. Indeed, such regularly updated opinion polls about the forthcoming European elections indicate a clear strengthening for movements beyond the mainstream.[2] These polls suggest that, overall, the eight transnational party groupings will remain the same; however, the traditional left and right could lose around 20 per cent or more. For example, it is predicted that the European People's Party will fall from 221 seats to 180; the Progressive Alliance of Socialists and Democrats from 191 seats to 135, while the Liberals might rise from 84 to 95 seats, and the Greens from 30 seats to 46. The big winners, however, will most likely be the Eurosceptic bloc (which includes the ENF and the EFDD) which is predicted to have a combined total of 119 seats (currently 78), rising from 10.4 per cent to 16.9 per cent (Psaledakis & Macdonald 2018; also Bertelmanns Stiftung 2016).

Moreover, the latest Eurobarometer from the spring of 2018 illustrates that 'immigration remains the leading concern at EU level, with 38 per cent of mentions, at 29 per cent terrorism remains in second

63

position, though it has lost ground since autumn 2017' (Standard Eurobarometer 89/2018: 4). Economic issues and unemployment lag behind, in third to fifth places in the hierarchy of important topics. Thus, it is not surprising that political parties that instrumentalize fears of immigration for their political interests are gaining votes. Accordingly, European institutions and their leading figures and programmes are likely to be influenced by these dramatic changes. As Falkner and Plattner (2018: 2) suggest, the EU in its everyday workings—which consist of very complex, multilayered decision-making procedures—will certainly be influenced by Eurosceptic voices, especially by parties which reject immigration and integration, and/or stand for greater protectionism and nativist nationalism.

Generally speaking, in spite of this obvious shift to the political right, and alongside the move to more so-called 'illiberal democracies', a range of different standpoints and positions exists among the EU leaders and governing parties. In examining the discursive-political changes and shifts that dominate European debates and developments, I will juxtapose two contrary visions for Europe and the EU, metonymically identified with Emanuel Macron and Victor Orbán respectively, in order to illustrate the huge tensions dominating the political debates.

May 2018 was the occasion of two remarkable speeches: Macron, the French President, was awarded the Charlemagne Prize in Germany, while Orbán, Hungary's Prime Minister, inaugurated his new government, having been re-elected with an impressive majority for his national-conservative party, Fidesz. Although both France and Hungary are EU member states, the two speeches staked out two significantly different positions on migration and diversity, on nationalism and globalization. They also offered two incommensurable visions on the future of European democracy and the EU, which is the subject of this article.

Macron made the case for a 'united Europe', stating that:

> Let's not be divided! The risk of extreme division tends to reduce most debates to overlapping nationalisms. Barbed wire is reappearing everywhere across Europe, including in people's minds. But our only solution is unity: divisions push us towards inaction … Each generation is required to harness all its strength and reinvent hope. (Macron 2018)

He argued against new walls and barriers ('barbed wire'), against divisive nationalisms which—as he maintained—were very dangerous for the EU, and, as he stated later, built upon a politics of fear instead of hope: 'Let's not be afraid; it means not being afraid of one another … We have got to fight for something which is greater than ourselves, a new stronger Europe again!' (Macron 2018).

By contrast, that same day, 10 May 2018, Orbán argued for a Christian-based, illiberal democracy, maintaining that everything should be done to ensure the 'survival' of the Hungarian nation. Of course, the two contexts were very different—Macron was speaking in a foreign country, Germany, and was reaching out to a huge international audience; while inversely, Orbán was primarily addressing his fellow Hungarians. Nevertheless, both politicians used the opportunity for programmatic, rhetorically well-polished, persuasive statements, and, crucially, to elaborate on their respective views of the future:

> In my view, the age of liberal democracy is at an end. Liberal democracy is no longer able to protect people's dignity, provide freedom, guarantee physical security or maintain Christian culture … We are Christian democrats and we want Christian democracy … The survival of Hungarians as a nation is not automatic. Hungarian policy should be predicated on the possibility that we could disappear, we could become extinct. Survival is a question of life force. We are a unique species. We have a language that is unique to us. There is a world which we alone see. (Orbán 2018)

Orbán here explicitly embraced the concept of an illiberal democracy; he defined Hungary (and the EU) as primarily Christian; and he endorsed both nationalism and uniqueness, not unity and diversity.

Even at first glance, it is apparent that the EU is polarized by these conflicting visions. Put simply, Europe is at the crossroads: either it will opt for necessary reforms, remaining a bulwark of liberal democracy and human rights, and fighting for solidarity, diversity, and more equality; or instead, it will redefine itself as a mainly economic, nationalistic federation of states, which would exclude all non-Christians and dismantle the very concept of liberal democracy. Of course, the reasons for such a polarization are manifold, historical, sociopolitical,

and economic, and influenced by global as well as glocal developments, which cannot be elaborated upon in this paper.[3] And equally
obviously, there are many in-between positions, apart from these two
totally polarized views (Plešu 2018).

Some sense can be made of these new developments from the
perspective of critical discourse studies, rhetoric, and argumentation
theory. For instance, Uitz (2015: 293 ff.) identifies the impossibility of
drawing upon the traditional conventions of dialogue, negotiation,
and compromise if one of the two partners does not want to comply
with the established rules of such language games (for example, Wodak
2015; 2017; 2018d). Uitz (2015: 294) argues that there can be no
'productive dialogue' in such instances. The Hungarian government,
and following it in its illiberalism, the Polish government, seem to
believe that these conventions do not apply to them. As Balcer notes,
'since Law and Justice (PiS) came to power in Poland in 2015, it has
implemented revolutionary changes in the legal system. According
to many prominent Western and Polish institutions and associations
(for example, Venice Commission) they aim at taking control of
the Polish judiciary in open defiance of the Constitution' (Balcer
2018). Furthermore, Balcer explains that these unprecedented hostile
takeovers constitute a crucial element of the so-called 'Good Change',
PiS's political programme. Indeed, the leader of PiS, Jarosław Kaczyński,
has frequently maintained that the Polish political system is based on
so-called legal impossibilism—in other words, in Kaczyński's opinion,
it is impossible for a democratically elected Polish government to fulfil
the 'nation's will' because of the checks and balances imposed on it by
the Polish Constitution.

What makes this rejection of dialogue possible is, I would argue, a
digital and narcissistic post-shame era. This is more than what many
scholars have held to be a post-truth era (for example, Scheff 2000;
Hahl et al. 2018; Fuchs 2018); namely, populist and exclusionary
rhetoric, symbolic politics, digital demagogy, 'bad manners', and
anti-politics, all of which help to construct non-compliant behaviour
among influential politicians. Against this background, anti-politics is
defined as a specific attitude and related discourse that systematically
undermine democratic institutions (Diehl 2017: 28–9). The state
itself, the entire political system, is challenged, as if it were reality TV:

shamelessness, the humiliation of other participants, defamation, lies, and ad hominem attacks dominate.[4]

Before elaborating on far-right populist performances and the manifold stages of transforming pluralistic democracies into illiberal and even authoritarian regimes, it is important to clarify the various concepts used. I will then proceed to illustrate some important discursive strategies used by far-right populist politicians in their front-stage and backstage rhetoric. The final section then provides a summary of what constitutes the process of normalization—the acceptance of far-right views, both in content and form, prominently supported by the tabloid media and catering to rich and powerful elites. Too often neglected by scholars of the contemporary far right, I argue that these ingredients form an integral part of the post-shame era.

Defining relevant concepts

There exists a vast amount of literature discussing possible definitions of right-wing populism, authoritarianism or neo-authoritarianism, especially in relation to other ideologies and social movements such as right-wing extremism, the radical right, the alt-right, far-right, populism, fascism, and left-wing populism. Moreover, opinions vary widely regarding concepts of illiberal democracy, managed democracy, neo-authoritarianism, competitive authoritarianism, and the like. Of course, it is beyond the scope of this chapter to discuss of all these concepts, which have helpfully been set out in some recent publications (Rydgren 2017; Mudde & Kaltwasser 2017; Pelinka 2018; Waring 2018; Rheindorf 2019; Wodak 2018d). In this article, I restrict myself to an overview of populism, right-wing populism, or populist right-wing extremism; authoritarianism or neo-authoritarianism; and illiberal democracy or managed democracy.

Populism

Obviously, there is no consensus over whether far-right populism and populist right-wing extremism count as an ideology (thin or thick) (Kriesi & Pappas 2015: 5), a philosophy (Priester 2007: 9), a specific media phenomenon (Pajnik & Sauer 2017), or an organizational method for right-wing extremists like the strategies used by inter-war fascists 1930s and 1940s (Salzborn 2018). Put another way, is populism a worldview, or is it a specific political style (Moffitt 2017; Brubaker 2017: 3) that manifests itself mainly in performance and communication?

For example, in his preface to the recent *Handbook of the Radical Right* (2017: 1–2), Rydgren claims that the term 'right-wing populism' has become obsolete. Rather, he argues, we are confronted with ethno-nationalist parties containing a populist element:

> Radical right parties and movements share an emphasis on ethno-nationalism rooted in myths about the past. Their programmes are directed toward strengthening the nation by making it more ethnically homogenous and—for most radical right-wing parties and movements—by returning to traditional values. They also tend to be populists, accusing élites of putting internationalism ahead of the nation and of putting their own narrow self-interest and various special interests ahead of the interests of the people. (Rydgren 2017: 1–2)

In contrast to these ethno-nationalist parties, he claims that properly radical right-wing parties are characterized by their rejection of the democratic system and its institutions. As this suggests, however, and as Rydgren concedes, the boundaries between ethno-nationalist, radical right parties or even extreme-right parties can easily become blurred. For example, clear and distinct categorizations of the Aktion für Deutschland (AfD) or the Lega prove difficult in this respect (for example, Giuffrida 2018). A similar argument has been advanced by Benjamin van de Cleen (2017: 8) (see also Deiwiks 2009: 1; Wodak 2018a; 2018b).

As a discourse analyst, it is important for me to stress that far-right populism or populist right-wing extremism should be seen not only as rhetorical style, nor as purely a media performance phenomenon (although the significance of rhetorical staging should, of course, never be underestimated). Underpinning communicative strategies, the ideological content so expressed remains crucial and demands rigorous attention. Indeed, following Pels (2012: 32), thinking that there is no substance behind this populist style is totally misleading; instead, it is precisely the dynamic mixing of content and form that has led to the success of far-right populist politics in contemporary democracies.

According to Mudde and Kaltwasser (2017), populism constitutes a thin ideology, which is realized in various discursive and material practices. Here, the authors draw upon Michael Freeden's notion of thin ideology, defined as a 'distinct set of ideas about the political which interact with the established ideational traditions of full ideologies' (Freeden 2008: 95). They emphasize three parameters for populism (Mudde & Kaltwasser 2017: 9–12): first, an opposition drawn between the people and the corrupt elite; second, a grounding in the *volonté générale*, or will of the people; and third, an eclecticism that does not constitute a coherent structure of beliefs but assembles diverse political elements. As they do not restrict their definition to right-wing populism—meaning that populists can also be from the left—the notion of 'the people' refers to both a polity as sovereign (the demos) and as allegedly commonplace views. Moreover, populism can refer to the people as an ethnos, or ethnonational community. Juxtaposed with populism is the notion of an elite that is differentiated into those with cultural, economic or social power; or elites defined on ethnic grounds. Finally, the *volonté générale* is equated with a general national outlook or sense, as first characterized by Jean-Jacques Rousseau. It is this frequently quoted, rather general definition that I would argue must be supplemented with several crucial considerations (Wodak 2015: 20–2, 25–33):

Nationalism, nativist nationalism, or anti-pluralism: Far-right populist parties identify a seemingly homogenous ethnos, a *populum* (community, *Volk*), which is arbitrarily defined, often in nativist (blood-related) terms. Such parties value the homeland or Heimat (or heartland, if an internal distinction within the nation is located), which requires protection from dangerous interlopers. In this way, threat scenarios are constructed, with the homeland, or the 'we', threatened by 'others': strangers within society and/or from outside, whether migrants, refugees, Turks, Jews, Roma, bankers, Muslims, and so on.

Anti-elitism: Such parties share an anti-intellectual attitude—an 'arrogance of ignorance', for example (Wodak 2015)—which at least in Europe is associated with strong EU-scepticism. According to these parties, democracy should essentially be reduced to the majoritarian principle, meaning the rule of an (arbitrarily defined) people. In this construction, there is no need for experts, who merely confuse the issues.

Authoritarianism or hierarchical leadership: A saviour is worshipped, alternating between the roles of Robin Hood (protecting the welfare state, taking back from the rich to give to the poor) and strict father, the repository of paternalistic values (Lakoff 2004). Such charismatic leaders require a hierarchically structured party and authoritarian structures to guarantee what they see as law and order and security.

Historical mythologizing: Far-right populist parties represent traditional, conservative values (for example, traditional gender roles and family values), and insist on preserving the status quo or a return to the good old days. The aim of protecting the homeland also builds upon a shared narrative of the past, in which 'we' are cast either as heroes or as victims of evil (the targets of a conspiracy, or of the enemies of the fatherland, etc.). This revisionism transforms past suffering or defeat into stories of the people's success, or into stories of betrayal and treachery by others. Social care, in the resulting welfare chauvinism, should only be extended to so-called true members of the (ethnic) community.

Although not all far-right populist parties endorse the above characteristics, when realized in specific combinations they are nevertheless the typical ideologemes of the far right. In cases where such parties advocate sociopolitical change, this entails moving away from an allegedly highly dangerous path that would lead straight to an apocalyptic end.

Illiberal democracy

The distinction between liberal or constitutional democracies and illiberal democracies is nothing new; in fact, the term 'illiberal democracy' first gained currency in the work of the political scientist Fareed Zakaria in 1997. He maintains that, while 'democracy is flourishing, constitutional liberalism is not' (Zakaria 1997: 23). Furthermore, Zakaria argues that 'in countries not grounded in constitutional liberalism, the rise of democracy brings with it hyper-nationalism and war-mongering' (1997: 38). Hence, a salient criterion for the existence of a liberal democracy is an expansive constitutionalism, viewed as a system of checks and balances designed to protect state and society from abuses of power. According to Zakaria (1997: 23–4), illiberal democracies have increased around the world since the end of the Cold War, and are dramatically limiting the freedoms of the people they represent—civil liberties of speech, religion, and so on. Despite its political science heft, however, the term 'illiberal democracy' remains a contested concept (for example, Krastev 2006).

In 2014, the Hungarian Prime Minster Victor Orbán, leader of the far-right or national-conservative party Fidesz, appropriated the term 'illiberal democracy'. In this way, it followed the interwar term totalitarianism, which was coined by the Catholic politician Luigi Sturzo as a descriptor of Italian Fascism, but was soon adopted by Mussolini as a positive attribute of PNF rule in the 1920s. Likewise, 'illiberal democracy' has entered everyday discourse, both as a political characterization *and* as a model to be emulated, while remaining a political system to be vehemently rejected by others. In a speech of 30 July 2014, Orbán maintained that

> the new state that we are constructing in Hungary is an illiberal state, a non-liberal state. It does not reject the fundamental principles of liberalism such as freedom, and I could list a few more, but it does not make this ideology the central element of state organization, but instead includes a different, special, national approach. (Orbán 2014)

Here, Orbán characterized his form of illiberal democracy as rejecting the toleration of minorities, while supporting existing forms of democratic majoritarianism. He reiterated his beliefs in nationalism (Hungary's uniqueness vis-à-vis the EU and the other EU member states) and ethnic separatism. The Hungarian Constitution, which was revised and accepted by the Hungarian Parliament on 25 April 2011, reflects Fidesz's illiberal values: curtailing freedom of the press, reforming the electoral system in unfair ways, and curbing checks and balances by undermining the independence of the judiciary (Uitz 2015: 285–8; Grabbe & Lehner 2017a).

Poland is seeing similar developments to the Hungarian trajectory under the national-conservative government of the PiS Party and its leader Jarosław Kaczyński (Grabbe & Lehner 2017b; Kerski 2018). Indeed, Sutowski (2018: 17–18) labels the new Polish way as 'neo-authoritarianism'.

Authoritarianism and neo-authoritarianism

Mudde draws upon the Frankfurt School in critiquing ideological constructions, even though he subscribes to a more socio-psychological tradition. He thus defines authoritarianism as 'a general disposition to glorify, to be subservient to and remain uncritical toward authoritative figures of the ingroup and to take an attitude of punishing outgroup figures in the name of some moral authority' (2007: 22) (see, for example, Adorno et al. 1969: 228). Yet in defending this view, Mudde also points to Juan Linz's influential work, which defined authoritarianism as a form of government featuring strong central power and limited individual freedoms. For Linz (1973), four dimensions represent key, interlocking elements for an authoritarian government: limited political pluralism, entailing constraints on political parties, interest groups, and NGOs. Second, legitimacy is hugely dependent upon emotions, and upon emotive identification with the regime. A third feature is suppression of the opposition, which can take either parliamentary or extra-legal forms, whether by violence or censorship. Finally, Linz highlights a vague and non-transparent definition of the powers of the executive.[5] Obviously, these criteria overlap with more recent approaches to illiberal democracy mentioned above. Furthermore, Levitsky and Way (2002) point to another relevant concept—competitive authoritarianism—whereby

> elections are regularly held and are generally free of massive fraud, but nevertheless incumbents routinely abuse state resources, deny the opposition adequate media coverage, harass opposition candidates and their supporters, and in some cases, manipulate electoral results. Journalists, opposition politicians, and other government critics may be spied on, threatened, harassed, or arrested. Members of the opposition may be jailed, exiled, or—less frequently—even assaulted or murdered. Regimes characterized by such abuses cannot be called democratic. (2002: 60)

Competitive authoritarianism is therefore qualitatively different to so-called 'façade' electoral regimes (also labelled pseudo-democracies, virtual democracies, or electoral authoritarian democracies); that is, regimes in which electoral institutions exist but provide for no meaningful competition for power (such as Egypt, Singapore, and Uzbekistan in the 1990s). Such regimes are generally classified as authoritarian. Under the rule of Vladimir Putin, Russia, on the other hand, is in keeping with the category of competitive authoritarianism. That said, Krastev (2006) prefers the label of 'managed democracy' for contemporary Russia (and challenges Zakaria's approach to illiberal democracies) (for Russia since 1989, see Nisnevich & Ryabov 2017). A managed democracy, Krastev argues, functions like an autocracy, but remains on paper a democratic government. Thus, governments are legitimized by elections, but elections exert no influence upon the state's policies and agenda.

As even this pared-down list makes clear, we are confronted with an abundance of labels for, and definitions of, illiberal democracy, authoritarianism, and populism. These sometimes overlap, sometimes complement one another, and sometimes exclude one another. Therefore, context-dependent, detailed, interdisciplinary research is of utmost importance in understanding specific sociopolitical developments, discursive shifts, and structural changes (for example, Uitz 2015) both across Europe and in national polities beyond.

The micropolitics of the far right

By using populist frames, far-right politicians seek to cultivate an image of themselves as the true representatives of the people, in direct contrast to the untrustworthy political classes. In these parties' efforts to substantiate their claims, their discourse becomes

> magically non-falsifiable, as only factual statements could be verified or falsified. Right-wing populist communication style creates its own 'genre' as a mix of scandal, provocation, transgression, and passion. (Sauer et al. 2018: 28)

In other words, far-right populists strategically cultivate their beliefs, threat scenarios, and nationalistic–nativist identities. In this section, I turn to the micropolitics of far-right political parties, and how they produce and reproduce their ideologies and exclusionary politics in everyday politics, in the media, when campaigning, on posters, in slogans and in speeches, while employing the framework of the discourse-historical approach (see Wodak 2015). Below, several widely used discursive strategies and performative elements of the far right are analysed, which are characteristic of genres such as party programmes, political speeches, campaign rallies and events, posters and slogans, websites, social media posts and tweets, television and radio interviews, and of course public debates.

The people, the elites, and the others

Far-right political rhetoric relies upon specific narratives of threat and betrayal, accusing the Establishment of having pursued their own interests, and having ignored the obvious anxieties of 'the people'. In manifold ways, this narrative arbitrarily constructs two opposing groups via texts and images. Such a Manichean opposition portrays these two groups as vehemently opposed to each other and forming two epistemic communities, one defined as powerless, the other as powerful; one described as good, innocent and hard-working, the other as bad, corrupt, criminal, lazy and unjustly privileged. For far-right populists, immigration constitutes a threat to the constructed identity of the people and their traditional values. This traducing of 'the other' varies according to nationally specific conditions. In Hungary, for example, the targets include Roma and Jewish minorities, while Trump and his allies focus upon Muslims, Mexicans, and other immigrants from Latin America.

Mechanisms of scapegoating constitute an important feature of such parties' discourse. Sometimes, the scapegoats are ethnic or religious minorities, sometimes capitalists, socialists, career women, NGOs, the European Union (EU), the United Nations (UN), the US or left-wingers, the governing parties, the elite, the media, and more. 'They' are foreigners, defined by race, religion, language or even politics. They are elites, not only within any given country but also on the European stage ('Brussels') or at the global level ('financial capital'). Important divides within society, such as class, caste, religion, and gender, may be neglected in focusing on such others when expedient, viewed through the prism of elitist conspiracy. These and other ad hominem arguments and their attendant fallacies include the straw-man fallacy (advancing a false opposing view) or the hasty generalization fallacy (an intentionally deceptive argument). Politicians tend to deny or justify even obvious failures (euphemistically labelled mistakes) and quickly find somebody else to blame; when pressured, ambiguous, evasive, and insincere apologies may be made, or no apologies offered at all (Wodak 2017; 2018b) (for us and them in the populist mindset, see Figure 3.1).

Bad manners (Moffitt 2017: 61–3; Montgomery 2017: 632; Wodak 2017: 559–60) also play an outsized role, as do deliberate rudeness, lies, insults, destructive (eristic) argumentation, and intentional breaches of taboos on racist, sexist, homophobic, or antisemitic remarks. Norms of political correctness are not merely violated, but explicitly challenged as restricting free speech, thus offering identification with an anti-elitist politics (Scheff 2000). The breaching of norms facilitates what I have called *calculated ambivalence* (Engel & Wodak 2013). The latter is understood as a phenomenon whereby one utterance carries at least two more-or-less contradictory meanings, oriented towards at least two different audiences. This not only increases the overall audience, but also enables the speaker or writer to deny responsibility: after all, 'it wasn't meant that way'. The former leader of the Austrian Freedom Party, Jörg Haider, employed this strategy cleverly on numerous occasions, for example, when referring to the allegedly powerful Jewish lobbies in New York with the term 'East Coast'. It was obvious who he was pointing to; however, when confronted, he denied having said anything antisemitic and maintained that 'East Coast was simply a geographic notion' (Pelinka & Wodak 2002).

Some far-right populist parties have become more explicitly racist (anti-Muslim, antisemitic, and anti-Zionist). These parties tend to highlight alleged violence by immigrants, while also vindicating violence against immigrants (for example the AfD). They deny the discrimination to which immigrants are subjected, but simultaneously maintain that the native population is subjugated (Fennema 2004). Such victim blaming may end up by denying the social and historical reality altogether, as the history of Holocaust denial shows (Wodak 2015). Moreover, Fennema (2004: 9) argues that if a party characterizes immigrants as criminals or targets asylum seekers as their one and only agenda, then this party may be labelled racist, even if their public statements—if regarded in isolation—are not explicitly racist. In distinguishing them from the extreme right and even neo-Nazi groups

DIVIDING THE WORLD

Decent, honest, good industrious, dutiful, charismatic, honourable, noble, brave trustworthy, incorruptible		Amoral, deceitful, lazy without conscience, evil, bad, cowardly, criminal

The good The true The upright The victims	**WE**	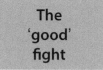 **The 'good' fight**	**The OTHERS**	The bad The fake The liars The perps

'The true people'. represented by the populists

'The others' are a threat to us! We must fear the 'others'! We have the right to defend ourselves against 'the others'

Those up there
The elites, politicians, upper classes, the 'east coast', fake media

Those out there
Asylum seekers, economic refugees, 'welfare tourists'

Those down there
'Spongers', 'parasites', the work-shy

Figure 3.1. Conceptual map of the far-right mindset.

(such as Golden Dawn, Nationaldemokratische Partei Deutschlands, the British National Party, or Jobbik), Fennema (2004: 15) concludes that far-right populist parties conscientiously screen front-stage activities (public speeches, TV appearances, and so forth), while explicitly racist activities (talk, texts, and images for party members only) take place backstage, usually hidden from public view (for example, Richardson 2018; Rheindorf & Wodak 2019).

Conspiracy theories

Constructing conspiracy theories necessitates unreal scenarios whereby some perpetrators (lobbies, parties, bankers and the 'other') allegedly pull the strings; their actions are frequently exaggerated or simply invented. Lies and rumours are spread which denounce, trivialize and demonize others. Rheindorf (2019) maintains that while 'Donald Trump may be credited with popularizing the term "fake news" … he was certainly not the first populist to pursue it.' Due to their globalized reach, online platforms and social media have been instrumental in circulating conspiracy theories, for such networks are predicated upon the kind of unmediated immediacy between populist actors and 'the people' (Moffitt 2017: 88–94; Fuchs 2018). Information does not seem to require mediatization via traditional media and professional journalists anymore. Moreover, as Krzyżanowski and Ledin (2017) argue, the 'antagonistic sphere' and lack of accountability of the Internet supports an uncivil society of conspiracism, incitement, or abuse, lending them to populism's polarization of politics and society.

Conspiracy theories also draw on the traditional antisemitic world-conspiracy stereotypes which characterized Nazi and fascist ideologies before 1945. For example, Hungarian Prime Minister Victor Orbán published a list of 200 so-called 'Soros mercenaries' who are trying to help refugees in Hungary (Deutsche Welle 2018), including scholars, journalists, intellectuals, and NGOs that allegedly supported the Jewish Hungarian-American philanthropist. Indeed, Soros has been demonized using all the traditional antisemitic tropes, and subsequently in all four Visegrad countries (Czechia, Slovakia, Hungary, and Poland) and even further afield, in order to shift the blame for the complexities of the refugee movement and immigration onto a Jewish *Feindbild*, a notorious coping strategy that I have labelled the *Iudeus ex machina* strategy (Wodak 2015; 2018c).

To quote one of many examples from the Italian Interior Minister and head of the radical, extreme right LEGA, Matteo Salvini: on 13 June 2018 he described NGO rescue boats as tools of a sinister conspiracy (launched by Soros) against the Italian people (for example, ESI 2018: 5):

> It is not possible that some private NGOs paid by nobody knows whom decide the speed and times of immigration. I love every kind of generosity and voluntarism, I am a blood and organs donor myself, but when I read that behind certain initiatives there is the Open Society Foundation of George Soros, I start having doubts about how spontaneous this kind of generosity is. (Italian Senate 2018)

Salvini, who excels in demonizing ethnic and religious minorities, then stated that Italians were people of love and compassion: 'in terms of generosity, kindness, and solidarity Italians have nothing to learn from anyone else.' As both an Italian and a father, moreover, he was 'sick and tired of children dying in the Mediterranean because somebody is deceiving them.' He then promised, to a standing ovation:

My aim is to save lives and to make sure that these children grow up in the best possible manner, without having to flee their villages and cities to get into rubber dinghies, which human traffickers let depart already half deflated, knowing that somebody will come and save these unfortunates. (Italian Senate 2018)

On this point, recent research has shown that far-right populists systematically identify looming crises that threaten the people (Rheindorf & Wodak 2018; 2019; Mazzoleni 2008; Triandafyllidou et al. 2009). Conspiracy theories lend themselves to these apocalyptic scenarios, particularly regarding a continuous state of siege of the homeland (Müller 2016: 43). Ultimately, such dark prophecies advocate strong leadership as a method for overcoming the supposed crises, while creating hope and promising change (Wodak 2015). In this way, they reconfigure the political agenda as simple binary choices (Müller 2016).

Charisma, leadership, and mediatization

The form of the performance is only one, albeit important, part of the far-right populist habitus. In such rhetoric, several vital ingredients are combined: the specific topics addressed; specific ideologies, which constitute both utterances and performances; strategies of calculated ambivalence and provocation, which are used to either create or deescalate intentionally provoked scandals; and a continuous campaigning style, providing for a wider antagonistic habitus, which does not comply with the conventional rules of negotiation and compromise (Diehl 2017; Kienpointner 2009). Taken together, these elements of anti-politics constitute the deliberate breaking of taboos, thus providing identification and de-stigmatization, fallacies, eristic (destructive) arguments, conspiracy theories (and, related to them, continuous victimhood), and the rejection of dialogue, politeness, and conversational maxims with which to construct an alternative discourse-world.

In this way, far-right party leaders often instrumentalize the media, attempting to come across as genuine and forthright. Such authenticity presupposes that they represent, know, and understand how their 'normal and true' fellow nationals feel. This implies that they are part of the in-group, neither elitist nor intellectual but firmly rooted in common-sense opinions and beliefs. They visit the same pubs as everyone else; they travel to similar places, drive similar cars; have similar problems in their family lives, and, above all; speak the same language. Simultaneously, they are also constructed as being tribunes for ordinary people, having the necessary courage to say what the woman or man in the street thinks but dares not say: they dare to oppose the powerful in direct and explicit language, circumventing the rules of political correctness and standards of decency (Wodak 2015: 132).

Euphemisms are frequently used in media reporting, often with the effect of making restrictive new migration policies seem acceptable. To take a recent example, at a meeting of EU heads of state in Brussels on 28 June 2018, the Austrian Chancellor, Sebastian Kurz, and his allies Orbán and Salvini, launched new linguistic terms such as 'regional disembarkation platforms' (rather than 'camps') for non-European refugees. Moreover, facts about the plight of refugees were challenged and expert opinions neglected. For example, on 22 June 2018, in an interview with the German weekly, *Die Zeit*, the editor-in-chief Giovanni Di Lorenzo asked Kurz what he felt when confronted with images of children who had been separated from their parents at the US–Mexico border (Di Lorenzo 2018). Kurz suggested that these accounts may have been 'fake news': 'I don't want to speculate, but I have devoted myself a lot to migration. I know that frequently the mistake is being made, that something is represented differently than it is.'[6] As Hannah Arendt (1971) asserted long ago, politicians can transmogrify facts into opinions that one can then oppose—quite shamelessly—with alternative viewpoints. In this way, she argues, scholarly and factual evidence can be negated (1971: 55).

In recent decades the political stage has obviously moved to television, social media, YouTube and similar platforms, a phenomenon termed the mediatization of politics, or even Berlusconization (Forchtner et al. 2013). This development may be one reason why far-right populism has entered mainstream politics, because many far-right populist parties have been at the forefront in creating their own Facebook pages, homepages, and YouTube and TV channels (Wodak 2015: 10–12, 134 ff.). It may also relate to how the media chooses to cover scandals, for sensationalist angles are likely to receive greater coverage, which often plays directly into the hands of populists (Deiwiks 2009; Greven 2016).

Media-savvy politicians with political charisma should thus be linked to the audience's recognition of the 'right' set of social or cultural capital (habitus), situated within the 'right' context. Charisma is invariably socially constructed and publicly recognized (Wodak 2015: 131–4). Eatwell conceptualizes charisma with four leadership traits, all of which have to be fulfilled by the politician in question:

> Charismatic leaders have a mission, posing as saviors of the people.
> Charismatic leaders portray themselves as ordinary men merely obeying the wishes of the people, thus also as having a symbiotic relationship with the people whom they represent.
> Charismatic leaders target and indeed demonize enemies.
> Charismatic personalities have great personal presence, which is frequently described as 'magnetism'. (Eatwell 2007: 6–11)

Individual studies on far-right ideologies have consistently described the persona and rhetoric of specific leaders as the 'Le Pen effect' (Christofferson 2003), the 'Haider phenomenon' (Wodak & Pelinka 2002) or 'Trumpism' (Fuchs 2018; Moffit 2017: 6), the latter being additionally linked to the celebrity image that some far-right populists have drawn upon.

Despite its obvious mendacity, as in the case of Trump's many thousands of lies as the US president, this frequently resonates as 'authentic' in the eyes of ardent followers, thus providing a means for positive identification as well as de-stigmatization (Wodak 2015: 126). As Lamont (2018: 422) has poignantly illustrated by analysing 73 of Trump's electoral speeches, Trump not only systematically appealed to white working-class voters, he also repeatedly points to globalization *tout court* in order to explain economic problems. Moreover, he provided a scapegoat ('illegal immigrants'), and raised workers' status and dignity by strategically addressing the recognition gap: by, for example, emphasizing their salient roles as protectors and providers for women and children (Lamont 2018: 423).

By means of constant provocation, attention is drawn to the respective leader and their political agenda—what I describe as a right-wing populist *perpetuum mobile* (Wodak 2013a; 2013b) (see Figure 2). This dynamic suggests that right-wing populist parties strategically manage their media debates. In response, other parties and politicians are forced to continuously react to an endless parade of freshly staged scandals. Few opportunities remain for the presentation of other frames, values, or counterarguments. In this way, far-right populist parties often dominate media and public debates through inflammatory language. Importantly, the dissemination of discriminatory rhetoric and fake news is continuously reproduced. As we have seen, due to their own information industry and the so-called message control, far-right populist parties circumvent the control through professional investigative journalism—they construct their own information, media and discourse worlds and neglect or downplay official channels (Horaczek & Wiese 2018).

- A scandal is first denied.
- Once evidence is produced, the scandal is redefined and equated with different phenomena.
- The provocateurs then claim the right of free speech for themselves ('Why can one not utter critique?' 'One must be permitted to criticize Turks, Roma, Muslims, Jews—!' or 'We dare to say what everybody thinks').
- Such utterances trigger another debate—not related to the original scandal—about freedom of speech and levels of political correctness.
- Simultaneously, victimhood is claimed by the original provocateur, while the event is exaggerated.
- This leads to conspiracy theorizing—somebody must be 'pulling the strings' against the original producer of the scandal—and scapegoats (for example, Muslims, Jews, Turks, Roma or foreigners) are quickly discovered.
- Once an accused member of the targeted minority finally receives a chance to present substantial counter-evidence.
- Finally, a quasi-apology may follow if a 'misunderstanding' has occurred, and the entire process starts all over again. Or, in the post-shame era, a new scandal might be launched without any preceding apology.

Figure 3.2. The right-wing populist *perpetuum mobile*.

Figure 3.3. Facebook post by Strache, 13 February 2018
(www.facebook.com/HCStrache, accessed July 12017).

As part of a wider project of illiberalism, the Hungarian, Polish, and more recently Austrian governments have launched programmes to 'reform' the media—a euphemism for continuous attacks on established journalists and moderators. The attacks on the media by the Austrian Freedom Party (FPÖ) exemplify this (see Figure 3.3), in this case using the rhetorical strategy of calculated ambivalence on social media. This strategy conveys distinct messages to multiple audiences (for example, the party's extreme-right base backstage and the public front stage) while maintaining plausible deniability through the cultivation of ambiguity (Engel & Wodak 2013). In this case, a meme posted by H. C. Strache, the Austrian Vice-Chancellor, was headed with the label 'Satire!' alongside an emoticon smiley (see Wodak & Rheindorf 2019). The image showed the internationally renowned journalist and moderator, Armin Wolf, host of the main news programme for the Austrian public broadcaster the ORF. In the background to the right, the text reads: 'There is a place where lies become news. That is the ORF. The best of Fake News, lies, and propaganda, pseudo-culture and involuntary fees. Regional and international. On television, radio, and the Facebook profile of Armin Wolf.'

In response, Armin Wolf and the ORF sued Strache for libel and won. Strache had to apologize publicly and pay €10,000 to Armin Wolf, who donated the money to the Dokumentationsarchiv des Österreichischen Widerstandes (DÖW), an NGO which documents neo-Nazi and extreme-right activities. Meanwhile, the FPÖ has continued to publicly campaign for the downsizing or privatization of the ORF, while backchannel pressure on editors and journalists has increased since the FPÖ joined the ruling coalition in 2017 (Klenk 2018).

Simultaneously, the Austrian government has implemented their own version of 'message control' (John & Mittelstaedt 2018). Each week, a specific topic is launched in a press conference and elaborated on for one week, until being replaced with a new agenda seven days later. For example, while discontent and strikes were contemplated against a new law allowing for 12-hour working days and 60-hour working weeks if employees voluntarily comply with their employer's request (implemented with 1 September 2018), the government launched various news items about a ban of headscarves for Muslim girls in kindergarten and pre-school. In this way, the government pleased their electorate with anti-Muslim and anti-immigration agendas, while being aware that the core electorate of the FPÖ would be enraged by such new labour laws, which were upsetting the post-war consensus of the social welfare state. The media have thus been kept busy debating 'the headscarf', while being distracted from other relevant news stories. Moreover, access to information is being severely restricted in Austria and in illiberal democracies in Europe: government employees have been frequently forbidden to speak with the press. Such rules come close to the managed democracies and their press policies defined above.[7]

Shameless normalization—
Paving the way to illiberalism

In illiberal democracies, most breaches of the constitutional order, such as freedom of opinion, assembly, the press, and the independence of the legal system (especially in Poland and Hungary) are not announced explicitly. Instead, they are secured in small and seemingly unimportant steps, such as intervening in the Supreme Court in Poland, where the replacement of lifetime judges was implemented through a bland paragraph about retirement age—just as the Polish Constitution sets a fixed term for Supreme Court Judges.[8] In this case, some of the Supreme Court judges resisted, leading to this incident making international headlines (ORF 2016). However, after a ruling of the European Court of Justice, which ordered Poland to suspend the measures and reinstate those judges who had lost their jobs, PiS proposed a legislative amendment on 21 November 2018, backtracking on controversial reforms it had made to lower the retirement age of Supreme Court judges. In this case, international critique and massive resistance by civil society was successful in opposing blatantly undemocratic measures (Wax 2018).

As Grabbe and Lehner (2017b: 3) argue, undemocratic changes imply 'mind-closing narratives', which are obviously 'gaining force as formerly liberal politicians run after populists'. Indeed, Uitz (2015: 296) concludes that the far-right governments in Poland and Hungary are driven 'by the urge to establish exceptions, in the spirit of constitutional parochialism'. In other words, the context-dependent discursive strategies presented in this chapter, as well as the rejection of dialogue and subsequent denial or silence, dominate official communication, and thus result in ever more nationalism and even ethno-national nativism. Such a dynamic corresponds to what I have labelled shameless normalization (Wodak 2018a). The post-war European consensus has increasingly become obsolete, while the limits of the unsayable have shifted. The unsayable has frequently become accepted, normalized: even formal public apologies are not needed any more. In short, anything goes.

This can be seen not only in Central Eastern European countries but also in contemporary Austria, the UK, the Netherlands, Italy, and, beyond Europe, in Brazil, India, and the Philippines. The sidestepping of shared values and the yearning for national exceptionalism directly challenges the post-war European project, so passionately appealed to by Macron in his Karl's Prize speech quoted above. However, the rejection of reasoned dialogue, agreed norms, and established conventions seems to render discussion impossible, further paving the way for illiberalism and neo-authoritarianism.

Claus Leggewie (2018: 4) poses the challenging, if rhetorical, question of whether one should 'even consider resistance as long as the Orbáns, Trumps and Erdogans are winning absolute majorities and can thus claim democratic legitimacy?' Unsurprisingly, the answer is 'yes' because, as Leggewie states, 'whoever does not object to the victors in effect consents to them', quite apart from the need for a new vision of Europe, a democratic alternative 'to citizens flirting with the right' (2018: 4). Michèle Lamont, the President of the American Sociological Association, proposes a detailed research programme to 'gain a better understanding of the factors that foster solidarity ... and that would help bridge the ideological "silos" (or "bubbles") that have come to define the US public sphere' (2018: 434–5). She emphasizes the necessity of investigating what brings people together, which she calls 'ordinary cosmopolitanism', that could combat anti-immigrant and anti-poor rhetoric. Such a counter-discourse would be able to bridge the recognition gap quite differently than that suggested by Trump's shameless demagogy. Obviously, such a counter-discourse would also be needed outside of the US, indeed globally.

Thus, new narratives, new public spaces, new communication and participation modes, and—most importantly—new policies are, in turn, urgently needed to protect the achievements of the Enlightenment and the practice of pluralistic liberal democracies in Europe. Meanwhile, the results of the imminent European elections on 26 May 2019 will provide more information about the short- and mid-term trajectories opted for by European citizens and their respective governments.

Notes

1   I am very grateful to the anonymous reviewers and to Matthew Feldman, Pieter Bevelander, and Markus Rheindorf who read and commented on this chapter in draft. I am also very grateful to the Institute of Human Sciences, Vienna (IWM) where I was a senior fellow for the academic year of 2018–19 and was able to work on this chapter and the entire volume in a wonderful and very supportive environment.

2   For each EU member state, see Polls of Polls 2018; Eurobarometer 2018a, 2018b; MEUZ 2018. The important political parties at the EU level are the European People's Party (EPP, 227 seats); Progressive Alliance of Socialists and Democrats (S&D, 190 seats); European Conservatives and Reformists (74 seats); Alliance of Liberals and Democrats (ALDE, 70 seats); European United Left/Nordic Left (GUE, 52 seats); European Greens/European Free Alliance (50 seats); Europe of Freedom and Direct Democracy (EFDD, 45 seats); Europe of Nations and Freedom (ENF, 39 seats); and Non-Attached (NI, 14 seats). The right-wing and left-wing parties together come to some 301 Conservative MEPs and 292 Left-wing/Green MEPs, while the far right currently has 84 seats and the Liberals 70.

3   For a range of interdisciplinary approaches and numerous studies of the rise of populism and East–West and North–South differences, see, for example, Finchelstein 2014; Krastev 2017; Lamont 2018; Mouffe 2018; Müller 2016; Salzborn 2018; Snyder 2018; Stavrakakis & Katsambekis 2014; Wodak 2015.

4   Such shameless behaviour could be seen in several TV debates during the presidential election campaign in Austria in 2016, employed by the far-right populist candidate (FPÖ), Norbert Hofer (for example, Wodak 2017). Mastropaolo (2000: 36) mentions similar patterns of scandalization, 'politicotainment' and the decay of democratic procedures in Italian politics in the 1990s.

5   Gasiorowski (2006: 110–11) also mentions the distinction between personal authoritarian regimes—characterized by arbitrary rule and authority exercised 'mainly through patronage networks and coercion rather than through institutions and formal rules' (for example, in postcolonial Africa)—and populist authoritarian regimes—'mobilizational regimes in which a strong, charismatic, manipulative leader rules through a coalition involving key lower-class groups' (for example, Argentina under Peron, Venezuela under Chavez and Maduro, etc.).

6   'Ich will da jetzt nicht mutmaßen, aber ich habe mich sehr viel mit Migration beschäftigt. Ich weiß, dass oft sehr schnell der Fehler gemacht wird, dass etwas anders dargestellt wird, als es ist.'

7   As noted by Uitz (2015) of Orbán's Hungary, parliamentary procedures are

frequently ignored. Discussion and consultations with experts, the opposition, and journalists seem to be out of the question in Kurz's Austria (see Wodak 2018a, 2018b, 2018d). Thus, it seems that the new Austrian People's Party (ÖVP)—in its streamlined, strategically planned trajectory to power (at least in the sense of leading the new government)—has either ignored or quietly accepted some non-democratic practices (pushed by the FPÖ) they had aligned themselves with, thus normalizing the previously unsayable and unacceptable.

8 I am very grateful to Jan Grzymski for alerting me to this case.

References

Adorno, T. W., E. Frenkel-Brunswick, D. Levinson & R. N. Sanford. (1969), *The authoritarian personality* (New York).

Arendt, H. (1971), *Wahrheit und Lüge in der Politik*. (Frankfurt).

Balcer, A. (2018), 'Law and justice but what about Europe?' Wise-Europa German–Polish European blog, wise-europa.eu/en/2018/07/09/law-and-justice-but-what-about-europe/.

Bertelsmann Stiftung (2016), 'Fear not values: Public opinion and populist vote in Europe', *Eupinions*, 2016. 3.

Brubaker, R. (2017), 'Why populism?' *Theory & Society*, doi.org/10.1007/s11186-017-9301-7.

de Cleen, B. (2017), 'Populism and nationalism', in C. Rovira Kaltwasser, P. Taggart, P. Ochoa Espejo & P. Ostiguy (eds.), *Handbook of Populism* (Oxford).

Christofferson, T. R. (2003), 'The French elections of 2002: The issue of insecurity and the Le Pen effect', *Acta Politica*, 38/2: 109–23.

Deiwiks, C. (2009), 'Populism', *Living Reviews in Democracy*: 1–9.

Diehl, P. (2017), 'Antipolitik und postmoderne Ringkampf-Unterhaltung', *APuZ*, 67/44–45: 25–30

Deutsche Welle (2018), 'Hungary's Viktor Orban targets critics with "Soros mercenaries" blacklist', www.dw.com/en/hungarys-viktor-orban-targets-critics-with-soros-mercenaries-blacklist/a-43381963.

Di Lorenzo, G. (2018), '"Achse" ist mein Normaler Sprachgebrauch', www.zeit.de/politik/ausland/2018-06/wien-sebastian-kurz-giovanni-di-lorenzo-live.

Eatwell, R. (2007), 'The concept and theory of charismatic leadership', in A. C. Pinto, R. Eatwell & U. L. Stein. (eds.), *Charisma and Fascism in Interwar Europe* (London).

Engel, J. & R. Wodak (2013), '"Calculated ambivalence" and Holocaust denial in Austria', in R. Wodak & J. E. Richardson (eds.), *Analysing fascist discourse: European fascism in talk and text* (London).

ESI (2018), 'European stability initiative', *ESI Newsletter* 7/2018.

Eurobarometer (2018a), europa.eu/cultural-heritage/news/eurobarometer–2018-results-have-been-published_EN.

— (2018b), 'Aktuelle Umfrage', www.europarl.europa.eu/news/de/pressroom/20180430IPR02826/eurobarometer–2018-aktuelle-umfrage-des-europaischen-parlaments.

Falkner, G. & G. Plattner (2018), 'EU Policies and Populist Radical Right Parties' Programmatic Claims: Foreign Policy, Anti-discrimination, and the Single Market', working paper, EIF, University of Vienna.

Fennema, M. (2004), 'Populist parties of the Right', ASSR Working paper 04/01 (Amsterdam School for Social Science Research).

Finchelstein, F. (2014), 'Returning populism to history', *Constellations*, 21/4: 467–82.

Forchtner, B., M. Krzyżanowski & R. Wodak (2013), 'Mediatisation, right-wing populism and political campaigning: The case of the Austrian Freedom Party (FPÖ)', in M. Ekström & A. Tolson (eds.), *Media Talk and Political Elections in Europe and America* (Basingstoke).

Freeden, M. (2008), 'Thinking politically and thinking about politics: Language, interpretation, and ideology', in D. Leopold & M. Stears (eds.), *Political Theory: Methods and Approaches* (Oxford).

Fuchs, C. (2018), *Digital demagogue: Authoritarian capitalism in the age of Trump and Twitter* (London).

Gasiorowski, M. (2006), 'The Political Regimes Project', in A. Inketes (ed.), *On measuring democracy* (New Brunswick).

Giuffrida, A. (2018), 'Gifts for Fascist Friends', *The Guardian*, www.theguardian.com/world/2018/dec/27/gifts-for-fascist-friends-mussolinis-calendar-comeback.

Grabbe, H. & S. Lehner (2017a), *Defending EU values in Poland and Hungary* (Brussels).

— — (2017b), *The closing of the European mind—And how to reopen it* (Brussels).

Greven, T. (2016), *The rise of right-wing populism in Europe and the United States* (Washington, DC).

Hahl, O., M. Kim & E. W. Zuckerman Sivan (2018), 'The authentic appeal of the lying demagogue: Proclaiming the deeper truth about political illegitimacy', *American Sociological Review*, 83/1: 1–33.

Horaczek, N. & S. Wiese (2018), *Informiert Euch: Wie du auf dem Laufenden bleibst ohne manipuliert zu werden* (Vienna).

Italian Senate (2018), 'Informativa del Ministro dell'interno sulla vicenda della nave Aquarius e conseguente discussione', 13 June.

John, G. & K. Mittelstaedt (2018), *Wie Türkis-Blau Widersprüche wegredet*, derstandard.at/2000075143822/Wie-Tuerkis-Blau-Widersprueche-wegredet.

Kerski, B. (2018), 'Was uns trennt, verbindet uns', *APuZ*, 68/10–11: 4–8.

Kienpointner, M. (2009), 'Plausible and fallacious strategies to silence one's opponent', in F. van Eemeren (ed.), *Examining argumentation in context: Fifteen studies on strategic manoeuvring* (Amsterdam).

Klenk, F. (2018), *Ein Knickserl vor der FPÖ*, www.zeit.de/kultur/2018–06/orf-oesterreich-rundfunk-fpoe-journalisten-entlassung-pressefreiheit (accessed 28 June 2018).

Krastev, I. (2006), 'Democracy's "Doubles"', *Journal of Democracy*, 17/2: 52–62.

— (2017), *Europadämmerung: Ein Essay* (Frankfurt).

Kriesi, H. & T. S. Pappas (eds.) (2015), *European populism in the shadow of the great recession* (Colchester).

Krzyżanowski, M. & P. Ledin (2017), 'Uncivility on the web: Populism in/and the borderline discourses of exclusion', in special issue, *Journal of Language and Politics*, 16/4: 566–81.

Lakoff, G. (2004), *Don't think of an elephant: Know your values and frame the debate* (White River Junction, VT).

Lamont, M. (2018), 'Addressing recognition gaps: Destigmatization and the reduction of inequality', *American Sociological Review*, 83/3: 419–44.

Leggewie, C. (2018), 'Resist, don't reminisce', *Eurozine*, www.eurozine.com/resist-dont-reminisce/.

Levitsky, S. & S. Way (2002), 'The Rise of Competitive Authoritarianism', *Journal of Democracy*, 13/2: 51–65.

Linz, J. (1973). 'An authoritarian regime: The case of Spain', in R. A. Dahl (ed.), *Regimes and Oppositions* (New Haven) (first pub. 1964).

Macron, E. (2018), Speech at Karls-Prize Ceremony, de.ambafrance.org/Festakt-zur-Verleihung-des-Internationalen-Karlspreises–2018-an-Emmanuel-Macron.

Mastropaolo, A. (2000), *Antipolitica: All'origine della crisi italiana* (Naples).

Mazzoleni, G. (2008), 'Populism and the media', in D. Albertazzi & D. McDonnell (eds.), *Twenty-First Century Populism* (London).

MEUZ (2018), *Model European Union*, meuz.eu/news/political-groups-european-parliament/.

Moffitt, B. (2017), *The global rise of populism: Performance, political style, and representation* (Stanford).

Montgomery, M. (2017), 'Post-truth politics? Authenticity, populism and the electoral discourses of Donald Trump', *Journal of Language and Politics*, 16/4: 619–639.

Mouffe, C. (2018), *Für einen linken Populismus* (Frankfurt).

Mudde, C. (2007), *The Populist Radical Right Parties in Europe* (Cambridge).

— & C. R. Kaltwasser (2017), *Populism* (Oxford).

Müller, J.-W. (2016), *What is populism?* (Philadelphia).

Nisnevich, Y. A. & A. V. Ryabov (2017), 'Modern authoritarianism and political ideology', *Basic Research Program Working Papers*, WP 44:PS.

Orbán, V. (2014), Speech at Hungarian Youth Camp. hungarianspectrum. org/2014/07/31/viktor-Orbáns-speech-at-the-xxv-balvanyos-free-summer-university-and-youth-camp-july–26–2014-baile-tusnad-tusnadfurdo/.

— (2018), *Victor Orbán: Osteuropas Anti-Macron?* www.dw.com/de/viktor-orb%C3%A1n-osteuropas-anti-macron/a–43789383.

ORF (2016), *Aufbegehren gegen Einschnitte*, orf.at/stories/2328900/2328903/.

Pajnik, M. & B. Sauer (eds.) (2018), Populism and the web: communicative practices of parties and movements in Europe (London).

Pelinka, A. (2018), 'Identity politics, populism and the far right', in R. Wodak & B. Forchtner (eds.), *The Routledge handbook of language and politics* (London).

Pelinka, A. & R. Wodak (eds.) (2002), *'Dreck am Stecken'. Politik der Ausgrenzung* (Vienna).

Pels, D. (2012), 'The new national individualism—Populism is here to stay', in E. Meijers (ed.), *Populism in Europe* (Linz).

Plešu, A. (2018), 'The anti-European tradition of Europe', *Eurozine*, www. eurozine.com/anti-european-tradition-europe/.

Poll of Polls (2019), *Wahlen zum Europäischen Parlament 2019*, de.pollofpolls. eu/EU.

Priester, K. (2007), *Populismus: Historische und aktuelle Erscheinungsformen* (Frankfurt).

Psaledakis, D. & A. MacDonald (2018), 'Polls suggest Far-Right to gain ground in 2019 EU vote' www.reuters.com/article/us-eu-election-polls/polls-suggest-far-right-to-gain-ground-in–2019-eu-vote-idUSKCN1LS16F.

Rheindorf, M. & R. Wodak (2018), 'Borders, fences and limits: Protecting Austria from refugees. Metadiscursive negotiation of meaning in the current refugee crisis', *Journal Immigrant & Refugee Studies*, 16/1.

Rheindorf, M. (2019, in press), 'Populism, rhetoric, discourse', in A. da Fina (ed.), *Handbook of discourse analysis* (Oxford).

— & R. Wodak (2019, in press), 'Austria First' revisited: A diachronic cross-sectional analysis of the gender and body politics of the extreme right', *Patterns of Prejudice*.

Richardson, J. E. (2018), 'Fascist Discourse', in J. Flowerdew & J.E. Richardson (eds.), *The Routledge handbook of critical discourse studies* (London).

Rydgren, J. (2017), 'The radical right: An introduction', in J. Rydgren (ed.), *The Oxford handbook of the radical right* (Oxford).

Salzborn, S. (2018), 'Right-wing populism as a strategy of the radical right', Center for the Analysis of the Radical Right, www.radicalrightanalysis. com/2018/05/21/right-wing-populism-as-a-strategy-of-the-radical-right/.

Sauer, B., A. Krasteva & A. Saarinen (2018), 'Post-democracy, party politics and right-wing populist communication', in M. Pajnik & B. Sauer (eds.), *Populism and the Web* (London).

Scheff, T. (2000), 'Shame and the social bond: a sociological theory', *Sociological Theory*, 18/1: 84–99.

Snyder, T. (2018), *The Road to Unfreedom* (New York).

Stavrakakis, Y. & G. Katsambekis (2014), 'Left-wing populism in the European periphery: The case of SYRIZA', *Journal of Political Ideologies*, 19/2: 119–42.

Standard Eurobarometer 2018/4. (eb_89_first_en.pdf)

Sutowski, M. (2018), '"Guter Wandel" zum "Neuen Autoritarismus"—und wie weiter?' *APuZ*, 68/10–11: 15–18.

Triandafyllidou, A., R. Wodak & M. Krzyżanowski (eds.) (2009), *The European public sphere and the media: Europe in crisis* (Basingstoke).

Uitz, R. (2015), 'Can you tell when an illiberal democracy is in the making? An appeal to comparative constitutional scholarship from Hungary', *I.Con*, 13/1: 279–300.

Waring, A. (ed.) (2018), *The New Authoritarianism, vol. I: A risk analysis of the US alt-right phenomenon* (New York).

Wax, E. (2018), 'Poland rows back on controversial Supreme Court law. The Law and Justice party will comply with an ECJ ruling', www.politico.eu/ article/poland-rows-back-on-controversial-supreme court-law/.

Wodak, R. & A. Pelinka (eds.) (2002), *The Haider phenomenon in Austria* (New Brunswick).

— (2013a), '"Anything goes!"—The Haiderization of Europe', in R. Wodak, M. KhosraviNik & B. Mral (eds.), *Right-Wing Populism in Europe: Politics and Discourse* (London).

— (2013b), 'The strategy of discursive provocation: A discourse-historical analysis of the FPÖ's discriminatory rhetoric', in Feldman, M. & P. Jackson (eds.), *Doublespeak: The Rhetoric of the Far Right Since 1945* (Stuttgart).

— (2015), *The politics of fear: What right-wing populist discourses mean* (London).

— (2017), 'The "Establishment", the "Élites", and the "People". Who's who?' *Journal of Language and Politics*, 16/4: 551–65.

— (2018a), 'Vom Rand in die Mitte—"Schamlose Normalisierung"', *Politische Vierteljahres Zeitschrift*, 75, doi: 10.1007/s11615-018-0079-7.

— (2018b), 'The revival of numbers and lists in radical right politics', *CARR: Center for the Analysis of the Radical Right*, www.radicalrightanalysis. com/2018/06/30/the-revival-of-numbers-and-lists-in-radical-right-politics/.

— (2018c), 'Antisemitism and the Radical Right', in J. Rydgren (ed.), *Handbook of the radical right* (Oxford).

— (2019), 'Entering the "Post-Shame era": The rise of illiberal democracy, populism and neo-authoritarianism in Europe: The case of the turquoise-blue government in Austria 2017/2018', special issue, *Global Discourse*, ed. R.

Foster & J. Grzymski, *The Limits of Europe*, doi.org/10.1332/20437891 9X15470487645420.

— & M. Rheindorf (2019, in press), 'The Austrian Freedom Party', in A. Waring (ed.), *The New Authoritarianism vol. II: A Risk Analysis of the Alt-Right Phenomenon* (New York).

Zakaria, F. (1997), 'The Rise of Illiberal Democracy', *Foreign Affairs*, 76/6: 22–43.

CHAPTER 4

Six theories and six strategies concerning right-wing populism

Floris Biskamp

In this chapter, I discuss six different theoretical perspectives on right-wing populism.[1] Each of them aims at a different level, offering different explanations and implying different strategies against right-wing populism.[2] Following a trajectory from the political through the psychological, the social, and the cultural back to the political and eventually to the economic, these six perspectives are (*i*) a model of democratic representation and its gaps; (*ii*) a theory of authoritarian resentment; (*iii*) an approach focusing on racializing power and hegemony; (*iv*) the hypothesis of a new cultural cleavage; (*v*) a theory of depoliticization and re-politicization; and (*vi*) a critical theory of democratic capitalism. Rather than discussing these perspectives in isolation, or deciding for one while discarding the others, I will demonstrate that each of them highlights not only specific aspects of right-wing populism, but also the blind spots and weaknesses of other perspectives.

In considering these perspectives, I will follow a minimal definition of right-wing populism, building on Cas Mudde's work. I consider political actors populist, if they pursue an ideology that constructs a moralized notion of 'the pure people' as opposed to 'the corrupt elite', demanding full sovereignty of 'the people'. Further, I consider populism to be right wing where this ideology is combined with nativism and authoritarianism. In these cases, the notion of 'the people' is defined as a biologically, ethnically, or culturally more-or-less homogeneous entity, distinguished not only from 'the elites' but also from 'the others' usually construed in a racializing fashion. Being authoritarian, right-wing populism also prioritizes 'security' and 'order' over individual liberties (Mudde 2017: 3–5; Mudde & Rovira Kaltwasser 2017: 1–20). Both its nativism and its authoritarianism make it a threat to democracy.

My considerations are limited in scope in two senses. First, I have the case of (mostly Western) European and North American societies in mind. Second, most of the counterstrategies discussed in this chapter presume that there is still a majority of political and social actors who are opposed to right-wing populism. Few of these counterstrategies could work in countries that have long been under the rule of right-wing populists, such as Hungary or Turkey, and only some are viable in countries such as Switzerland or Austria, where right-wing populism is a firmly established part of political and public life.

The gap in representation

One common political explanation for the rise of right-wing populism centres on a gap in political representation. According to liberal or 'realistic' theories of democracy, the political system works by aggregating and representing the interests of different social groups. Parties and candidates compete for the roles as representatives in regular elections following democratic procedures. Just like all contenders for public office, populists are voted for by particular groups for particular reasons. What differentiates them from other actors is the ideological discourse framing the representation; a discourse that creates an image of 'the people' pitted against 'the elite', with all politicians except for the populists in question being part of 'the elite' and the populists being the only true representatives of 'the people'. Mobilization built around such an ideology has the best chances for success, if there are significant parts of the population that do not feel represented by traditional parties, and that do not believe they have much political influence through the standard civil-societal channels—in other words, such groups are particularly susceptible to a mobilization strategy that addresses them as 'the people', abandoned by 'the elite'. Such gaps can open up because of changes on the demand side or on the supply side, or both. On the demand side, social structure, lifeworlds, and political attitudes can transform in such ways that pre-existing social groups change or new groups emerge. On the supply side, parties can change their position—sometimes due to internal dynamics, sometimes for strategic reasons to adapt to changing opportunity structures. Both processes—which are oftentimes interrelated—can have the effect of leaving social groups without ties to a certain party, feeling unrepresented in the current party system, and thus susceptible to populist mobilization. Such explanations have long been deployed to explain the successes of the radical right in general and of right-wing populist parties in particular (Mudde & Rovira Kaltwasser 2017: 80–4, 101; Arzheimer 2017; Kitschelt 2017; Mair 2009: 17; Bieling 2017: 562–3).

When it comes to current right-wing populist successes in North America and Western Europe, the most common explanation is that parties on the mainstream left and the mainstream right have both shifted into the liberal centre in order to adapt to a new opportunity structure created by transformations of the social structure. The two groups that are typically said to have lost representation in this process are white or majoritarian blue-collar workers abandoned by the mainstream left, and groups with strongly conservative values abandoned by the mainstream right (Koppetsch 2018: 387–8; Biskamp 2017: 92–3; Patzelt 2015; Eribon 2013). In the formerly socialist democracies of Central and Eastern Europe, the gap in representation cannot be described this way, since the traditional bonds between political parties and specific social groups known in the Western European countries do not exist there (Minkenberg 2017).

The counterstrategy: Close the gap

If the cause of right-wing populism is a gap in representation, one obvious counterstrategy is to close that gap. Political parties that are not right-wing populists would have to address the issues, interests, and grievances of the groups who do not feel represented, thereby denuding the right-wing populists of their support (for example, Patzelt 2015).

Yet, the feasibility and effectiveness of such strategy is questionable. The strategy might be plausible, were the mainstream parties to shift to the centre because of internal party dynamics—then they could simply reconsider their choice. However, if they were to do so for the strategic reason that gains in the centre are more important for electoral success than losses on the margins, and were these calculations to remain valid, then such a strategy would be less plausible. It might still weaken support for right-wing populists, but possibly at the cost of losing elections—a bargain few parties would willingly make.

More importantly, there are many cases in which the attempt of mainstream conservative parties to regain lost ground on the right failed spectacularly, and produced significant victories for right-wing populism—two of them very recent. Prior to Brexit, the Conservative Party adopted the strong Euroscepticism advocated by right-wing populist UKIP, promising a Brexit referendum in the event of a victory. The Tories did indeed win the ensuing general election; however, rather than stopping the dynamics of right-wing populism, they forced their own hand into launching a Brexit process. Adopting UKIP's issues did not stop the dynamic of right-wing populism, but rather granted it a political victory. However, as a party, UKIP then lost influence after the implementation of this strategy. While their share of the vote had risen from 3.1 per cent in 2010 to 12.6 per cent in 2015—when the Tories promised a Brexit referendum—it plummeted to 1.8 per cent in the post-Brexit snap election of 2017 (McGowan & Phinnemore 2017).

The Austrian parliamentary elections in 2017 provide even less evidence of success. The conservative ÖVP now running as List Sebastian Kurz—The New People's Party did their very best to mimic the position of the right-wing populist FPÖ, which had surged in the polls in between the elections. Notably, the conservatives pushed the issue of immigration, promising an uncompromising stance on the 'refugee crisis'. With this strategy, they did indeed improve their result from 24 per cent in 2013 to 31.5 per cent in 2017. However, the FPÖ did the same, going from 20.5 per cent to 26 per cent and becoming the second-strongest party. Even if one takes into account that the two right-wing parties BZÖ (3.5 per cent in 2013) and Team Stronach (5.7 per cent in 2013) did not run in 2017, this can hardly be considered a blow to right-wing populism. On the contrary, it must be noted that just as with Brexit, the very positions that make the FPÖ a right-wing populist party have been magnified, since they are now supported by the two strongest parties in parliament, who rule together in a coalition government (Wodak 2018). These cases suggest that the strategy of closing the gap on the right might transfer some votes from right-wing populists to conservatives, but when it comes to policy, it seems to foster the very same agendas that make right-wing populists right-wing populists. Such victories are pyrrhic at best.

This does not per se disqualify the approach of addressing the grievances and issues of groups who do not feel represented, and are susceptible to right-wing populist mobilization. Rather, it suggests that the model of democracy as a representation of social groups and their interests by political actors must be qualified in three ways. First, it must be acknowledged that social groups, interests, and grievances are not pre-politically given and then simply represented in politics. Rather, politics and political representation contribute to the formation of the very groups, interests, and grievances that are represented. If major parties address certain issues, these issues can gain traction. Second, one must differentiate between different ways of addressing the grievances of those who do not feel represented. Some ways will reinforce the distinction between 'the people' and 'the others' so central to the right-wing populist discourse, others will not. Third and last, one must distinguish between the various sorts of grievances. While some—the fear of social decline, say, or a perceived deficit in recognition—can be addressed and represented in a democratic way, others may spring from resentment or racism, making it impossible to represent them politically without undermining democracy (Biskamp 2017).

Authoritarian resentment

One approach to distinguishing grievances that are democratically representable from grievances that by themselves constitute a danger to democracy is the theory of authoritarianism. This theory was formulated in the 1930s and 1940s to explain the rise of fascism and Nazism, or more specifically to explain the fact that the masses in Germany and other European states acted in a way that seemed to contradict their very own rational (class) interest, as the theorists of authoritarianism saw it. Building on psychoanalytic theories, Erich Fromm (1994), Leo Löwenthal (1987), and Theodor W. Adorno et al. (1950) developed a theory of the authoritarian personality. This personality is defined by its aspiration to become an identical part of a strong collective under clear authoritarian leadership, typically connected to ideals of purity as well as traditional norms of gender and masculinity. Since such a pure collective is imaginary and does not have a correlate in social reality, it can only be defined by demarcation against others—by prejudice, in other words. The one collective is then identified with positive, desirable traits, while negative, undesirable traits are projected onto the others, who are seen as the cause for the problems the favoured collective is facing. The sheer presence or existence of these others is then perceived as a problem.

Approaches based on the theory of authoritarianism have long been used to address the radical right in general and right-wing populism in particular (Milbradt 2018; Arzheimer 2017: 279; Kitschelt 2017: 360–1). According to this approach, individuals with an authoritarian stance are likely to be susceptible to right-wing populist mobilization. The theory of authoritarianism also offers an explanation for the detrimental effects that the conservative parties' strategy of adopting right-wing populist issues often have: if authoritarianism means being bound by authority, it also means that the willingness to act upon one's resentment depends on whether or not this resentment is sanctioned by the authorities. Thus, established conservative parties which take up the positions of right-wing populists might convince some of the right-wing populist voters to vote conservative. However, at the same time it will legitimize and thereby foster authoritarian resentment.

There is evidence that authoritarian attitudes and the prejudices linked to it are disproportionately strong among the supporters of right-wing populism (for example, Brähler et al. 2016; MacWilliams 2016). Yet, its explanatory value when it comes to electoral behaviour has long been contested—the correlation between traditional scales of authoritarianism and support for right-wing parties is less than clear (Kitschelt 2017: 360–1).

There is a particular problem in trying to explain the recent rise of right-wing populism with the concept of authoritarianism: in Germany, several research projects regularly measure authoritarian attitudes among the population, and the results have remained broadly constant over the years (Heitmeyer 2012; Decker et al. 2016; Zick 2016).

No sharp upsurge corresponding to the recent electoral successes of the AfD has been registered. Since changes in one variable cannot be explained with a constant, the dynamics of right-wing populist successes cannot be explained with authoritarian attitudes. Still, the theory of authoritarianism can have some explanatory value. First, it can explain how right-wing populist mobilization works; in particular it can help tackle what Arlie Russell Hochschild (2016: 8–16) calls 'the great paradox', the fact that subjects can be mobilized for politics that apparently violate their own rational self-interest. This way, the concept of authoritarianism can be deployed to explain why changes in other variables (for example, social structure) are processed in a way that fosters right-wing populism. Second, the study of authoritarianism could be used to predict which parts of the population are the most likely to be mobilized by right-wing populism and estimate the mobilization potential.

But even given this limited role, making authoritarian attitudes among the population an independent, explanatory variable begs the question of what the causes of these attitudes might be. The classic authors referred to family relations to explain authoritarianism. However, it would be important to discuss which social constellations and transformations on a structural level foster or hinder the production of authoritarian personalities. Does post-Fordism produce more, less, or different kinds of authoritarianism than Fordism? What are the effects of a larger public sector and stronger welfare states, or of the transformation of family and gender relations, and so on? Kitschelt and others argue that there is a relation between type of occupation and support for right-wing populism (Kitschelt 2017; Kitschelt & Rehm 2014). Yet, in order to make the theory of authoritarianism count, more such research is required.

The counterstrategy: Selective representation, repression, and education

If one does not ask for therapeutic or educational measures but for political strategies in the narrower sense, the main takeaway from the theory of authoritarianism is the distinction between *rational* interests and grievances and *authoritarian* resentment (which, of course, can only be a heuristic and analytic distinction). If one assumes that any public legitimation of authoritarian positions will strengthen authoritarianism and undermine democracy, the strategy of closing the gap in representation must be qualified accordingly. Only those interests and grievances that have a rational core should be addressed emphatically and represented by democratic parties; authoritarian resentment should not. Ambiguous grievances should only be addressed in ways that does not legitimize and foster resentment. For example, if certain groups are afraid of losing jobs in the context of migration, this grievance should be addressed as an issue of job security rather than as a discourse about dangerous migrants taking away jobs. These qualifications do not imply that certain subjects or groups should not have political representation. No individual subject or group is defined by one interest or grievance alone, authoritarian or otherwise. Usually, all bearers of an authoritarian personality also have reasonable grievances. These should be emphatically addressed and represented; their authoritarianism should not. On the contrary, approaches based on authoritarianism suggest that public utterances of these resentments should be scandalized, just as processes of de-scandalization should be countered (Biskamp 2017).

Such a strategy is of course questionable from a democratic perspective. There might be good, rational grounds for the claim that certain authoritarian, anti-egalitarian 'interests' should not be represented. Yet, such a claim in itself runs counter to the very idea of representative democracy.

Racialization, hegemony, and marginalization

The perspective of authoritarianism is partial and overgeneralized if addressed in isolation. Authoritarian personalities can and do emerge in all social groups. Yet, since right-wing populism is defined by its nativist notion of 'the people' explicitly excluding certain 'others', it can mostly mobilize the authoritarian tendencies within certain groups—those groups framed as parts of 'the people'. The definitions of 'the people' and 'the others' made by right-wing populist actors, as well as the exclusions and inclusions implied by them, are contingent but not arbitrary. They attach to pre-existing discourses and distinctions. While regional populisms do exist and minority populisms are conceivable, right-wing populist actors in most cases align with hegemonic discourses defining a national majority as 'the people' and racialized minorities as 'the others'—usually this is the only kind of right-wing populist mobilization that promises electoral success on a national level. Therefore, right-wing populist mobilization should not be seen as a mobilization of authoritarian resentment in general, but rather as a mobilization of the authoritarian resentments of certain, typically majoritarian and/or hegemonic groups aligning with pre-existing hegemonic discourses. Thus, the analysis of right-wing populism should include the concepts of hegemony and racialization (Biskamp 2017: 96–8; Biskamp 2018).

Most important among these discourses are racializing discourses against ethnic and migrant minorities who are the main objects of right-wing populist othering.[3] The critical analysis of right-wing populism must take racializing discourses against these minorities into account—the pre-existing discourses to which populist mobilization attaches, as well as the populist discourses themselves (Biskamp 2018). All right-wing populist actors also have an agenda concerning gender and sexuality—in some cases one that is distinctively anti-egalitarian and anti-feminist, in others one championing 'moderate' forms of equality and emancipation, pitted against 'exaggerated' or 'radical' forms feminism and an anti-egalitarian Islam on the other (Mudde & Rovira Kaltwasser 2015; Lang 2017; Mayer et al. 2018). In both cases, their understanding of 'the people' is gendered as well as sexed and pitted against corresponding 'others'. Yet, when it comes to the exclusion of marginalized groups from 'the people', racializing discourses against minorities are crucial.

The counterstrategy: Empowerment

This also opens another perspective on the attempts of mainstream parties to engage right-wing populism by addressing the (authoritarian) grievances within the population. Just like the right-wing populist mobilization they seek to counter, these strategies routinely focus on the grievances of hegemonic and/or majority populations, ignoring and in effect exacerbating those of minorities. If one takes these dynamics into account, effective counterstrategies must include an additional differentiation: if the aim is to counter right-wing populism by addressing the grievances among groups who do not feel represented, one must not only reflect on the different kinds of grievances (authoritarian–rational), but also on the different groups whose grievances are addressed (hegemonic–marginalized, majority–minority). Of course, the counterstrategy cannot cater to authoritarian impulses among minorities in order to balance things out, yet the stigmatizing discourses reinforced by right-wing populism create additional, specific grievances among the affected groups. These grievances should also be addressed and represented by democratic actors. Moreover, if power differentials between a hegemonic majority construed as 'the people' and marginalized minorities stigmatized as 'the others' are among the factors that enable a right-wing populist mobilization, it is those power differentials that must be addressed. At that point, not only the destabilization of right-wing populist discourses, but also the empowerment of the racialized, ethnic, sexual, cultural, or religious minorities targeted by these discourses should be among the counterstrategies (Biskamp 2017, 2018).

A new cultural cleavage in politics

Just like theories of gaps in representation, cleavage theories have long been deployed to explain the successes of radical right-wing parties. The argument then goes that these parties mobilize along specific cleavages, offering them an advantage over mainstream parties. In recent years, various authors have argued that the emergence of one or more *new* cleavages is behind the recent successes of right-wing populism (Inglehart & Norris 2016; Bieling 2017: 563).

One formulation of this hypothesis has been advanced by cultural sociologist Andreas Reckwitz (2016). Reckwitz argues that the defining political conflict of our time is indeed a cultural clash, yet one that is entirely different from the one Samuel Huntington described. According to Reckwitz, the clash is not between distinct world civilizations, but rather between two distinct culturalization regimes present in most societies. Reckwitz dubs these two regimes 'hyperculture' and 'cultural essentialism'. The conflict between these culturalization regimes is not caused by the fact that they are 'culturally different', but that they are at odds about the very question of what culture is. In both regimes, culture is a valorization of social life, but the valorization takes very different forms. Hyperculture valorizes the diversity of individual lifestyles. Workplaces, living spaces, relationships, vacations, bodily practices, etc. are aestheticized and these aesthetic innovations are understood as a pursuit of the good life. Hypercultural lifestyles inter-relate in a peaceful competition of 'diversity', which is considered to be a political virtue. Hyperculture is individualistic and cosmopolitan, spreading within the networks of global cultural capitalism. Cultural essentialism, on the other hand, valorizes a community with a clear moral identity. Culture is deployed as a defence of the community by (re)inventing traditions, whether ethnic, national, or religious. Within cultural essentialism, culture is not understood as an individual life style in a diverse market, but as a community in conflict with other communities—and with hyperculture. It does not aim at innovation but at (imaginary) preservation. Reckwitz identifies this second cultur-alization regime with a variety of movements such as different (ethnic) nationalisms in different parts of the world, but also with religious movements such as Evangelicalism or Salafism (Reckwitz 2016: 2–7).

Viewed from this angle, right-wing populism aligns with and is part of the second, essentialist culturalization regime. The cause of its success, however, cannot be reduced to cultural essentialism and its supporters alone. Rather, the conflict of the two culturalization regimes should be considered the cause. The rise of right-wing populism can only be understood in the context of the conflictual dynamics of cultural essentialism *and* hyperculture, producing a new cleavage and so enabling populist mobilization.

This approach is less normative than the theory of authoritarianism, which comes with advantages as well as disadvantages. The main dis-advantage is that the theory of cultural cleavage does not offer answers to the question of which grievances or interests can be democratically addressed or represented, and which cannot. The main advantage is that it opens a wider perspective on the problem, locating the source not only among the supporters of right-wing populism, but within a dynamic among both its supporters and its opponents. Thereby it is in less danger of being paternalistic or overly normative. It even casts

EUROPE AT THE CROSSROADS

doubt on certain forms of scandalizing authoritarian resentment and empowering marginalized minorities: if this happens in a way that valorizes the lifestyles of hyperculture while ridiculing cultural essentialism, it might strengthen the very cleavage that right-wing populist mobilization builds on. Yet, the scandalization of authoritarianism and the empowerment of minorities must also be qualified.

The counterstrategy: Deculturalization

Reckwitz himself does not propose a counterstrategy. He only sets out the ways in which the two regimes can interrelate—relations of confrontation or coexistence (Reckwitz 2016: 7–10). Towards the end of his essay, however, he presents the problem in a way that hints at a possible strategy. He notes that both culturalization regimes *are* culturalization regimes, that they both contribute to the overall culturalization of politics (Reckwitz 2016: 10), and thereby to the creation of the cleavage that fosters right-wing populist mobilization. This implies that one possible way to avoid a conflict between two culturalization regimes fostering right-wing populism would be to deculturalize politics. This might mean that political conflict and mobilization should be less concerned with the cultural valorization of society one way or another.

Depoliticization and re-politicization

One possible candidate for such politics of deculturalization is the left-wing populism proposed by Chantal Mouffe. Like the gap-in-representation argument above, Mouffe's explanation for the rise of populism is based on a political theory of democracy. However, her approach is quite different in being decidedly constructivist and agonistic. As a constructivist, she emphasizes that political interests and identities represented in parliament are honed by political discourse and political representation. As an agonistic theorist, she promotes a model of democracy based on a (wilfully eclectic) reading of Carl Schmitt. In Mouffe's model, democracy is not about finding a consensus in reasonable deliberations. Rather, she holds that political conflicts cannot be decided by reason since they are by (her) definition based on irreducible differences. These differences should not be blurred or overcome in rational discourse but clearly politicized. Contrary to Schmitt, she does not want political opponents to become enemies in a fight potentially pursued with deadly force. Rather, conflicts should be conducted in an agonistic play represented in parliament. Democracy, then, requires clear and visible conflict lines between political opponents. In this model, politicians and parties have the task of presenting clear alternatives to the public, thereby contributing to the construction of the opposing political and social identities they can represent in parliament (Mouffe 2005: 1–63; 2018: 10–26).

Given this, Mouffe argues that Western democracies have witnessed a process of depoliticization, undermining democracy. She specifically blames the parties of the moderate left. In the name of the 'reasonable' politics of a 'third way' and with the justification of intellectuals such as Ulrich Beck in Germany and Anthony Giddens in Britain, these parties reacted to the rise of neoliberalism by abandoning their positions on the left and moving towards the liberal centre. The classic conflict between left and right, framed in economic terms, was abandoned, and the established liberal parties of the centre-left and centre-right no longer offer a choice between these clearly distinguishable alternatives. This post-democratic, post-political situation created an opportunity for right-wing populists, who can claim—with some legitimacy—that all the other parties have become indistinguishable. Right-wing populists offer a clear political alternative by politicizing issues such as immigration or ethnic difference. Although Mouffe sees politicization as the defining mark of democracy, she does not welcome but rather denounces this right-wing populist politicization for its anti-egalitarianism (Mouffe 2005: 35–89; 2018: 10–38).

Mouffe's approach offers insights into some of the points I have already discussed. Her constructivist and agonistic outlook offers a more differentiated explanation for the gap in representation. According to her, the problem is not so much that certain groups or interests are no longer properly represented; it is rather that the loss of a clear left–right distinction undermines the formation of clear political identities and positionalities that could be democratically represented. This also offers a new perspective on the representation of authoritarian subjects. If these subjects are offered a clear, politicized representation of their economic position, their authoritarian stance concerning immigration or cultural minorities might still exist, but would lose its political relevance (Eribon 2013: 140–54). Finally, her approach offers an explanation for the culturalization of politics that Reckwitz discusses, in whose perspective, politics became culturalized because the cultural became politicized as an *Ersatz* for the depoliticization of the old left–right distinction focused on economic questions. However, Mouffe certainly does not endorse any wholesale criticism of 'identity politics'. On the contrary, she argues that the failure to connect the economic agenda of the old left to the struggles of new social movements was the core shortcoming of leftist strategy in the 1970s and 1980s (Mouffe 2018: 27–30).

The counterstrategy: Re-politization

The corresponding counterstrategy is obvious: the left should seize the 'populist moment' opened by the current crisis of neoliberalism, and engage in its own project of re-politization, connecting the struggle against economic inequality (neglected by the centre-left in recent decades) with the struggle introduced by the new social movements, thereby creating an alternative, egalitarian politicization and clear political conflict lines. Mouffe (2016, 2018) explicitly endorses left-wing populism as the best possibility for such a re-politicization, and argues that the left should not hesitate to claim their position as that of 'the people' against 'oligarchs', and to speak to emotions rather than to reason alone.

At first glance, this strategy might appear a solution to all the aforementioned problems. It shifts public attention away from the discriminatory discourses of the populist right; it closes the gaps in representation produced by the left's shift to the liberal centre; it represents subjects within an egalitarian project rather than in their authoritarian affects; it destabilizes racist discourses; and it counters the culturalization of politics. However, there are two caveats. First, Mouffe's demand to pursue a populism of the left, building on affect and emotion, can itself have highly problematic effects, even if one adheres to a non-rationalist understanding of democracy. There is no guarantee that inciting the emotions of the masses as 'the people' against neoliberal 'oligarchs' will not itself stoke resentment and have a detrimental effect on democratic culture, a risk should at the very least be reflected on rather than brushed aside. Second, Mouffe has framed the problem in a voluntarist fashion. In her narrative, it seems as if the left simply changed its agenda because it made wrong decisions based on wrong theories—decisions that could then simply be reversed by further decisions, this time based on better theories. She does not really discuss whether these decisions were a reaction to changes in the political economy or the social structure that made the old leftist strategies infeasible.[4] In other words, her political theory remains rather vague when it comes to social theory and political economy.

A theory of democratic capitalism

To fill some of the blanks Mouffe leaves, I would suggest complementing her argument with a political economic perspective, namely Wolfgang Streeck's discussion (2014, 2016) of the developments leading up to the Great Recession and the Eurozone crisis.[5] Streeck describes a cascade of crises caused by an inherent tension between two principles of resource allocation, those of capitalism and democracy:

> one operating according to marginal productivity, or what is revealed as merit by a 'free play of market forces': and the other based on social need or entitlement, as certified by the collective choices of democratic politics. (Streeck 2016: 75)

Immediately after the Second World War, both principles appeared to exist in a harmony of democratic capitalism: Western societies witnessed continually high profit rates, growth rates, and an expansion of mass welfare guaranteed by rising wages, expanding social rights, and state intervention. However, the two principles collided in the late 1960s and early 1970s, when capital owners considered the progressing welfare-state expansion as a threat to the profitability of their investments. This led to what Streeck dubs an 'investment strike', in which capital owners decided to refrain from further investment, exerting political pressure on the state not to implement any further reforms expanding the welfare state. To cater to the demands of democracy and capitalism, the governments turned to one strategy after the other, each of which resolved the tension on one level by shifting it to another, not solving the problem but only 'buying time' (Streeck 2014: 40). First, the recession was overcome by expansive monetary policy resulting in an inflation crisis; then, inflation was overcome by policies based on tax-cuts and public spending resulting in a public debt crisis; then, public debt was combatted in neoliberal reforms maintaining mass welfare by an expansion of private household debt through 'financial innovation', finally resulting in the multiple crisis of the Great Recession (Streeck 2014: 34–54; 2016: 73–90).

In summary, Streeck describes a cascade of crises in which the inherent tension in democratic capitalism keeps on building in one area until it is no longer tenable, and then is released by deflecting it to another area—a process that appears to be finite. Without being 'economistic', deterministic, or reductionist, one can connect this economic argument with the perspectives discussed above. If one accepts Streeck's argument, Mouffe's must be reassessed. The process in which the left abandoned its traditional economic positions no longer appears simply to be a wrong decision informed by misleading theories of democracy and politics. Rather, it appears to be a reaction to an economic and social situation in which the old position was no longer tenable. Since the 1970s, the temporary harmony between high profit rates and an expanding welfare state, and therefore the apparent harmony between capitalism and democracy, could no longer be sustained or re-established. The subsequent shift towards cultural issues and the politics of recognition came in the hope of finding new rallying grounds after the old ones were lost.

The counterstrategy: New Left Keynesianism

Streeck himself argues for a left-wing populist programme similar to that of Mouffe;[6] yet, his own economic argument casts doubt on the sustainability of this strategy. For left-wing populist platforms focused on the economy to be a successful antidote to right-wing populism, they would have to present an economic programme with which a large proportion of the population could identify in the hope of it bettering their situation. Due to the fractured class structure of most contemporary democracies, this is by no means a trivial demand. But as the relative successes of Syriza, Podemos, La France Insoumise, Bernie Sanders, and Jeremy Corbyn demonstrate, it is possible at least in some countries. However, such economic populism could bind voters in the long run only, if it delivers on some of its promises. First, this would demand winning national elections, and overcoming the institutional obstacles elected governments might face—and as the example of Syriza in Greece dramatically shows, these obstacles can be too great to be overcome. Even if such projects win elections and are not obstructed by institutional barriers, Streeck's description of the cascade of crises and the finite process of buying time makes it seem doubtful that a left–Keynesian programme could recreate the post-war successes of democratic capitalism. The causes he gives for the multiple crisis of the great recession are systemic, which is why the successor to his book *Buying Time* is titled *How Will Capitalism End?* A populist strategy of Mouffe's making would either have to come up with an economic programme to overcome the crisis in capitalism, or a democratic form for the end of capitalism. Mouffe's conception (2018: 47–51) is explicitly open to both interpretations, yet these aspects should be elaborated on in formulating an actual strategy.

Conclusion

Each of the theoretical perspectives discussed in this chapter offers specific insights into the causes and dynamics of right-wing populism, and each of them presents a different outlook on possible counter-strategies: closing the gap in representation, distinguishing authoritarian resentment from rational grievances, and scandalizing the former and representing the latter; empowering marginalized minorities; overcoming the culturalization of politics; re-politicizing economic questions; or addressing the possible end of capitalism. Yet, none of these strategies comes close to offering a silver bullet, which becomes particularly clear in light of the other approaches. If the recent successes of right-wing populism have a foundation in the dynamics of political economy, and the transformations in social structure and political representation connected to it, no short-term political strategy will be able to overcome right-wing populism. This, however, is not a case for defeatism. Rather, the limitations of existing theories and strategies show the need for a deeper understanding of why representative democracy in these advanced political systems is no longer delivering non-populist representation that satisfies voters.

Notes

1 I wish to thank the editors, the anonymous reviewers, and the participants of the workshop 'Contesting the Populist Challenge: Beyond "Orbánism" and "Trumpism" and the Normalization of Exclusion' for their valuable feedback on draft versions.

2 The premise here is that in a normative perspective, right-wing populism is held to be a danger to democracy and that the search for counterstrategies is imperative.

3 The notions of race, racialization, and racism used here refer to Guillaumin (1995) and Hall (1980, 1986).

4 In her latest book on left-wing populism, Mouffe (2018: 26–7) briefly mentions the economic crisis of the 1970s but does not elaborate. At a later point, she argues that there can be no return to the economics of the post-war consensus. Yet, her main argument is ecological rather than economic (Mouffe 2018: 52).

5 Most recently Mouffe (2018: 25-6) herself cites Streeck, but only to describe the post-war consensus, not to address his analysis of the crisis dynamics of the last five decades.

6 However, the version of populism he is inclined to credit has far less to do with the struggles of the new social movements, which Mouffe wants to include.

References

Adorno, T. W., E. Frenkel-Brunswik, D. Levinson & N. Sanford (1950), *The Authoritarian Personality* (New York).

Arzheimer, K. (2017), 'Electoral Sociology: Who votes for the extreme right and why—and when?', in C. Mudde (ed.), *The Populist Radical Right: A Reader* (New York) (first pub. 2012).

Bieling, H. (2017), 'Aufstieg des Rechtspopulismus im heutigen Europa: Umrisse einer gesellschaftstheoretischen Erklärung', *WSI-Mitteilungen*, 8: 557–65.

Biskamp, F. (2017), 'Angst-Traum Angst-Raum: Über den Erfolg der AfD, die "Ängste der Menschen" und die Versuche, sie "ernst zu nehmen"', *Forschungsjournal Soziale Bewegungen*, 30/2: 91–100.

— (2018), 'Populism, religion, and distorted communication: Public discourse, Islam, and the anti-Muslim mobilization of the alternative for Germany', *Zeitschrift für Religion, Gesellschaft & Politik*, 2/2: 247–76.

Brähler, E., J. Kiess & O. Decker (2016), 'Politische Einstellungen und Parteipräferenz: Die Wähler/innen, Unentschiedene und Nichtwähler 2016', in O. Decker, J. Kiess & E. Brähler (eds.), *Die enthemmte Mitte: Autoritäre und rechtsextreme Einstellungen in Deutschland* (Gießen).

Decker, O., J. Kiess & E. Brähler (eds.) (2016), *Die enthemmte Mitte: Autoritäre und rechtsextreme Einstellungen in Deutschland* (Gießen).

Eribon, D. (2013), *Returning to Reims* (Cambridge, MA).

Fromm, E. (1994) *Escape from freedom* (New York) (first pub. 1941).

Guillaumin, C. (1995), *Racism, sexism, power and ideology* (New York).

Hall, S. (1980), 'Race, articulation, and societies structured in dominance', in UNESCO (ed.), *Sociological Theories: Race and Colonialism* (Paris).

— (1986), 'Gramsci's relevance for the study of race and ethnicity', *Journal of Communication Inquiry*, 10/2: 5–27.

Heitmeyer, W. (ed.), 2012. *Deutsche Zustände 10* (Berlin).

Hochschild, A. R. (2016), *Strangers in their own land: Anger and mourning on the American right* (New York).

Inglehart, R. & P. Norris (2016), 'Trump, Brexit, and the rise of populism: Economic have-nots and cultural backlash', faculty research working paper, Harvard Kennedy School.

Kitschelt, H. (2017), 'The contemporary radical right: An interpretative and explanatory framework', in C. Mudde (ed.), *The Populist Radical Right: A Reader* (New York) (first pub. 1995).

Kitschelt, H. & P. Rehm (2014), 'Occupations as a site of political preference formation', *Comparative Political Studies*, 47/12: 1670–1706.

Koppetsch, C. (2018), 'Rechtspopulismus als Klassenkampf? Soziale Deklassierung und politische Mobilisierung', *WSI-Mitteilungen*, 71/5: 382–91.

Lang, J. (2017), '"Wider den Genderismus!" Extrem rechte Geschlechterpolitiken', in B. Milbradt et al. (eds.), *Ruck nach rechts? Rechtspopulismus, Rechtsextremismus und die Frage nach Gegenstrategien* (Opladen).

Löwenthal, L. (1987), *False prophets: Studies on authoritarianism* (New Brunswick) (first pub. 1949).

MacWilliams, M. (2016), *The rise of Trump: America's authoritarian spring* (Amherst, MA).

Mair, P. (2009), 'Representative versus Responsible Government', MPIfG working paper.

Mayer, S., I. Šori, B. Sauer & E. Ajanović (2018), 'Mann, Frau, Volk: Familienidylle, Heteronormativität und Femonationalismus im europäischen rechten Populismus', *Feministische Studien*, 36/2: 269—285.

McGowan, L. & D. Phinnemore (2017), 'The UK: Membership in crisis', in

D. Dinan, N. Nugent & W. E. Paterson (eds.), *The European Union in Crisis* (London).

Milbradt, B. (2018), Über autoritäre Haltungen in 'postfaktischen' Zeiten (Opladen).

Minkenberg, M. (2017), 'The radical right in postsocialist Central and Eastern Europe: comparative observations and interpretations', in C. Mudde (ed.), *The Populist Radical Right: A Reader* (New York) (first pub. 2002).

Mouffe, C. (2005), *On the political* (New York).

— (2016), *In defence of left-wing populism*, theconversation.com/in-defence-of-left-wing-populism–55869.

— (2018), *For a left populism* (London).

Mudde, C. & C. Rovira Kaltwasser (2015), 'Vox populi or vox masculini? Populism and gender in Northern Europe and South America', *Patterns of Prejudice*, 49/1–2: 16–36.

— (2017), 'Introduction', in C. Mudde (ed.), *The populist radical right: A reader* (New York).

— & C. Rovira Kaltwasser (2017), *Populism: A Very Short Introduction* (Oxford).

Patzelt, W. (2015), 'Die Sorgen der Leute ernst nehmen!', *Aus Politik & Zeitgeschichte*, 65/40: 17–21.

Reckwitz, A. (2016), *Zwischen Hyperkultur und Kulturessenzialismus*, soziopolis. de/beobachten/kultur/artikel/zwischen-hyperkultur-und-kulturessenzialismus/.

Streeck, W. (2014), *Buying time: The delayed crisis of democratic capitalism* (London).

— (2016), *How will capitalism end?* (London).

Wodak, R. (2018), 'Vom Rand in die Mitte: "Schamlose Normalisierung"', *Politische Vierteljahresschrift*, 59/2: 323–35.

Zick, A. (2016), *Gespaltene Mitte: Feindselige Zustände: Rechtextreme Einstellungen in Deutschland 2016* (Bonn).

CHAPTER 5

The rise of neo-nationalism

Maureen A. Eger & Sarah Valdez

Support for Western European radical right parties has increased in recent years, prompting the need for new research on these parties.[1] Especially important are studies that investigate their ideology and how it has changed over time. After describing their recent electoral gains at the national and European levels, we make the case that neo-nationalism—a form of nationalism occurring when nation-state boundaries are settled, but perceived to be under threat—is the underlying ideology of contemporary radical right parties. Analyses of Manifesto Project data show that contemporary parties increasingly make nationalist claims; indeed, the issues most important to these parties are consistent with the notion that the sovereignty and autonomy of modern nation-states are under threat from external forces (Eger & Valdez 2015; 2018). When framing their opposition to globalization, supranational organizations, and multiculturalism, they cite negative economic, sociocultural, and political consequences for the nation-state. Our analyses also show that nationalism not only increasingly characterizes radical right parties, but also distinguishes them from other major party families.

Table 5.1 reports the electoral results from the last two general elections for parties in fourteen Western European countries, along with the results from the last two European Parliament (EP) elections. Figure 5.1 depicts the rise of these parties in both European and national settings by illustrating the change in support between these last two elections. With the exception of the Swiss People's Party (SVP/UDC) and the Austrian Freedom Party (FPÖ), which have garnered high levels of support for decades, few of these parties reached 10 per cent

Country	Party	Most recent national election		Previous national election		European parliamentary election	
		Year	% vote	Year	% vote	% vote 2014	% vote 2009
Austria	Freedom Party (FPÖ)	2017	26.0	2013	20.5	19.7	12.7
Belgium	Flemish Interest (VB)	2014	3.7	2010	7.8	4.3	9.9
Switzerland	People's Party (SVP/UDC)	2015	29.4	2011	26.6	—	—
Denmark	Danish People's Party (DF)	2015	21.1	2011	12.3	26.6	14.8
Finland	True Finns (PS)	2015	17.6	2011	19.0	12.9	9.8
France	National Front (FN)	2017	13.2	2012	13.6	24.9	6.3
Germany	Alternative for Germany (AfD)	2017	12.6	2013	4.7	7.1	—
Greece[a]	Golden Dawn (XA)	2015 II	7.0	2012 II	6.9	9.4	0.5
	Independent Greeks (ANEL)	2015 II	3.7	2012 II	7.5	3.5	—
	Popular Orthodox Rally (LAOS)	2015 II	—	2012 II	1.6	2.7	7.2
Italy	Northern League (LN)	2018	17.4	2013	4.1	6.2	10.2
	Brothers of Italy (FDI)	2018	4.4	2013	2.0	3.7	—
Luxembourg	Alternative Democratic Reform (ADR)	2018	8.3	2013	6.6	7.5	7.4
Netherlands	Party for Freedom (PVV)	2017	13.0	2012	10.1	13.3	17.0
Norway	Progress Party (FrP)	2017	15.2	2013	16.3	—	—
Sweden	Sweden Democrats (SD)	2018	17.5	2014	12.9	9.7	3.3
United Kingdom	United Kingdom Independence Party (UKIP)	2017	1.8	2015	12.6	26.8	16.1

Sources: Parties and Elections in Europe (http://www.parties-and-elections.eu) and European Parliament Election Results (http://www.europarl.europa.eu/).

[a]There were two elections in Greece in 2012 and 2015. The results of the second elections are included here.

114

Figure 5.1. Changes in radical right vote share, previous two elections.

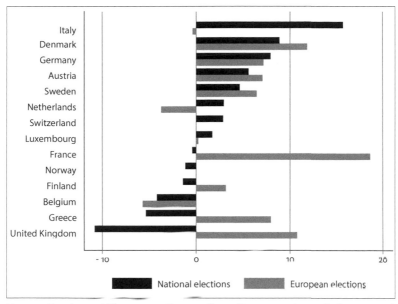

National elections   European elections

Sources: Parties and Elections in Europe (http://www.parties-and-elections.eu) and European Parliament Election Results (http://www.europarl.europa.eu/).

Note: Countries sorted by largest increase in share of national vote by radical right.

of the national vote in the early 2000s. This has changed. Indeed, in most countries, these parties are enjoying historic levels of support, and their growing popularity has made it increasingly difficult for other party families to formally exclude them (a cordon sanitaire). Support for some parties, such as Italy's Lega Nord (LN) recently rebranded Lega, has grown exponentially between elections, while other parties, such as the Sweden Democrats (SD), have steadily increased their share of electorate at each election this century. Only one country, Belgium, has seen a decline in support in both types of elections.

With these gains in mind, this chapter explores changes in the underlying ideology of parties described as radical right. It is generally agreed that opposition to immigration is the single most important issue

Table 5.1. Electoral results of Western European radical right parties in national and European elections.

to radical right parties (Hainsworth 2008; Van der Brug & Fennema 2007; Arzheimer 2008), so, unsurprisingly, scholars tend to attribute electoral outcomes to the threat that native-born citizens perceive from increasing immigration and potential competition for jobs and social welfare benefits (Lubbers et al. 2002; Arzheimer & Carter 2006; Norris 2005). Recent research sees these perceived threats as features of a more comprehensive nationalist ideology (Gingrich & Banks 2006; Halikiopoulou et al. 2012; Eger & Valdez 2015; 2018).

Using data from the Manifesto Project, we assess levels of nationalism in 134 radical right election-year manifestos between 1970 and 2015. For the purposes of comparison, we also measure nationalism in 1,363 party platforms across 7 other major party families. We find that contemporary radical right parties have become more nationalist in recent decades, and these changes increasingly set them apart from other major party families. Given the rise in nationalism among contemporary parties, we would argue that contemporary parties are better described as neo-nationalist (Eger & Valdez 2015; 2018). To advocate a change in terminology is not to divorce these parties from their historical context or heritage; however, recognizing shifts in the underlying ideology of these parties is critical to understanding their recent electoral gains. Thus, it is important to use terminology that correctly identifies what drives these parties and the sentiments that motivate their voters.

Nationalism

Nationalism[2] is a political ideology primarily concerned with congruence between nation and state (Gellner 1983; Hechter 2000). Arguably, one of the most powerful belief systems of the nineteenth and twentieth centuries, nationalism remains a potent political force in contemporary democracies (Hjerm & Schnabel 2010; Smith 2010). According to Gellner (1983), nationalist sentiments arise when the congruence between nation and state is violated. Threats to sovereignty and self-determination, such as other nation-states or ethnic groups (Triandafyllidou 1998), activate national identities and mobilize nationalist sentiment (Hechter 2000).

We contend that, for contemporary radical right parties, nationalism is the primary political concern and the lens through which policy preferences are determined. Indeed, issues important to radical right parties are consistent with the notion that the sovereignty and autonomy of modern nation-states are under threat, socially, politically, and economically. For example, opposition to immigration is consistent with the idea that diversity threatens the nation-state. Betz and Johnson (2004: 323) argue that 'radical right-wing populist ideology is a response to the erosion of the system of "ethno-national dominance", which characterized much of the history of modern nation-states. Thus, parties' ardent opposition to immigration and multiculturalism reflects an ethnocentric notion of the nation, and an effort to preserve or return to an ethnically homogenous nation-state (Betz 1994; Mudde 2007; Hainsworth 2008). Rydgren (2007: 244) calls this ideology ethno-pluralism, which 'states that to preserve the unique national characters of different peoples, they have to be kept separated.' Mudde (2010: 1173), meanwhile, calls this nativism, 'an ideology which holds that states should be inhabited exclusively by members of the native group ("the nation") and that non-native elements (persons and ideas) are fundamentally threatening to the nation-state's homogeneity.' While Mudde (2010: 1174) states that 'all references to national self-determination are [not] necessarily expressions of nativism', he implies that nativism is an expression of nationalism, as without immigration or ethnic minorities, native-born and the nation are conceptually equivalent.

Contemporary radical right parties also express opposition to the EU and European integration (Luther 2009; Vasilopoulou 2009; Berezin 2009; Halikiopoulou et al. 2012) citing the supranational body as a threat to ethnic and cultural homogeneity (Minkenberg 2002; Hainsworth 2008) and to the political autonomy of nation-states (Kriesi et al. 2008). Yet, the EU, which began as the European Economic Community (EEC), is first and foremost an economic union. With its single market and European currency, the EU is representative of economic globalization. However, it is important to note that radical right parties were not always opposed to a single market or free trade among European countries. Mudde (2007: 159) singles out the 1992 Maastricht Treaty as an ideological turning point.

Kriesi et al. (2012: 23) argue that those dissatisfied with globalization identify more with the nation-state, believing it to be 'the only legitimate and appropriate level for decision-making or for politics.'

Accordingly, contemporary radical right parties aim to mobilize the 'losers' of globalization (Kriesi et al. 2008; 2012). Although radical right parties most often frame their opposition to globalization as cultural (Gingrich & Banks 2006), they also frequently cite economic concerns about labour and social security (Höglinger et al. 2012: 247). Just as immigrants may be perceived not only as cultural but also economic threats (Olzak 1992; Quillian 1995), globalization, and the EU in particular, may be thought threatening in multiple dimensions.

Some scholars call contemporary radical right parties neo-nationalist. Elsewhere, we describe neo-nationalism as 'a subset of nationalism that can be considered a boundary-maintenance project rather than a nation-building project' (Eger & Valdez 2015: 127). We argue that neo-nationalism occurs in contexts where national boundaries are settled and widely accepted—both nationally and internationally—but are nevertheless perceived to be under threat. Gingrich and Banks (2006: 2) explicitly connect neo-nationalism to contemporary 'global and transnational conditions.' They define neo-nationalism as a reaction against the current phase of globalization and its economic, political, and sociocultural effects.

As research on contemporary political parties has identified nativist, ethnocentric notions of European nation-states (Hainsworth 2008; Mudde 2010) and nationalism (Betz & Johnson 2004; Halikiopoulou et al. 2012; Höglinger et al. 2012; Eger & Valdez 2015) as central to the ideology of the radical right, we have investigated these parties' level of nationalism relative to other major party families and show how it has changed over time.

Data and methods

To study levels of nationalism[3] we have used the Manifesto Project Dataset (Volkens et al. 2016), which codes election-year party manifestos and reports their positions on political issues as a percentage of the space each occupied on their election platform. Thus, the data allow for comparisons of not only party positions, but also the salience and relative importance of those issues. The dataset includes parties that won any legislative seats in a democratic election in 56 countries from 1945 to 2015. Our sample consists of election manifestos from 18 Western European countries: Austria, Belgium, Denmark, Finland,

France, Germany, Greece, Iceland, Ireland, Italy, Luxembourg, the Netherlands, Norway, Portugal, Spain, Sweden, Switzerland, and the UK. In total, our sample includes 1,497 party manifestos in 225 elections between 1970 and 2015. During this period, the majority of these countries have had electorally successful radical right parties (the exceptions being Iceland, Ireland, Portugal, and Spain).

We have relied on scholarly descriptions of parties and include any Western European parties described in the literature as 'radical right' or 'populist radical right'. The majority of these parties are coded either as 'nationalist' or 'special issue' parties in the dataset, and a smaller percentage either 'agrarian' or 'ethnic–regional.' Table 5.2 lists the 134 radical right party manifestos in our sample by country, party name, and election year (party splits and name changes are not uncommon in radical right parties, so although 29 party names are listed, they represent only 24 parties in the dataset). The details are provided in the notes to Table 5.2, and Table 5.3 provides the frequencies by country and decade. We have relied on the coding in the dataset for the other major party families in our analysis. Frequencies for the entire sample by party family and decade are found in Table 5.4.

To construct a measure of nationalism for each manifesto, we adapt the methodology employed by the Manifesto Project (Budge et al. 2001; Klingemann et al. 2006) in their construction of the core indicator 'rile' and other composite scores. Our measure of nationalism is the sum of nationalist statements (social, political, and economic) minus the sum of globalist statements (social, political, and economic) contained in a party's manifesto. Thus, we generate a score for each party in each election year, where negative numbers indicate a globalist position and positive numbers reflect a nationalist position. To identify variables that capture different elements of nationalism, we follow an analytical strategy similar to Halikiopoulou et al. (2012), and from the data identify the economic, social, and political issues that are theoretically representative of nationalist or globalist sentiments.[4]

Nationalism:

Σ[social(*national way of life: positive* (per601)+*multiculturalism: negative* (per608))+political(*internationalism: negative* (per109)+*European Community/Union: negative* (per110)+*military/defence: positive* (per104))+economic(*protectionism: positive* (per406)]

– Σ[social(*national way of life: negative* (per602)+*multiculturalism: positive* (per607))+political(*internationalism: positive* (per107)+*European Community/Union: positive* (per108)+*military/defence: negative* (per105))+economic(*protectionism: negative* (per407))]

We use stances on multiculturalism and national way of life to capture the social or cultural dimension of nationalism. Used previously to measure elite articulation of nationalism (Hjerm & Schnabel 2010), positive statements related to a national way of life include favourable mentions of the country's nation and history, including appeals to nationalism, patriotism, established national ideas, and pride in citizenship. Negative statements, indicative of globalism, are unfavourable mentions of any of the above, such as opposition to nationalism, the existing nation-state, national pride, or national ideas. Nationalist sentiments related to multiculturalism are appeals for cultural homogeneity and the cultural integration of immigrants, as well as opposition to indigenous and minority group rights. Positive statements about multiculturalism, which reflect globalist sentiments, are favourable mentions of cultural plurality, immigrant diversity, and indigenous and minority group rights. The only economic factor in the dataset that is indicative of nationalism or globalism is protectionism. Favourable statements related to extending or maintaining the protection of internal markets, including tariffs, quotas, and export subsidies, indicate a nationalist position, while statements in support of open markets, free trade, and the abolition of protectionism indicate a globalist position.

We have also included three issues that are unequivocally political and speak directly to the issues of national sovereignty and self-determination. The first is internationalism, which captures stances on the nation-state and global order. Unfavourable mentions of international cooperation and favourable mentions of national sovereignty, isolationism, and unilateralism reflect nationalism; favourable mentions of international cooperation, global governance, international courts, and supranational organizations like the UN indicate globalist sentiments. The second issue is the EEC/EU. Nationalist sentiments are negative mentions of membership in, the territorial expansion of, or the power of the EU. These may include opposition to specific policies or to the member state's financial contributions to the EU. Globalist sentiments include positive mentions of the EEC/EU in any of these regards. Finally, we also include stances on the armed forces. Favourable mentions of external security, border defence, military spending, and national self-defence constitute nationalist sentiments, whereas negative mentions of any of the above and the use of military power to resolve conflicts are taken to reflect a globalist stance.

Results

In this chapter, we identify nationalism in radical right platforms and how levels have changed over time.[5] Figure 5.2 shows the average level of nationalism in election manifestos by social, political, and economic components. Positive values on the y-axis represent the average share of election manifestos devoted to nationalist positions net of globalist positions. A negative value denotes that the average stance was globalist, which was the case for political stances on internationalism and the EEC in the 1970s. Otherwise, all other average positions were nationalist and increase over time.[6] Radical right parties increasingly articulate support for a national way of life and opposition to multiculturalism, internationalism, and the EU. Further, support for economic protectionism increased over time. The largest increase was between the 1990s and 2000s, when the average share of nationalism seen in radical right manifestos more than doubled.

Because multiple issues contribute to two of our three components, we provide a more detailed picture of the political and social aspects of nationalism. Figure 5.3 shows that radical right parties have consistently taken pro-military stances when it comes to national self-defence. In fact, only one party, PVV in the 2010 Dutch election, made more anti-military than pro-military statements. Among all radical right parties, the average share of pro-military rhetoric has also increased over the years. Levels of internationalism and anti-EU sentiment have varied, however. In earlier decades, parties were favourable towards both international cooperation and supranational organizations, including the EEC. Consistent with the notion of the Maastricht Treaty being a watershed moment (Mudde 2007: 159), anti-EU statements make up an increasing proportion of election manifestos from the 1990s on.

Figure 5.2. Nationalism in radical right election manifestos, 1970–2015.

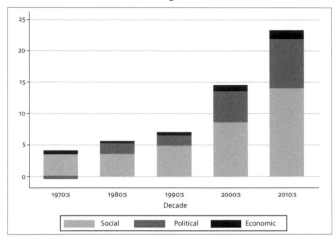

Source: Manifesto Project (MRG/CMP/MARPOR), Version 2016b.

Notes: Positive values on the *y*-axis represent the average share of election manifestos devoted to nationalist positions net of globalist positions. A negative value indicates that the average stance is globalist.

Figure 5.3. Nationalism in radical right election manifestos, political components.

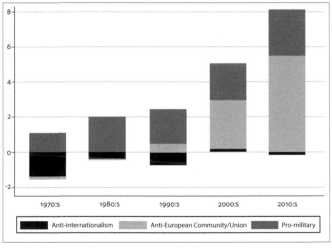

Source: Manifesto Project (MRG/CMP/MARPOR), Version 2016b.

Notes: Positive values on the *y*-axis represent the average share of election manifestos devoted to nationalist positions net of globalist positions. A negative value indicates that the average stance is globalist.

Figure 5.4. Nationalism in radical right election manifestos, social components.

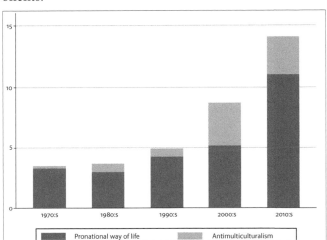

Source: Manifesto Project (MRG/CMP/MARPOR), Version 2016.

Notes: Positive values on the *y* axis represent the average share of election manifestos devoted to nationalist positions net of globalist positions. A negative value indicates that the average stance is globalist.

Figure 5.4 shows that while manifestos have always made appeals to nationalism, the share of these sentiments has increased over time. Explicit opposition to multiculturalism, immigrant diversity, and ethnic minority rights also increased over time.

We examine levels of nationalism among radical right parties compared to other major party families. While most party families make some nationalist claims, globalist positions make up a much larger proportion of manifestos. Except for the conservatives in the 1970s, whose manifestos contained an average of 1.45 per cent nationalist statements net of globalist statements, all other party families have held, on average, globalist positions (Figure 5.5). Given that radical right parties have become more nationalist over time, it is clear that it was nationalism that increasingly set the radical right parties apart from all other party families.

Finally, we compare levels of nationalism in Western European radical right parties by EP group in the Eighth European Parliament (2014–2019). As of December 2018, the radical right parties

Figure 5.5. Nationalism in Western European party politics by party family, 1970–2015.

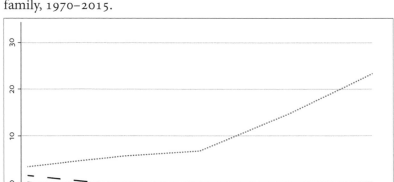

Source: Manifesto Project (MRG/CMP/MARPOR), Version 2016b.

Notes: Positive values on the y-axis represent the average share of election manifestos devoted to nationalist positions net of globalist positions. A negative value indicates that the average stance is globalist.

belonged to either European Conservatives and Reformists (ECR), established in 2009, Europe of Freedom and Direct Democracy (EFDD), established in 2014, or Europe of Nations and Freedom (ENF), established in 2015. We rely on data from the most recent round of the Manifesto Project, updated with five relevant elections, which was released on 21 December 2018 (Volkens et al. 2018). As Figure 5.6 demonstrates, there was some variation within parliamentary groups, but the pattern did not differ much across groups. In each group, on average, 13 per cent of manifestos were devoted to nationalist claims that were social and 6 per cent to nationalist stances that were political. Averages for the economic dimension were lower; in the elections, the only parties to make these claims were the AfD (1.2 per cent) and FN (5.4 per cent).

Figure 5.6. Nationalism in Western European radical right election manifestos, by European Parliamentary group.

Europe of Freedom and Direct Democracy

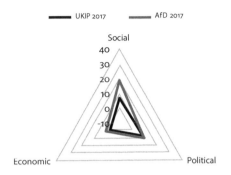

Europe of Nations and Freedom

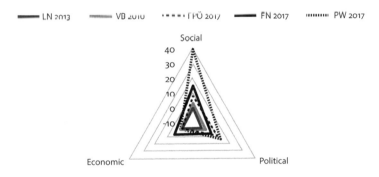

European Conservatives and Reformists

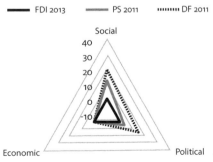

Source: Manifesto Project (MRG/CMP/MARPOR), Version 2018b.

Notes: Positive values represent the share of election manifestos devoted to nationalist positions net of globalist positions. A negative value indicates that the stance is globalist.

Conclusions

Our analyses show that, between 1970 and 2015, radical right parties increasingly made nationalist claims. They articulated greater opposition to multiculturalism, internationalism, and the EU, while promoting a 'national way of life'. Support for economic protectionism also increased over time. Our analyses also demonstrate that nationalist concerns increasingly distinguished these parties from all the other major party families, whose average positions consistently reflected globalism. Our claim that nationalism not only characterizes these parties but also sets them apart from alternatives is consistent with other recent research that shows that national identification and national pride increases the likelihood of voting for a European radical right party (Lubbers & Coenders 2017).

Based on these analyses and our previous work, which shows that contemporary radical right parties have largely abandoned right-wing economic stances (Eger & Valdez 2015), we argue that contemporary parties are better described as neo-nationalist rather than radical right. First and foremost, the neo-nationalist label identifies the parties as fundamentally nationalist. Indeed, the issues most important to these parties are consistent with the idea that external forces pose a threat to the sovereignty and autonomy of modern nation-states. Parties cite negative economic, sociocultural, and political consequences for the nation-state when framing their opposition to economic globalization, supranational organizations such as the EU and the UN, and increasing multiculturalism and insecurity due to immigration. 'Neo-' denotes a sub-type of nationalism occurring within the context of settled boundaries. Thus, this term also distinguishes them from nationalist parties that promote state-building or separatist movements.

Second, this term helps differentiate the economic stance of contemporary parties from other party families, left and right, including the economically right-wing radical right parties of the 1970s, 1980s, and 1990s. While the descriptor 'right-wing' is often used to refer to authoritarian or socially conservative positions, it is more traditionally used to indicate where one stands on an economic scale, where right refers to economic liberalism or neoliberalism. Although these parties have largely abandoned right-wing economic preferences, they differ from traditional left-wing parties that favour inclusive or universal social welfare policies. Instead, contemporary parties are welfare chauvinists, meaning they seek to preserve welfare benefits for native-born and restrict immigrants' access to the national welfare state (Andersen & Bjørklund 1990; Betz & Johnson 2004). For example, they often seek to increase social spending on pensioners while decreasing benefits to asylum seekers. Thus, the label neo-nationalist distinguishes them from parties, past or present, that are or were economically right wing. without conflating them with traditional parties of the economic left.

Most scholarship contends that sociocultural issues matter most to the radical right (Rydgren 2007; Kriesi et al. 2012); thus, given the low prominence given to economic issues, it possible for these parties to attract voters who hold a range of economic preferences (Ivarsflaten 2005). However, anti-immigrant parties with rightist economic preferences and anti-immigrant parties with leftist economic preferences occupy distinct political spaces, leaving them broadly able to compete for different types of voters. Given these parties increasing popularity, especially among those dissatisfied with globalization, we would argue that the economic message of these parties should not be discounted. Instead, it is important to assess how their economic stances fit into to the parties' underlying ideology.

As the election results illustrate, neo-nationalism is increasing across Western Europe, although somewhat paradoxically, it is not confined to the national sphere. Some have called the European Parliament election of 2014 an 'earthquake', because it was marked by a surge in far-right Eurosceptic parties (Halikiopoulou & Vasilopoulou 2014). Yet, elections are more than a single event, as they may have long-term consequences not only for policy, but also for norms and values. For example, UKIP received nearly 27 per cent of the national vote in the 2014 European Parliament election. In the 2015 general election, the party garnered 12.6 per cent of the vote, and a year later voters chose to leave the EU in a referendum championed by UKIP.

Despite their increased popularity, however, it is not clear what sort of influence neo-nationalist parties have at the European level. These parties have long sought affiliation in the EP, but not always with other parties described as the populist radical right (Mudde 2007: 177). Where possible, some have chosen strategic alliances in an attempt to gain legitimacy in their national systems. McDonnell and Werner

(2018) describe these alliances as 'respectable marriages' that MEPs hope will legitimize them and help overcome cordons sanitaires at home. However, some Eurosceptic MEPs, referred to as 'absentees' (Brack 2015), do not seek active participation or responsibility in the EP. Their focus on nationalism means that they hold national concerns to be paramount, even if it limits their effectiveness as MEPs, and their emphasis on national politics may have helped prevent these parties from forming a grand coalition. However, according to Mudde (2019), this could change in the 2019 EP election, especially if these parties make electoral gains.

Our analyses make clear that it is in their embrace of nationalism that the neo-nationalist parties increasingly differ from other party families. Indeed, neo-nationalists are staking their political future on the idea that people want a strengthening of national borders to protect against external social, economic, and political forces, as well as domestic elements perceived as weakening national institutions, culture, and way of life. Not only do the results of recent national elections indicate that this ideology increasingly resonates with voters, but recent survey data confirms that significant proportions of EU voters are concerned about the very issues on which these parties campaign. According to the November 2018 Eurobarometer survey, voters identify immigration, terrorism, the member state's public finances, and the economic situation as the most important issues facing the EU. Immigration was mentioned most frequently by respondents in all member states except Portugal and Sweden, which ranked immigration second most important (European Commission 2018). Thus, an explicit rejection of globalist ideology could mean even greater gains for these parties in the 2019 election.

Notes

1 This research was supported by the Marianne and Marcus Wallenberg Foundation (MMW) Grant No. 2014.0019; the Swedish Foundation for Humanities and Social Sciences (RJ) Grant No. P14-0775:1; and the Swedish Research Council for Health, Working Life and Welfare (FORTE) Grants No. 2016-07177 and the Swedish Research Council grant (2018-05170).

2 Reproduced with permission of Springer Nature, this section is taken from Eger & Valdez 2018, duly modified.

3 Reproduced with permission of Springer Nature, this section is taken from Eger & Valdez 2018, duly modified.

4 Halikiopoulou et al. (2012) refer to these components as ethnic, cultural, territorial, and economic. We use social to describe the ethnic and cultural elements and political to refer to what they call territorial.

5 Reproduced with permission of Springer Nature, this section is taken from Eger & Valdez 2018, duly modified. Figure 5.6 and its accompanying text are entirely new.

6 Greek election manifestos constitute a third of the sample between 2010 and 2015, but this does not explain the increase in nationalism. The average share in the 2010s is 23.36. Excluding all Greek manifestos, the average share of nationalist sentiment is 20.74.

References

Andersen, J. G. & T. Bjørklund (1990), 'Structural changes and new cleavages: the progress parties in Denmark and Norway', *Acta Sociologica*, 33: 195–217.

Arzheimer, K. (2008), 'Protest, neo-liberalism or anti-immigrant sentiment: What motivates the voters of the extreme right in Western Europe?' *Zeitschrift für Vergleichende Politikwissenschaft/Comparative Governance & Politics*, 2: 173–97.

— & E. Carter (2006), 'Political opportunity structures and right-wing extremist party success', *European Journal of Political Research*, 45: 391–418.

Berezin, M. (2009), *Illiberal politics in neoliberal times: Cultures, security, and populism in a new Europe* (Cambridge).

Betz, H. G. (1994), *Radical right-wing populism in Western Europe* (Houndmills).

— & C. Johnson (2004), 'Against the current—stemming the tide: The nostalgic ideology of the contemporary radical populist right', *Journal of Political Ideologies*, 9: 311–27.

Brack, N. (2015), 'The roles of Eurosceptic members of the European parliament and their implications for the EU', *International Political Science Review*, 36/3: 337–50.

Budge, I., H.-D. Klingemann, A. Volkens, J. Bara, with E. Tanenbaum, R. C. Fording, D. J. Hearl, H. M. Kim, M. McDonald & S. Mendez (2001), *Mapping policy preferences: Estimates for parties, electors, and governments 1945–1998* (Oxford).

Eger, M. A. & S. Valdez (2015), 'Neo-nationalism in Western Europe', *European Sociological Review*, 31/1: 115–130.

— — (2018), 'From radical right to neo-nationalist', *European Political Science*, doi: 10.1057/s41304-018-0160-0.

European Commission (2018), *Standard Eurobarometer 90: Autumn 2018: Public opinion in the European Union, First results*, doi:10.2775/104.

European Union (2018). European Parliament, www.europarl.europa.eu/.

Gellner, E. (1983), *Nations and Nationalism* (Oxford).

Gingrich, A. & M. Banks (2006), *Neo-Nationalism in Europe and beyond: Perspectives From Social Anthropology* (New York).

Hainsworth, P. (2008), *The extreme right in Western Europe* (Oxfordshire).

Halikiopoulou, D., K. Nanou & S. Vasilopoulou (2012), 'The paradox of nationalism: The common denominator of radical right and radical left Euroscepticism', *European Journal of Political Research*, 51/4: 504–39.

— & S. Vasilopoulou (2014), 'Support for the far right in the 2014 European parliament elections: A comparative perspective', *Political Quarterly*, 85/3: 285–88.

Hechter, M. (2000), *Containing nationalism* (New York).

Hjerm, M. & A. Schnabel (2010), 'Mobilizing national sentiments: Which factors affect nationalist sentiments in Europe?' *Social Science Research*, 39/4: 527–39.

Höglinger, D., B. Wüest & M. Helbling (2012), 'Culture versus the economy: The framing of public debates over issues related to globalization', in H. Kriesi, E. Grande, M. Dolezal, M. Helbling, D. Höglinger, S. Hutter & B. Wüest (eds.), *Political Conflict in Western Europe* (Cambridge).

Ivarsflaten, E. (2005), 'The vulnerable populist right parties: No economic realignment fuelling their electoral success', *European Journal of Political Research* 44/3: 465–492.

Klingemann, H.-D., A. Volkens, J. Bara, I. Budge & M. McDonald (2006), *Mapping policy preferences, ii: Estimates for parties, electors, and governments in Eastern Europe, the European Union and the OECD 1990–2003* (Oxford).

Kriesi, H., E. Grande, R. Lachat, M. Dolezal, S. Bornschier & T. Frey (2008), *West European politics in the age of globalization* (Cambridge).

— — M. Dolezal, M. Helbling, D. Höglinger, S. Hutter & B. Wüest (2012), *Political conflict in Western Europe* (Cambridge).

Lubbers, M. & M. Coenders (2017), 'Nationalistic attitudes and voting for the radical right in Europe', *European Union Politics*, 18/1: 98–118.

Lubbers, M., M. Gijsberts & P. Scheepers (2002), 'Extreme right-wing voting in Western Europe', *European Journal of Political Research*, 41: 345–78.

Luther, K. R. (2009), 'The revival of the radical right: the Austrian parliamentary election of 2008', *West European Politics*, 32/5: 1049–61.

McDonnell, D. & A. Werner (2018), 'Respectable radicals: Why some radical right parties in the European Parliament forsake policy congruence', *Journal of European Public Policy*, 25/5: 747–63.

Minkenberg, M. (2002), 'The radical right in post-socialist Central and Eastern Europe: Comparative observations and interpretations', *East European Politics & Society*, 16/2: 335–62.

Mudde, C. (2007), *Populist radical right parties in Europe* (Cambridge).

— (2010), 'The populist radical right: A pathological normalcy', *West European Politics*, 33/6: 1167–86.

— (2019), 'Will the radical right consolidate power in the heart of the EU this year?' *The Guardian*, www.theguardian.com/world/commentisfree/2019/jan/11/radical-right-consolidate-power-heart-eu.

Nordsieck, Wolfram (2018), *Parties and Elections in Europe*, www.parties-and-elections.eu.

Norris, P. (2005), *Radical right: Voters and parties in the electoral market* (New York).

Olzak, S. (1992), *The dynamics of ethnic competition and conflict* (Stanford).

Quillian, L. (1995), 'Prejudice as a response to perceived group threat: Population composition and anti-immigrant racial prejudice in Europe', *American Sociological Review*, 60/4: 586–611.

Rydgren, J. (2007), 'The sociology of the radical right', *Annual Review of Sociology*, 33: 241–62.

Smith, A. D. (2010), *Nationalism* (2nd edn, Cambridge).

Triandafyllidou, A. (1998), 'National Identity and the "other"', *Ethnic & Racial Studies*, 21/4: 593–612.

van der Brug, W. & M. Fennema (2007), 'Causes of voting for the radical right', *International Journal of Public Opinion Research*, 19: 474–87.

Vasilopoulou, S. (2009), 'Varieties of Euroscepticism: The case of the European extreme right', *Journal of Contemporary European Research*, 5: 3–23.

Volkens, A., P. Lehmann, T. Matthieß, N. Merz & S. Regel (2016), *The manifesto data collection. Manifesto Project (MRG/CMP/MARPOR), Version 2016b* (Wissenschaftszentrum Berlin für Sozialforschung (WZB) Berlin), doi.org/10.25522/manifesto.mpds.2016b.

— W. Krause, P. Lehmann, T. Matthieß, N. Merz, S., Regel & B. Weßels (2018), *The Manifesto Data Collection: Manifesto Project (MRG/CMP/MARPOR), Version 2018b* (Wissenschaftszentrum Berlin für Sozialforschung (WZB), Berlin). doi.org/10.25522/manifesto.mpds.2018b.

Appendix

Table 5.2. Radical right parties included in analysis.

Country	Party	Years in dataset
Austria	Freedom Party (FPÖ)	1970, 1971, 1975, 1979, 1983, 1986, 1990, 1994, 1995[a], 1999, 2002, 2006, 2008
	Alliance for the Future of Austria (BZÖ)	2006, 2008
Belgium	Flemish Bloc (VB)	1978, 1981, 1985, 1987, 1991, 1995, 1999, 2003
	Flemish Interest (VB)	2007, 2010
Switzerland	People's Party (SVP/UDC)	1971, 1975, 1979, 1983, 1987, 1991, 1995, 1999, 2003, 2007, 2011
	National Action (NA/AN)[b]	1971, 1975, 1979, 1983, 1987
	Swiss Democrats (SD/DS)	1991, 1995, 1999, 2003
	Motorists' Party (AP)[c]	1987, 1991
	Freedom Party of Switzerland (FPS)	1995
Denmark	Progress Party (FP)	1973, 1975, 1977, 1979, 1981, 1984, 1987, 1988, 1990, 1994, 1998
	People's Party (DF)	1998, 2001, 2005, 2007, 2011
Finland	Finnish Rural Party (SMP)[d]	1970, 1972, 1975, 1979, 1983, 1987, 1991, 1995
	True Finns (PS)	1999, 2003, 2007, 2011
France	National Front (FN)	1986, 1988, 1993, 1997, 2002, 2007, 2012
Germany	Alternative for Germany (AfD)	2013
Greece	Popular Orthodox Rally (LAOS)	2007, 2012
	Golden Dawn (XA)	2012(2), 2015
	Independent Greeks (ANEL)	2012(2), 2015
Italy	Social Movement-National Right (MSI-DN)[e]	1972, 1976, 1979, 1983, 1987, 1992
	National Alliance (AN)	1994, 1996, 2001, 2006
	Northern League (LN)	1992, 1994, 1996, 2001, 2006, 2008, 2013
Luxembourg	Action Committee for Democracy and Pension Justice (ADR)[f]	1989[g], 1994, 1999, 2004
	Alternative Democratic Reform (ADR)	2009, 2013
Netherlands	List Pim Fortuyn (LPF)	2002, 2003
	Party for Freedom (PVV)	2006, 2010, 2012
Norway	Progress Party (FrP)	1973[h], 1977, 1981, 1985, 1989, 1993, 1997, 2001, 2005, 2009
Sweden	New Democracy (NyD)	1991
	Sweden Democrats (SD)	2010
United Kingdom	United Kingdom Independence Party (UKIP)	2001, 2015

Table 5.3. Radical right manifestos (election years), by country and decade.

Country	1970–1979	1980–1989	1990–1999	2000–2009	2010–2015	Total
Austria	4	2	4	5		15
Belgium	1	3	3	2	1	10
Denmark	4	4	4	3	1	16
Finland	4	2	3	2	1	12
France		2	2	2	1	7
Germany					1	1
Greece				1	7[a]	8
Italy	3	2	6	5	1	17
Luxembourg		1	2	2	1	6
Netherlands				3	2	5
Norway	2	3	2	3		10
Sweden			1		1	2
Switzerland	6	5	8	3	1	23
United Kingdom				1	1	2
Total	24	24	35	32	19	134

a. There were two elections in Greece in 2012. Golden Dawn (XA) and Independent Greeks (ANEL) are represented in this count two times each and the Popular Orthodox Rally (LAOS) only once. January 2015 election manifestos for XA and ANEL are also included in this count.

Source: Manifesto Project (MRG/CMP/MARPOR), Version 2016b.

a. Called the Freedom Movement in 1995.
b. Party renamed the Swiss Democrats (SD) in 1991; NA/AN and SD/DS treated as same party in the dataset.
c. Party renamed the Freedom Party of Switzerland (FPS) in 1994; AP and FPS treated as same party in the dataset.
d. Party renamed the True Finns (PS) in 1998; SMP and PS treated as same party in the dataset.
e. Party renamed the National Alliance (AN) in 1994; MSI-DN and AN treated as same party in the dataset.
f. Party renamed the Alternative Democratic Reform Party (ADR) in 2006; treated as same party in the dataset.
g. Called the Action Committee 5/6ths in the 1989 election.
h. Called the Anders Lange's Party (ALP) in the 1973 election.

Source: Manifesto Project (MRG/CMP/MARPOR), Version 2016b.

Table 5.4. Party manifestos (election years), by party family and decade.

Party Family	1970–1979	1980–1989	1990–1999	2000–2009	2010–2015	Total
Green	1	23	35	34	15	108
Socialist	48	50	47	52	31	228
Social Democratic	81	88	68	57	27	321
Liberal	55	43	38	40	22	198
Christian Democratic	57	51	58	45	20	231
Conservative	35	37	30	34	20	156
Ethnic–regional	26	22	22	31	20	121
Radical Right	24	24	35	32	19	134
Total	327	338	333	325	174	1497

Source: Manifesto Project (MRG/CMP/MARPOR), Version 2016b.

CHAPTER 6

The end of EU-topia and the politics of hate

Totalitarianism and the mainstreaming of far-right discourse in the Greek political scene

Salomi Boukala

Greece has dominated the international headlines during the past years due to its debt crisis and political turmoil. A Grexit possibility, the realignment of the Greek political scene and the electoral success of the radical left party Syriza made Greece the EU's political and financial scapegoat. The broad sweep of financial and political commentators of mainstream media have focused on Syriza's threat and largely ignored the extreme polarization, the resurgence of historical dichotomies and the mainstreaming of ultranationalist and totalitarian discourse in the public sphere. The new coalition government, which comprises Syriza and the ultranationalist party Independent Greeks (ANEL), has contributed to the political polarization, but those who orchestrated the divisive climate were the main opposition party—conservative New Democracy—and its recent leadership. A characteristic example of New Democracy's rhetoric was the political debate caused by the refusal of Greece's Justice Minister, Stavros Kontonis, to attend a conference on crimes committed by totalitarian regimes, which was organized by the Estonian presidency of the Council of European Union (23 August 2017). As the party's statement noted, 'The government's decision not to participate in the heritage in 21st-century Europe regarding the crimes committed by communist regimes offends Greeks and European citizens who have always defended democratic ideals and the universal human value of freedom.'[1] Thereafter, the author of the statement explicated that Kontonis' decision 'highlights the Greek peculiarity and leads us to a strange kind of European and international isolation'[2]. Moreover, Kontonis and Syriza's government were being criticized by several members of New Democracy as being 'communists' and 'totalitarians', emerging from the antithetical ideologies of two political poles, the left wing and the right wing, as expressed by the representatives of the two political parties—Syriza and New Democracy.

'Ideologies', writes Hannah Arendt in her book *The Origins of Totalitarianism* (2004: 604), 'pretend to know the mysteries of the whole historical process—the secrets of the past, the intricacies of the present, the uncertainties of the future—because of the logic inherent in their respective ideas.' Drawing upon Arendt's diachronic work on totalitarianism and focusing on her observations on the relation between ideology and history, and the ideology of terror, I attempt to study the mainstreaming of extreme-right discourse, the legitimation of political enmity and historical divisions in New Democracy's rhetoric. I assume that polarized rhetoric and the rediscovery of the communist or 'red menace' were intentionally used by the main opposition party, because, since the 2012 double-earthquake national elections, and due to Greece's debt and sociopolitical crisis, the politics of hate against the left and a new form of anti-communist rhetoric made the jump from far-right parties over to New Democracy's agenda.

In the following, I first review the pertinent aspects of Greece's divided past and the Greek political scene during the debt crisis (2010–2017), Syriza's governance, and the election of New Democracy's new leadership (2015). Having then presented a discourse-historical approach (DHA) to critical discourse studies as an adequate theory and methodology with which to analyse the mainstreaming of the far-right discourse, resurgence of the red threat' and historical, ideological divisions, I use a DHA approach to the concepts of Aristotelian topoi and fallacies and the argumentation strategies that I intend to explore, in order to chart how far-right rhetoric has been legitimized by the conservative party—using the archetypal 'communist enemy' in times of political crisis and while Greece's position in the EU was in question. In particular, I seek to examine how the 'ideology of terror' (Arendt 2004; Friedrich & Brzezinski 1956) as a mode of persuasion was used by New Democracy to stigmatize Syriza as a red menace to the Greek nation on the basis of political dichotomies. Moreover, I focus on the juxtaposition of Europe and Greece, and a the politics of hate against the left via an analysis of New Democracy's former leader (2009–2015) Antonis Samaras' pre-election campaigns (2012 and 2015) and the party's current leader Kyriakos Mitsotakis' statements on security and terrorism.

Hannah Arendt underlined the totalitarian lawfulness of Nazi Germany and Stalin's Soviet Union through the 'law of nature' and the 'law of history', respectively, and provided a systematic presentation of totalitarianism as a form of government. She argued that totalitarianism developed from the convergence of several economic and political trends such as the financial crisis and the rise of nationalism (Halberstam 1999). The Greek political system cannot be characterized as totalitarian, although Greece has been through totalitarian systems in recent history (1936–41 and 1967–74), and has faced social and political challenges as an aporia of the current debt crisis. However, as Arendt (2004: 138) argues, 'the road to totalitarian domination leads through many intermediate stages for which we can find numerous analogies and precedents'. Hence, Arendt's work on totalitarianism, lawfulness, and the function of propaganda remains timely and can be used to explicate the dystopian political present of Greece.

Rethinking political polarizations in Greece

Although this chapter is not concerned with Greek political history per se, a brief description of the political climate in Greece since Metaxas' dictatorship (1936–41) is needed to understand the political dichotomies that have dominated recent Greece. The Fourth of August Regime (1936–41), headed by Ioannis Metaxas, an obscure political figure, adopted an ethno-patriotic nationalism, which is generally recognized to have been authoritarian, autocratic, dictatorial, and conservative in tone (Kallis 2007; 2010): into the highly polarized ideological-political landscape of interwar Greece, Metaxas introduced an authoritarian, anti-communist regime rooted in Greek tradition, religion, and history.

This regime ended with Metaxas' death in 1941. Its last vestiges were crushed by the Nazi invasion of Greece a few months later. Metaxas' rejection of the ultimatum set by Benito Mussolini on 28 October 1940, demanding Greece allow Italian forces to invade Greek territory, gave Metaxas a mythic dimension as a political figure, and his regime is still memorialized by far-right parties such as Golden Dawn. Moreover, Ochi Day, 28 October, the anniversary of his 'No', was later made a public holiday in Greece, signifying Metaxas' ambiguous position in the modern history of Greece as dictator-cum-hero. With Konstantinos Maniadakis as undersecretary of public security, Metaxas embarked on an attempt to destroy the left in general and the Communist Party in particular; Maniadakis organized a witch-hunt against them, and cultivated anti-communist propaganda by representing the left as a national threat (Psarras 2014; Panourgia 2009). The deep divisions between the left and the right did not end with Metaxas' death though. Quite the contrary, they led to the Greek Civil War.

The Greek Civil War was fought from 1946 to 1949, between the coalition government's army, backed by the UK and the US, and the Democratic Army of Greece (the DSE), which was the military branch of the Greek Communist Party, and it ended with the final dominance of the Greek government army, the right-wingers, in the summer of 1949 (Margaritis 2009). After the civil war, political instability again characterized the Greek political situation in the 1950s and 1960s. Meanwhile, Greek society was still split between supporters of the right-wing government and those who felt nostalgic for the leftist National Liberation Front (EAM). The political tension continued (seen in eight national elections between 1950 to 1964) and was accompanied by violent struggles between police and anti-government protesters, the parliamentary 'elections of violence and fraud' (1961), and the growth of right-wing paramilitary groups determined to fight the 'communist enemy' (Linardatos 1977: 290), which participated in the murder of a number of leftist civilians and politicians, including the United Democratic Left (EDA) party's MP Grigoris Lambrakis in Thessaloniki in 1963 (Panourgia 2009). Hence, the organized terror against the left continued and led to a *coup d'état* on 21 April 1967 that legitimized a witch-hunt against the 'enemies of the Greek nation', the 'red peril' (Linardatos 1977: 430–42; Christopoulos 2014).

The 'white terror' that accompanied the persecution of the leftists dominated the Greek political scene after the end of civil war, and ended only with the transition to democracy (Metapolitefsi) in 1974. However, anti-communist ideology had taken root in the Greek state and the right. The Metapolitefsi period (1974–2010) was characterized by a two-party system (Vernardakis 2012)—including the conservative New Democracy and the Pan-Hellenic Socialist Movement (PASOK)—with its framework of consolidated mass clientelism and populism that transcended left–right divisions (Vasilopoulou & Halikiopoulou 2013; Vernardakis 2012; Verney 2015). This two-party system collapsed on 6 May 2012, when the combined voting share of the two parties in question, New Democracy and PASOK, plunged to 32 per cent. Meanwhile, the Radical Left Coalition, Syriza, tripled its vote, and thrust the left to the forefront of political stage (Verney 2014; Voulgaris & Nikolakopoulos 2014). A repeat election held six weeks later on 17 June 2012 tempered this result, and led to a fragile coalition government, new austerity measures, and mass protests.

At the same time, anti-communist ideology was revived in response to Syriza's electoral success, and duly dominated New Democracy's election campaign. The conservative party's rediscovery of the red menace continued after Alexis Tsipras, the Syriza leader, was sworn in as prime minister in September 2015, illustrating that anti-communist rhetoric is not limited to the far right of Greece's political spectrum. The reintroduction of the 'red threat' by New Democracy and its extreme-right political communications, based on the dichotomy of 'us', the patriots and Europeans, and 'them', the red traitors, reveals that modern Greek democracy is still shaped by the ruins of old political divisions. Moreover, it shows that totalitarian survival of the Greek past reappeared in a time of crisis, while a populist left-wing-based government challenged the political status quo of the country.

Speaking of methodology

DHA holds discourse to be 'context-dependent semiotic practices, as well as socially constituted and socially constitutive, related to a micro-topic and pluri-perspective' (Reisigl & Wodak 2016: 89). Hence, DHA can uncover the links between discursive practices, social variables, institutional frames, and sociopolitical and historical con-texts. For this reason, DHA is a useful theory and methodology with which to analyse and explain the complexities of the Greek political discourse against the background of the country's divisive past.

In the analysis below, I draw upon the discursive strategies of DHA (Reisigl & Wodak 2001), and especially its argumentation strategies and concepts of Aristotelian topoi and fallacies. DHA's argumenta-tion schemata illustrate prejudiced and binary discourses and play an important role in an in-depth analysis of the fallacious arguments usually employed by politicians in positive self- and negative 'other' representations (Reisigl & Wodak 2001; 2009), my assumption here being that Aristotelian dialectic and rhetoric will facilitate an in-depth study of the fallacious reasoning and strategies of political communi-cation employed by New Democracy's leadership.

The concept of topos—from Aristotle to the DHA

In his *Topics*, Aristotle (1992) defines a syllogism as 'an argument in which, when certain things are laid down, something different from these things follows necessarily by means of the things laid down' (Topics 100a 25–27). Topoi are those 'search formulas' that examine *endoxon*, or common knowledge, and comprise fallacious reasoning. Thus, topoi are integrated into the area of *dialectic*, which Aristotle calls *endoxon*. *Endoxon* refers to a previous, commonly accepted opinion, whose validity is examined by dialectic syllogism. It belongs to the realm of doxa (common opinion) (Amossy 2002). Aristotle uses the concept of *endoxon* to describe an opinion that can be accepted by the majority of people because it represents traditional 'knowledge'. In *Topics*, Aristotle does not define topos. However, he explains that a topos is a special extension of the general meaning of place or an analogy between a natural place and an intellectual/dialectic place (Topics 100b). Thus, Aristotelian dialectic topoi are the means and places for the development of dialectic syllogisms; they are the means by which a dialectician verifies *endoxa* and solves a dialectic problem through predicables, while topoi in Aristotle's *Rhetoric* (2004) are a means of persuasion.

In *Rhetoric*, Aristotle categorizes the topoi that apply to all subjects/

topics in common (Rhetoric B23). According to Rubinelli (2009: 84), these topoi are 'argument schemes, they are all devices for arriving at a certain conclusion about a case'. While they do not all have universal applicability, they can be applied to every rhetorical case (Rubinelli 2009). Aristotle (Rhetoric B23) provides a holistic classification of topoi that can be used by interlocutors to persuade an audience (though they might be named differently) of their argument. For this reason, topoi can be useful in a systematic analysis of various discourses. Aristotle also distinguishes between 'topoi of probative/real enthymemes' and 'topoi of fallacious enthymemes'; and as he explains via a number of examples, topoi are usually expressed by the proposition 'if one, then the other' (Rubinelli 2009). Thus, topoi are central to the analysis of seemingly convincing, but actually fallacious, arguments, which are widely adopted in prejudiced and discriminatory discourses (Reisigl & Wodak 2016; Wodak 2015; Boukala 2016).

False Reasoning—the concept of fallacy

In his *Sophistical Refutations*, Aristotle introduces various types of false reasoning and suggests resolutions to sophistical arguments. In its first lines, indeed, he provides an implicit definition of a fallacy by explaining that in this work he intends to discuss 'arguments that appear to be logical refutations, but in fact there are not; they are fallacies (paralogisms)' (Sophistical Refutations 164a 19–21). Thereafter, Aristotle provides a systematic classification of fallacies that seems to be diachronic, and this categorization can contribute to the recognition of fallacies that dominate contemporary political discourses. A wide variety of scholars and disciplines have focused on fallacies as means to serve the justification of discrimination and binary oppositions (see Reisigl & Wodak 2001). In particular, the study of fallacies, like the study of topoi, holds an important place in argumentation theory, Pragma-dialectics, and the DHA.

Van Eemeren and Grootendorst (1987) developed a set of norms for the identification of fallacies and the development of a critical discussion of false reasoning. Hence, in pragma-dialectics an argumentative tactic that violates any of the rules below is evaluated as fallacious. These rules can be described as follows:

1. Parties must not prevent one another from advancing or casting doubt on standpoints.
2. Whoever advances a standpoint is obliged to defend it if asked to do so.
3. An attack on a standpoint must relate to the standpoint that has already been advanced by the protagonist.
4. A standpoint may be defended only by advancing an argument relating to that standpoint.
5. A person can be held to the premises s/he leaves implicit. Conversely, antagonists must not be attacked on premises that cannot be inferred from their utterances.
6. A standpoint must be regarded as conclusively defended if the defence takes place by means of argumentation taken from the common starting point. A standpoint must be regarded as conclusively defended if the defence takes place by means of arguments in which a commonly accepted scheme of argumentation is correctly applied.
7. A standpoint must not be considered to be conclusively defended if the defence has not taken place by means of argumentation schemes that are plausible and correctly applied.
8. The argument used in a discursive text must be valid or capable of being validated by the explicitization of one or more unexpressed premises.
9. A failed defence must result in the protagonist withdrawing her or his standpoint, and a successful defence in the antagonist withdrawing her or his doubts about the standpoint.
10. Formulations must be neither puzzlingly vague nor confusingly ambiguous, and they must be interpreted as accurately as possible. (See Van Eemeren & Grootendorst 1987; Van Eemeren et al. 2009)

As Van Eemeren et al. (2009) further explain, if any of the above rules are violated, we are no longer dealing with topoi, but with fallacies. Fallacies are analysed in Pragma-dialectics 'as discussion moves which threaten the resolution of a dispute; they are violations of the rules of critical discussion' (Van Eemeren & Grootendorst 1987: 297).

DHA also serves to emphasize fallacies and false reasoning. As Reisigl and Wodak note:

The above ten rules for rational arguing should form the basis of a discourse ethics on which a political model of discursive, deliberative democracy can be grounded ... if one wants to analyse the persuasive, manipulative, discursive legitimation of racist, ethnicist, nationalist, sexist and other forms of discrimination, one encounters many violations of these ten rules. (Reisigl & Wodak 2001: 71)

Moreover, according to Reisigl and Wodak (2001; 2016), the lines between reasonable and fallacious argumentation cannot be drawn clearly in any case. Based on this observation, I would argue that the introduction of a DHA-informed systematic analysis of the Aristotelian tradition can contribute to an in-depth study of those arguments, which, in this case, reveal historical dichotomies that dominate the Greek political scene and are conducive to the discursive construction of the politics of hate in New Democracy's rhetoric.

Waking up the ghosts of a divided past

The 2012 national elections caused a political tumult in Greece. Syriza's anti-austerity, populist discourse led to the party's electoral success. By coming in second, Syriza challenged the political status quo—the two-party system. The radical left's predominance was already apparent due to the massive anti-austerity, anti-government protests and numerous opinion polls that noted Syriza's big lead over New Democracy. In this tense political climate, New Democracy's election campaign was based on a 'politics of fear' and the representation of Syriza as the main enemy (Boukala & Dimitrakopoulou 2016). In what follows, I present some characteristic examples of the speeches by the then Prime Minister and New Democracy leader, Antonis Samaras.

On 3 May 2012, Antonis Samaras mentioned during his final pre-electoral speech in Athens:

The last two years I had two enemies: PASOK's memorandum that caused all the financial problems and the left-wing that removed investments, kicked out tourists and supported hooded criminals... I'm going to fight against the left wing by introducing security measures and I will remove all the illegal immigrants, who became tyrants of this country.

So, do you want to be ruled by us, who fight against the illegal immigrants or by them, who tolerate illegal immigrants, support hooded men, and want to destroy Greece?

Could I leave them to destroy Greece? Yes, but I didn't do it because my priority is my country. One of the weapons in the fight against the crisis is security ... We have to stop the illegal immigrants and we have to get the hoods off those people who burn the cities and the citizens' properties. We need to protect our cities from the protests that destroy our economy and Greek people's lives ... The left wing does not present any solutions. It organizes protests and hooded criminals; that's why it is a threat against our kids' future.[3]

There were two opposing social actors here, the left wing that supports 'hooded criminals' and 'illegal immigrants' and organized protests, and Samaras' New Democracy, the conservative party that fights the country's enemies. Samaras openly characterized the left wing as an enemy of the nation and emphasized security issues. Hence, the then leader of New Democracy named the left wing as a threat to the Greek nation and its fortunes on a number of financial, ideological, and historical points to orchestrate a climate of terror. In particular, according to Samaras, the left was causing financial troubles for the country and its citizens due to protests that led to violent battles and property damage. They also spoilt the image of Greece as an ideal destination for tourists. Moreover, Samaras' references to leftist support for 'illegal immigrants' and 'hooded men' illustrate New Democracy's extreme political communication and its attempt to connect the left to lawlessness, criminality, and domestic terrorism. Here, I should also mention that 'hooded men' historically referred to Greek traitors—wearing hoods—who collaborated with the Nazis during the Second World War and betrayed EAM–ELAS partisans. In recent decades this historically and politically charged concept has been paraphrased by the mainstream media and politics and is usually applied to hooded youths who participate in riots. However, New Democracy restored the meaning of the concept to its historical context, but this time it was the leftists who were the traitors and enemies of the Greek nation.

Based on Aristotelian homonymy (Sophistical Refutations 165b 23–27), a linguistic fallacy producing the illusion of a logical argument within language or argumentum ad hominem (Reisigl & Wodak 2001: 72), Samaras here enlarged on an argument that implied that the left—and indirectly, Syriza—supports lawlessness, traitors, and criminals and, due to its actions, is a threat to the nation. Hence, left wing and threat become synonyms via a fallacy of homonymy (Sophistical Refutations 165b) that violates logical validity (rule 8) and correct reference to implicit premises (rule 5).

Another important point of Samaras' speech was its discursive construction of Syriza's lawlessness and criminality through the links between 'illegal immigrants' and 'hooded traitors', developed via a fallacy due to consequence (Sophistical Refutations 167b), which violates rule 7, given that the argument is not correctly applied. It is further developed by the Aristotelian topos of the consequential (Rhetoric B23 1398b) or the topos of threat (Reisigl & Wodak 2001); a topos which here relies on the conditional 'if the left wing supports "hooded men" and "illegal immigrants" who are considered to be a national threat, then the left wing is a national threat as well'. The characterization of immigrants as 'tyrants' illustrates the far right political agenda of the conservative party that was built on the basis of racism and terror. Racism, as Arendt (2004) shows, has proved to be a powerful ideology of imperialistic and totalitarian policies. By focusing on antisemitism, she argues that racism and the idea of a master race that has to be protected from inferiors are an essential justification for terror. Here, I would argue that Samaras followed the origins of totalitarian thought by turning against not only his political opponents but also immigrants supported by the left wing. By utilizing war metaphors, he presented himself as a warrior who will protect the country from its enemies through security measures. Security issues, indeed, dominate New Democracy's rhetoric, which underlines security, police and the exclusion of the 'other' as main subjects of the party's agenda through the prism of New Democracy's adoption of totalitarian thinking. Thus, Samaras creates an ingroup of 'us', the supporters of his party, Greek patriots and 'guards of the nation', and an outgroup of 'them'—the national enemies—'the red threat' that has to be fought in the name of national security.

EUROPE AT THE CROSSROADS

On 23 January 2015, a few days before the national election and the electoral success of Syriza, the leader of New Democracy, Antonis Samaras, addressed his party's supporters. As he noted in his main pre-election speech in Athens:

> A conflict between two worlds will take place on Sunday. These two worlds have huge differences.
> Our world focuses on security—we aim to secure our borders against illegal immigrants.
> In contrast, Syriza asks for open borders. They will drive us to anarchy, together with their communist allies in Europe. They will destroy Europe![4]

The significant nomination of Syriza's members as dangerous 'others', who oppose Europe and will destroy it with their communist allies, the resurgence of civil war, Cold War memories, and the emphasis on security that will be ensured by New Democracy, leads to a double distinction between a pro-European right wing and dangerous Eurosceptic left-wing Syriza. By employing the metaphor of conflict (Musolff 2006) and other linguistic devices, such as hyperbole and generalization, seen through the prism of historical divisions—references to communism—and introducing a fallacy that is not only based on division and historical misrepresentation, but also violates rules of logic (rule 8), Samaras summarized the two parties' ideological and political differences. In particular, he represented Syriza as a threat, a national enemy. This argument is further substantiated using the topos of opposites, which is set out by Aristotle with the argumentation scheme 'if the contrary of a predicate belongs to the contrary of a subject, then this predicate belongs to this subject' (Rhetoric B23 1397a). In this case, it relies on the conditional: 'if Syriza's government manages to do damage to Greece and Europe, then the Greeks should vote for New Democracy'.

According to Arendt (2004), propaganda and terror are connected and used by totalitarian regimes to win over the masses. As she puts it, propaganda is a psychological form of warfare that is used by totalitarianism while it struggles for power, while terror is the very essence of its form of government. Paraphrasing Arendt, who emphasizes totalitarian propaganda and the decline of common sense through the use of terror, I would argue that the demagoguery of terror is propagated through populism, can be linked to the theory of securitization and leads to the legitimation of a politics of exclusion and conflict.[5]

Europe and the relation between Europe and Greece also dominate New Democracy's election campaign. As Samaras mentioned in his pre-election speech on 23 January 2015:

> Development has returned to Europe. The EU offers us money; much-needed money for Greece; money that we can get, if there is a New Democracy government on Monday. However, as it starts raining money in Europe, Syriza holds an umbrella …
>
> The Others do not care about the country's development. They say No to the adjustment programmes, No to investment, No to new jobs. They bring back political and financial insecurity.
>
> They are a threat to our country's future and can lead us to a horrible accident … I openly accuse Syriza that undermines our country and its future. They will bring back recession and lead us to economic suffocation. This is the accident![6]

Syriza is defined here as 'the other', a 'threat' that can lead the country to a 'horrible accident'. By employing an allegory, 'as it starts raining money in Europe, Syriza holds an umbrella', and a metaphorical scenario (Musolff 2006) of the supposed danger of Syriza's policies (the horrible accident), Samaras highlights the opposition between New Democracy and Syriza, which is based on financial issues and also signifies the antithesis between pro-European and anti-European policies. Samaras' references to the hypothetical negative causes of Syriza's policies implicitly indicate a connection between the EU and the New Democracy government, a coexistence that could safeguard the economic future of the country. In contrast, Syriza is represented as anti-European and a threat to Greece's development and the EU-topia.[7] This argument is further developed via the topos of (Syriza's) threat that can be paraphrased as 'if Syriza becomes the next government, then Greece will face a financial catastrophe'. Thus, Samaras represents Syriza as a threat, and presupposes that New Democracy will ensure Greece's economic and political security and a better future for the country via a fallacy due to consequence (Sophistical Refutations 167b), which violates rule 8, insofar as the argument is not valid or capable of being validated by the explication of one or more unexpressed premises.

The conveying of Samaras' political agenda through his election campaigns can be seen as an attempt to ensure the people's consent on the basis of securitization and propaganda. The representation of Syriza as a threat to the country's EU-topia and a source of terror, and the resurgence of political dichotomies that are connected to obscure historical periods, reveal his attempts to decrease Syriza's forthcoming electoral success. Samaras' election campaign also highlights New Democracy's transition from centre-right to extreme right and legitimizes far-right discourse, insofar as the main values of totalitarianism are utilized by the then Prime Minister and leader of the conservative party.

From neoliberalism to totalitarianism— terror and the politics of hate

Since January 2016, Kyriakos Mitsotakis has been the president of New Democracy and the leader of the main opposition. In contrast to Antonis Samaras' nationalist and polarized agenda, Mitsotakis' election to the party's leadership was considered anti-populist, neoliberal, and EU-oriented. However, Kyriakos Mitsotakis soon adopted Samaras' political tradition by nominating Adonis Georgiadis, the spokesman of the far-right party Popular Orthodox Rally (LAOS) that joined New Democracy in 2012, as New Democracy's vice-president and cultivating political enmity and polarization. Security became the main issue of New Democracy's political communication and was linked to terrorism and lawlessness. As Kyriakos Mitsotakis mentioned in a POLITICO interview after a terrorist attack against the former Prime Minister, Lucas Papademos, in May 2017:

> It's very, very worrisome — it's worrisome for me in terms of my personal safety, and it's worrisome in general. It is an issue I deeply care about because I lost a member of my family back in 1989 to domestic terrorism.

We are the only country [in Europe] that has domestic terrorism that is promoted exclusively by the extreme left.
I haven't seen anything that convinces me that they [the Syriza government] have a real willingness or desire to address this issue.[8]

In the same climate, he said in parliament on 3 July 2017:

I will repeat it once again. Terrorism has its roots in the far left. Syriza's government supports terrorists. They do not attempt to solve the problem of criminality and they have established lawlessness in the country.[9]

Here, the leader of New Democracy intends to evoke compassion from his followers regarding the threat of 'far-left terror'. An appeal for compassion replaces relevant arguments that could explicate the escalation of violence and lead to false reasoning based on the synthesis of the Aristotelian fallacy due to consequence (Sophistical Refutations 167b), which draws on a false belief that one can convert the implication and claim that the argument is endoxic because its consequence is, or the argument ad misericordiam (Reisigl and Wodak 2001: 72) and the fallacy of homonymy (Sophistical Refutations,165b). Mitsotakis underlined his family tragedy in order to present himself as an expert on the issue of terrorism and stigmatizes the far left as a synonym of terrorism.[10] Furthermore, the absence of any references to far-right terror illustrates his one-dimensional approach to the issue of terrorism—carefully oblivious to the history of the 'white terror' against the left—and his attempt to accuse his political opponents. By synthesizing these above fallacies and the Aristotelian topos of the analogue consequence that relies on the conditional—'if the leftist Syriza government is unable to mitigate the risk of terrorism attacks, then terrorism has its source in the far left that is supported by Syriza'—Mitsotakis creates a discursive connection between Syriza and terrorism in an attempt to increase people's feeling of insecurity. This strategy seems to be reused by New Democracy after every guerrilla attack.

It is worth considering Mitsotakis' statements made after visiting a police station in Pefki-Attica, which was petrol bombed on 26 October

2017, and after the 'Rubicon' guerrilla group's paint attack on the Council of State on 22 May 2018.

> Example 6.1: This incident is added to a series of other phenomena that have a common reference point and shows the government's provocative indifference to tackling incidents of law-and-order disruption. Upholding the law and the safety of citizens is an agenda without ideological poles. Freedom cannot exist without security, and I am personally determined to restore law and order to the country. Example 6.2: Every form of violence wherever it comes from is unacceptable. It undermines the Republic ... Neither the country, nor justice, nor the citizens are allowed to become the waif of every Rubicon or other terrorist groups, which the government, of course, knows very well. Mr Tsipras has to realize that his divisive words only cause damage to the country. He has to ensure, as he ought, law and order, the security and cohesion of society and the functioning of institutions.[11]

The dogma of law and order dominates Mitsotakis' rhetoric, as he underlines once again the necessity of security, and blames the government for 'provocative indifference' to face lawlessness. The other important point here (Example 6.1) is not his personal decisiveness in restoring and guaranteeing law and order, but the correlation between freedom and security, and the neutralization of the law-and-order dogma beyond 'ideological poles', an argumentation scheme that implicitly leads to the theory of securitization and the ideology of terror. According to Arendt (2004: 599), 'the chief aim of terror is to make it possible for the force of nature or history to race freely to mankind, unhindered by any spontaneous human action'. Mitsotakis personalizes terror through references to a 'Rubicon' group and Syriza's government that allegedly supports terrorists. Hence, the government is transformed into the 'objective enemy' (Arendt 2004), which is neither interested in people's security nor ensures the functioning of institutions. Mitsotakis' argumentation is further substantiated via the fallacy of homonymy and the topos of threat. This intends to seek the Greek people's consent to a law-and-order strategy and also implies historical oblivion regarding totalitarian regimes and their consequences for the country.

The emphasis on law and order and security is part of New Democracy's communication agenda, which reappeared in Mitsotakis' statement regarding the transfer to Korydallos prison—located in Athens—of the anarchist and hunger striker Konstantinos Yatzoglou, who had been charged with the terrorist attack on the former Prime Minister, Lucas Papademos. On 5 March 2018, Kyriakos Mitsotakis commented,

> The government negotiates with terrorists and eventually does what they are asking for. This is a serious blow to democratic legitimacy and the rule of law. Violence and lawlessness, unfortunately, extend from the centre of Athens to other cities in the country. Citizens feel insecure as they themselves and their properties are at risk due to hooded men ... For us citizens who feel unprotected this is a challenge, but I guarantee that this situation will be stopped immediately by the next New Democracy government ... The Greek state will not tolerate acts or threats of violence. Citizens will be protected. The police have the operational capability to guarantee citizens' security. We will provide police with political support to fulfil their mission ... the prisons of Korydallos will cease to be a source of criminals and terrorists. The terrorists will be transferred to high-security prisons. Greek citizens require security. They can trust us, because we will make it happen.[12]

Here, Mitsotakis proceeds with an explication of the law-and-order dogma and how it will be applied under his future governance: there will be political support for police actions and high-security prisons. He also expresses his confidence that he has the people's consent to apply law-and-order and security measures, and assures them that his plans will be put into practice. In addition, Mitsotakis blames the government for negotiating with terrorists, and simplifies or intentionally ignores the courts' decisions in order to construct a discursive analogy between terror/ terrorism and Syriza's government. However, this argument is developed on the basis of the fallacy of ignoratio elenchi that violates rule 3, insofar as it consists of discussing a standpoint that is not the standpoint in question (Reisigl & Wodak 2001: 73), which here is Yatzoglou's transfer to Korydallos prison due to his hunger strike while a trial was still pending.

As Arendt (2004) claims, repetition is very important for convincing the masses and establishing belief in state propaganda, and it seems that Mitsotakis' decision to focus on law and order, and to repeat security issues and the connection between Syriza and terrorism, is not accidental. Rather, it is a strategy that illustrates how propaganda can be used by the leader of the opposition, who attempts to ensure the people's consent, given that he highlights the supposed threat through repetitions and hyperboles that dominate his political statements and lead to the establishment of a totalitarian, anti-leftist political agenda.

Syriza's connection to terror and terrorism is also defined by Mitsotakis in his frequent references to the Exarcheia district in Athens, a district in the city centre surrounded by universities that played and still play a significant role in the cultural and political life of modern Greece. Riots between anarchists—described by the mainstream media and political parties as 'hooded men'—and the police are usual in this district, and dominates New Democracy's political communication as expressed by its leader's statements on the 'Exarcheia issue':

> The government cannot face the anti-authoritarians. The police are not allowed to use force and clean up Exarcheia. As the next Prime Minister, I will clean up the region within a month and I will create the highest-security prison. As the next government we will finish with Exarcheia.[13]

In the last few days, public buildings and vehicles have been burnt, citizens and members of political parties have been beaten, fully armed anarchists have walked in Exarcheia, policemen have been beaten up by terrorists. Especially, Exarcheia has been transformed into a no-go area for the police.[14]

By highlighting Exarcheia, Kyriakos Mitsotakis implicitly presents leftism/anarchism and terrorism as synonyms, using the fallacy of homonymy. Moreover, he explicates that the rise of criminalization and terrorism is connected to the Syriza government's decision to establish a lawless state and defend its ideological allies. Furthermore, by introducing a fallacy of division (Sophistical Refutations 169a 33) that violates rule 7—the standpoint is not conclusively defended—and the topos of (Syriza's) threat (see above), he underlines the political divisions between New Democracy and Syriza. In particular, New Democracy's leader presents a totalitarian model that is based on security and suppression in the name of the Greek people's safety and euphoria. Finally, Mitsotakis portrays Exarcheia as avaton or no-go area,[15] a cliché widely used by the Greek media and the right wing, and in this way at the same time gives a negative but also sacred tone to a district that historically identifies as leftist.

Mitsotakis' decision to adopt the extreme political communication established by his predecessor, Samaras, confirms New Democracy's turn from the centre-right to the far right as aporia in a time of crisis. The two leaders' arguments are based mainly on the topos of (Syriza's) threat and fallacies that contribute to the cultivation of terror, as developed using historical falsifications and divisive simplifications. Totalitarianism and populism pervade the two leaders' rhetoric in an attempt to highlight Syriza's inability to keep Greek citizens safe and Greek institutions functioning.

Conclusion

The Greek debt crisis and the sociopolitical crisis caused by austerity policies suspended the myth of the Greek EU-topia that had been cultivated by the two-party system under PASOK and New Democracy. Greece's position in the EU and the Eurozone was called into question as the threat of a possible Grexit increased. Euroscepticism and nationalism also challenged the political status quo of the two-party system, which was delegitimized by Radical Left Coalition's and Syriza's election successes in 2012. Syriza's anti-austerity, populist rhetoric together with the party's electoral 'revenge' on the traditional state of affairs led to a dystopian climate of extreme political communication and political enmity, orchestrated by the far right and the right wing. Drawing on long-silenced stories of Greece's divided past that had remained untold during the era of EU-topia, the resurgence of the red menace and the analogy between terror/terrorism and Syriza in a climate of a politics of hate, the leaders of the New Democracy party attempted to stigmatize Syriza and the left in general. Of course, Syriza and its ultranationalist partner in government—the Independent

Greeks (ANEL)—also contributed to the divisive climate; however, it was New Democracy that pushed extreme polarization and revived the ghosts of past political dichotomies.

Drawing on Arendt's work on totalitarianism, I would argue that the resurgence of Greece's divided past and the discursive convergence between the right-wing party New Democracy and the extreme right can be explicated on the basis of the ideology of terror and the discursive construction of antithetical political and historical identities—the left and the right. By employing DHA, especially its argumentation analysis, and the Aristotelian tradition of topos and false reasoning, I show the discursive distinction between 'us', the patriots who ensure the people's safety and the country's European process, and 'them', the traitors who support terrorists and imply lawlessness. Terror and the topos of (Syriza's) threat thus function as 'common sense', and dominate the two New Democracy leaders' rhetoric, which is based on security and law-and-order dogma.

Totalitarianism is not limited to a particular form of government known by the name of totalitarian dictatorship (Friedrich & Brzezinski 1956; Arendt 2004). Totalitarian methods of government, as distinguished from democracy and autocratic regimes (Friedrich and Brzezinski 1956) and totalitarianism's social and historical aspects, have been described widely (Pomian 1995; Halberstam 1999). What makes Arendt's work timely is her systematic effort to describe totalitarianism not only as a form of autocratic governance, but also as an aporia of liberalism's inadequacies, and to explicate the propagation of racism and antisemitism in times of crisis (Halberstam 1999). As Arendt (2004; 1998) noted, the destruction of European institutions and traditions by the First World War and the growth of racial and ethnic consciousness led to a moral destruction of community and the cultivation of totalitarianism. Greece's multiple crises (debt, financial, sociopolitical) challenge the country's European process, and create a dystopian political climate that is based on populism and the convergence between the right wing and the extreme right powers' rhetoric.

As Arendt wrote, 'terror is the essence of totalitarian domination' (2004: 599). The result of the next election in Greece will prove if New Democracy's signposting of terror and the red menace can be successful. What we are watching now is the mainstreaming of extreme polarization and a politics of hate, and the legitimation of a far-right discourse that signifies Greece's political scene.

Notes

1 All translations from the Greek are by the author.
2 Regarding the debate, see https://vouliwatch.gr/news/article/sto-koinovoylio-metaferetai-i-syzitisi-peri-exisosis-kommoynismoy-nazismoy-erotisi-gia-ti-mi-symmetohi-tis-elladas-sto-synedrio-tis-e.
3 https://www.youtube.com/watch?v=kBZoU8goUWg.
4 https://www.youtube.com/watch?v=4KWaSJKppbg.
5 The complicated relation between 'existential threats' and 'security issues' is linked to the influence of Carl Schmitt's political theory. Drawing upon Schmitt's work (1932) the Copenhagen School developed the theory of securitization in order to explain the discursive construction of security by political elites; a theory that contributes to the analysis of the discursive opposition as 'us' and 'them' (see McDonald 2008; Balzacq 2005). According to Balzacq 'securitization is a rule-governed practice, the success of which does not necessarily depend on the existence of a real threat, but on the discursive ability to effectively endow a development with such a specific complexion' (2005: 179).
6 https://www.youtube.com/watch?v=4KWaSJKppbg.
7 EU-topia implies that Greece's financial, social and political prosperity is connected to the country's access to the EU; it is antithetical to Grexit— Greece's posited exit from the EU due its debt crisis.
8 https://www.politico.eu/article/greece-fears-revival-of-far-left-violence.
9 http://www.iefimerida.gr/news/348178/haos-sti-voyli-otan-o mitsotakis eipe i-tromokratia-cihe-proeleysi-apo-ti-mitra-tis.
10 Kyriakos Mitsotakis was the brother-in-law of the late Pavlos Bakoyannis, who was assassinated by the far left terrorist group 17 November in 1989.
11 https://www.youtube.com/watch?v=q4UvYXy6T5Y; https://www.protagon.gr/epikairotita/mitsotakis-o-dixastikos-logos-tsipra-mono-zimia-proka-lei-ston-topo-44341624994.
12 https://www.xrimaonline.gr/article/politiki/62738-nees-boles-mitsotaki-gia-ti-metafora-giatzoglou-ston-korydallo.
13 https://www.cnn.gr/news/politiki/story/62226/synenteyxi-kyriakoy-mit-sotaki-tha-kathariso-ta-exarxeia.
14 http://www.naftemporiki.gr/story/1203542/erotisi-kur-mitsotaki-gia-tin-eg-klimatikotita-kai-to-abato-ton-eksarxeion.
15 Avaton in Greek means a place or a sacred area to which access is forbidden.

References

Amossy, R. (2002), 'How to do things with doxa: Toward an analysis of argumentation in discourse', *Poetics Today*, 23/3: 465–87.

Arendt, H. (1998), *The human condition* (Chicago).

— (2004), *The origins of totalitarianism* (New York).

Aristotle (1992), *Topics* (Athens).

— (1994), *Sophistical refutations* (Athens).

— (2004), *Rhetoric* (Thessaloniki).

Balzacq, T. (2005), 'The three faces of securitization: Political agency, audiences and context', *European Journal of International Relations*, 11: 171.

Boukala, S. (2016), 'Rethinking topos in the discourse historical approach: Endoxon seeking and argumentation in Greek media discourses on "Islamist terrorism"', *Discourse Studies*, 18/3: 249–68.

— & D. Dimitrakopoulou (2016), 'The politics of fear vs the politics of hope: Analysing the 2015 Greek election and referendum campaigns', *Critical Discourse Studies*, 14/1: 39–55.

Christopoulos, D. (2014), 'The political venture of the far right extremism mapping in the Greek state', in D. Christopoulos (ed.), *The deep state in Greece and the far right* (Athens).

Friedrich, C. & Z. Brzezinski (1956), *Totalitarian dictatorship and autocracy* (Cambridge).

Halberstam, M. (1999), *Totalitarianism and the modern conception of politics* (New Haven).

Kallis, A. (2007), 'Fascism and religion: The Metaxas regime in Greece and the "Third Hellenic civilisation": Some theoretical observations on "fascism", "political religion" and "clerical fascism"', *Totalitarian Movements & Political Religions*, 8/2: 229–46.

— (2010), 'Neither fascist nor authoritarian: The fourth of August regime in Greece (1936–1941) and the dynamics of fascistisation in 1930s Europe', *East Central Europe*, 37: 303–30.

Linardatos, S. (1977), *From the Civil War to Junta*, i, v (Athens).

Margaritis, G. (2009), *History of the Greek civil war 1946–1949*, i (Athens).

McDonald, M. (2008), 'Securitization and the construction of security', *European Journal of International Relations*, 14/4: 563–87.

Mitsotakis, Kyriakos (2017a), statement, 17 January, www.cnn.gr/news/politiki/story/62226/synenteyxi-kyriakoy-mitsotaki-tha-kathariso-ta-exarxeia.

— (2017b), statement, 10 February, www.naftemporiki.gr/story/1203542/erotisi-kur-mitsotaki-gia-tin-egklimatikotita-kai-to-abato-ton-eksarxeion.

— (2017c) interview, 26 June, www.politico.eu/article/greece-fears-revival-of-far-left-violence/.

— (2017d), addresses the Greek Parliament on terrorism, 4 July, www.iefimerida.

gr/news/348178/haos-sti-voyli-otan-o-mitsotakis-eipe-i-tromokratia-eihe-proeleysi-apo-ti-mitra-tis.

— (2017e), statement, 26 October, www.youtube.com/watch?v=q4UvYXy6T5Y.

— (2018a), statement, 5 March, www.xrimaonline.gr/article/politiki/62738-nees-boles- mitsotaki-gia-ti-metafora-giatzoglou-ston-korydallo.

— (2018b), statement on terrorism, 22 May, www.protagon.gr/epikairotita/mitsotakis-o-dixastikos-logos-tsipra-mono-zimia-prokalei-ston-topo-44341624994.

Musolff, A. (2006), 'Metaphor scenarios in public discourse', *Metaphor & Symbol*, 21/1: 23–38.

Panourgia, N. (2009), *Dangerous citizens: The Greek Left and the Terror of the State* (New York).

Pomian, K. (1995), 'Totalitarisme', *Vingtième Siècle: Revue d'histoire*, 47: 4–23.

Psarras, D. (2014), 'Constantine Plevris and the 4th of August party', in ASKI, *Far right in the light of history* (Athens).

Reisigl, M. & R. Wodak (2001), *Discourse and Discrimination* (London).

— (2016), 'The Discourse Historical Approach', in R. Wodak & M. Meyer (eds.), *Methods of Critical Discourse Analysis* (London) (first pub. 2009).

Rubinelli, S. (2009), *Ars Topica: The Classical Technique of Constructing Arguments from Aristotle to Cicero* (Berlin).

Samaras, Antonis (2012), pre-election speech, 3 May, www.youtube.com/watch?v=kBZoU8goUWg.

— (2015), pre-election speech, 23 January, www.youtube.com/watch?v=4K-WaSJKppbg.

Schmitt, C. (1932), *The Concepts of the Political* (Chicago).

Van Eemeren, F. & R. Grootendorst (1987), 'Fallacies in pragma-dialectical perspective', *Argumentation*, 1/3: 283–301.

— Gerssen, B. & B. Meuffels (2009), *Fallacies and judgments of reasonableness: Empirical research concerning the pragma-dialectical discussion rules* (Berlin).

Vasilopoulou, S. & D. Halikiopoulou (2013), 'In the shadow of Grexit: The Greek election of 17 June 2012', *South European Society & Politics*, 18/4: 523–42.

Vernardakis, C. (2012), 'From Mass Parties to Cartel Parties: The evolution of the structure of political parties in Greece through changes in their statutes and systems of financing', working paper series in the legal regulation of political parties, 27.

Verney, S. (2014), '"Broken and can't be fixed": The impact of the economic crisis on the Greek party system', *International Spectator: Italian Journal of International Affairs*, 49/1: 18–35.

— (2015), 'Waking the 'sleeping giant' or expressing domestic dissent? Mainstreaming Euroscepticism in crisis-stricken Greece', *International Political Science Review*, 36/3: 279–95.

Voulgaris, Y. & I. Nikolakopoulos (2014), 'The 2102 election earthquake', in

Y. Voulgaris & I. Nikolakopoulos (eds.), *The 2012 double election earthquake* (Athens).

Wodak, R. (2015), The politics of fear: *What right-wing populist discourses mean* (London).

CHAPTER 7

Articulations of climate change by the Austrian far right

A discourse-historical perspective on what is 'allegedly manmade'[1]

Bernhard Forchtner

As climate change has become an ever more present topic in public debate, political camps too have positioned themselves on the phenomenon, reproducing their political identity by taking a stance. And while, historically, the far right has in many cases shown an ideological affinity with environmental protection (Forchtner 2019a), its stances on climate change appear to vary. Indeed, while people and land are interwoven in far-right ethno-nationalist thought, resulting in a view on environmental protection as homeland protection, research on far-right stances on manmade climate change has found acceptance and, more prevalent, varying degrees of scepticism towards the thesis of manmade climate-change (Gemenis et al. 2012; Voss 2014; Forchtner & Kølvraa 2015; Forchtner et al. 2018; Lockwood 2018). However, while research on, for example, conservatives in the US and conservative newspapers in Europe have indicated higher levels of climate-change scepticism than amongst their liberal counterparts (for example, Carvalho 2007; McCright & Dunlap 2011; Campbell & Kay 2014; Kaiser & Rhomberg 2016; Painter & Gavin 2016), little is known about climate change communication by far-right actors, ranging from radical right populists such as the Danish People's Party, to extreme-right parties such as the National Democratic Party of Germany (NPD). Indeed, the stance of these actors on, for example, immigration has been researched extensively, but few studies have investigated far-right contributions to the discourse about climate change.

Existing research, then, has shown that the situation is not uniform (Forchtner 2019c). Gemenis et al. (2012) note that at least the Greek Popular Orthodox Rally agrees with it, and Voss (2019; 2014), having studied party documents and legislative motions, claims that the Freedom Party of Austria (FPÖ) too accepts the thesis. At the same time, members of the party, including its chairman (Strache 2013; 2015; 2017; 2018) and the FPÖ's then environmental spokesperson (Winter 2015), have casted doubt on human influence. In fact, it was even noted in the influential Austrian far-right weekly *Zur Zeit* (Sailer 2007: 25) that one of the 'well-cherished false messages' within the 'right' is that climate change is an invention of 'left–green fanatics'—a view the author rejected. Still, about a decade later, a survey amongst readers of *Zur Zeit* showed almost two-thirds of the respondents agreeing with the statement that 'The withdrawal [of the US from the Paris Climate Agreement] is reasonable—no manmade climate change exists' (Zur Zeit 2017).

Against this background, this chapter addresses far-right climate change communication in general and the case of Austria in particular. That is, the chapter contributes insights into elements of far-right climate change communication in general, and, more specifically, the seemingly puzzling case of the Austrian far right. Given that the FPÖ has already been studied, and that the wider Austrian far right is often, in one way or another, connected to the FPÖ, I shed light on the heterogeneous Austrian case by analysing paradigmatic 'satellite actors'—actors that do not officially belong to the party, but which are nevertheless closely connected to it, such as the monthly *Die Aula*, the Internet blog *unzensuriert.at* and the aforementioned *Zur Zeit*. I do so by adopting a discourse-analytical perspective, drawing eclectically on the discourse-historical approach (DHA) (Reisigl & Wodak 2009) in critical discourse studies (CDS) applied to samples taken from these three sources. In so doing, I set out the dominant discursive strategies of argumentation—of justifying and legitimizing far-right stances on the thesis of manmade climate change—and, to a lesser degree, the strategies of nomination and predication, in order to illustrate the role that climate change communication plays for the far right.

I turn briefly to the (Austrian) far right and existing research on climate-change scepticism. This is followed by a section on data and method utilised in this chapter. I subsequently analyse this corpus of far-right texts on climate change before ending my argument with a comprehensive conclusion.

The far right, environmental protection and climate change communication

To talk about the far right in Austria is impossible without at least briefly recapitulating the status of the FPÖ. The latter prides itself on representing the so-called *Drittes Lager* (third camp), which is neither the social- nor the Christian-democratic segment of the Austrian electorate, but rather the German-national/national-liberal one (see Bailer & Neugebauer 1994; Wodak & Pelinka 2002; Rheindorf & Wodak 2019). After the Second World War, the forerunner of the FPÖ, the Association of Independents, was founded, providing a home for this segment, including Nazis. Following an internal crisis, the FPÖ emerged in 1955/56 as 'a German nationalist, far to the right party in which former, in part seriously incriminated National Socialists took leading functions' (Schiedel & Neugebauer 2002: 16). And while more liberal voices rose to prominence after the 1960s, 1986 saw Jörg Haider become party chairman, marking the forceful return of far-right views to the forefront of the party. The party was part of the national government between 2000 and 2005, but ultimately experienced internal turmoil, a split, and a severe crisis (emerging out of the FPÖ, the far-right Alliance for the Future of Austria was in government from 2005 to 2007,). Under Heinz-Christian Strache, who became party chairman in 2005, the party has recovered, and since 2017 has been back in the national government (again, with the conservative Austrian People's Party). Under Strache, far-right fraternities have seized key positions and are now clearly shaping the party's ideological core (Scharsach 2017).

In Austria and Germany, extreme right ideology comprises (to varying extents, depending on the actor in question) ethno-nation-alist convictions; ethnocentrism, ethnopluralism and xenophobia; anti-liberalism, anti-pluralism and authoritarianism; anti-socialism, anti-Americanism and antisemitism; the demand for a strong state; a proclivity for scapegoating; and an apologetic view of history, potentially including Holocaust denial and the relativizing of war guilt (Holzer 1994). Some of these ideological elements have also been connected to the natural environment (Forchtner 2019b). For example, nature is viewed as providing the ultimate assurance of what is authentic, providing a stable blueprint for how the social order is supposed to work vis-à-vis the zeitgeist (Kedourie 1966: 57). Furthermore, the natural environment, to the extent that it becomes 'the homeland', enters into a symbiotic relationship with the people (Smith 2009: 49–50). Viewing the natural environment along these lines unifies ecologism and nationalism in a rebellion against 'the levelling perversion of the universal and [in] defence of the particular as a diversifier' (Barcena et al. 1997: 302).

This 'rebellion' has long been present among the German-speaking far right, and can be traced back to the Romantic revolt against the Enlightenment. In fact, Olsen (1999: 28) notes that far-right ecology is 'a distinct right-wing form of modern environmentalism, one that is grounded in hostility to Enlightenment universalism characteristic of ultra-nationalism.' Looking specifically at the FPÖ, already its 1968 party programme briefly mentions opposition to environmental pollution, while its manifesto of 1973 includes a relatively detailed section on 'Man and his environment'. In fact, the party adopted environmentalist positions early on. Concerning this stance, one well-known party member, Andreas Mölzer, links environmental protection to a 'typical German tradition of nature-awareness' in a revealing publication by the FPÖ training institute, stating that

> Who speaks of homeland, means historically grown culture within specific spaces and these spaces are composed of field and meadow, of mountain and river, of lakes and grassland, of humans and animals. In short: the identity-conscious man is necessarily also an ecoconscious one. (Mölzer 1994: 16)

Similarly, a widely circulating slogan in the German-speaking far right, 'Environmental protection is homeland protection' (sometimes 'Nature protection is homeland protection'), is also noted by FPÖ cadres (for example, Strache 2018; for Germany, see Forchtner 2019b). Unsurprisingly, Turner-Graham (2013) is thus able to illustrate how the FPÖ's youth wing has connected national identity and national environment in the online world—using the latter to imagine a pure homeland. Similarly, Voss (2014; 2019) identifies a strong link between nation and environmental protection when it comes to the far-right party family. And while he identifies climate change as a divisive issue within the far-right party family, according to Voss (2014: 163–5; 2019), the FPÖ is one of those parties that warns that humans contribute to climate change. As sources investigated in this chapter are closely linked, both personally as well as ideologically, to the FPÖ (Doew 2017), one might therefore hypothesize that these sources are (largely) in line with the stance of the FPÖ.

However, as even prominent party members have voiced climate-change scepticism (Strache 2013; 2015; 2017; 2018; Winter 2015), the link between land and people has apparently not always led far-right actors to accept the thesis of manmade climate change. In fact, studies on the far right and climate change in general (Lockwood 2018), on Germany (Forchtner et al. 2018) and Denmark and the UK (Forchtner & Kølvraa 2015), for example, indicate the prevalence of climate-change scepticism amongst such actors. Similarly, Gemenis et al. (2012) point to further European parties which reject the thesis of manmade climate change. More recently, Schaller & Carius (2019: 27–30, 63–4) recorded the often negative voting behaviour concerning mainstream climate change policies by many far-right parties in the European Parliament. And a study of Norway focuses on attitudes towards climate change amongst conservative white males, and, more specifically, identifies a variable that measures xenophobic views as increasing climate-change scepticism (Krange et al. 2018).

Scepticism about climate change has been famously conceptualized by Rahmstorf (2004) along the lines of trend scepticism (the denial of climate change happening at all), attribution scepticism (the denial of climate change's anthropogenic cause), and impact scepticism (a changing climate might not be a bad thing). This typology has been expanded by Van Rensburg (2015), who speaks of, first, evidence scepticism (covering Rahmstorf's three types) as well as two concomitant classes of arguments: that is, second, process scepticism (scepticism concerning knowledge generation and decision-making processes in the context of climate change), and, third, response scepticism (scepticism about policy responses to climate change). In the following, I adopt this typology (see Table 7.1, where to increase legibility, only those categories with at least one occurrence are kept while additions I have made are in italic).

Numerous studies (for a review, see Krange et al. 2018) have illustrated the link between climate-change scepticism and contemporary conservatism in Europe, the US, and beyond, and that elements evident in far-right climate change communication at times resemble conservative scepticism. However, due to different ideological elements and foci, far-right climate-change scepticism should not be viewed as a simple extension of contemporary conservative scepticism (Forchtner et al. 2018: 590). In addition, the far right itself is not a homogeneous bloc, as the aforementioned ideological elements are present to different degrees, in different historical and societal contexts, and vary according to genre, such as party manifestos and nominally independent far-right magazines. We thus need to look at more cases—if possible, comparatively—so that far-right climate-change scepticism is explored comprehensively.

Data and method

This chapter does not draw on official party-political material, but rather on texts produced by sources close to the FPÖ. In fact, all three sources—the Internet blog *unzensuriert.at*, the weekly *Zur Zeit*, and the monthly *Die Aula*—have been shaped by members of the party. *unzensuriert.at* was founded in 2009 on the initiative of the then third National Assembly Speaker Martin Graf (FPÖ). The Documentation Centre of Austrian Resistance (Doew) calls the platform a 'disinformation project at the right-wing fringe' (Doew 2017). The blog claims to report about topics mainstream media do not cover (or only do so in an allegedly biased way), and, according to the blog's masthead, it is accessed 2 million times a month.

More traditional than *unzensuriert.at* is the weekly *Zur Zeit*. Founded in 1997, the newspaper grew out of the Austrian edition of the German far-right weekly *Junge Freiheit*, though cooperation between the two papers ceased to exist in 2007 after the latter's editor objected to contacts between the NPD and one of the founding editors of *Zur Zeit*. This editor, Mölzer, is a former FPÖ Member of the European Parliament and high-profile party member, and currently co-edits the paper with another politician of the FPÖ, Walter Seledec. According to their website, *Zur Zeit* has a print run of 22,000.

Finally, *Die Aula* was founded in 1951. Its first editor, Josef Papesch, was an early member of the NSDAP (since 1934 when the party was still illegal in Austria) and the magazine's final editor was Martin Pfeiffer (2004–2018). Its final issue was printed in June 2018; in December 2018, its successor, *Freilich*, was first published. *Die Aula* was a key publication of the Austrian far right and published by the Arbeitsgemeinschaft Freiheitlicher Akademikerverbände Österreichs, the association of academics close to the FPÖ. The magazine was accused of open racism, anti-Americanism, and antisemitism, and of historical revisionism; and while, for example, online media such as *unzensuriert.at* have proved increasingly influential, *Die Aula* did continue to connect the FPÖ to the non-parliamentarian extreme right (Doew 2017; see also Gärtner 1994). According to Doew, *Die Aula* had a circulation of about 9,000 in its later days.[⁴]

The source material analysed here thus consists of texts (articles, features, editorials, a small number of book recommendations, comic strips, and one front page) from the three sources which treat climate change or CO_2 as a main topic (as signalled by a headline and/or lead paragraph, see Van Dijk 1991: 131) and were published between 2007 and 2017. I have thus excluded pieces which mention climate change, but primarily deal with topics such as chemtrails, energy security, renewable energy sources, and energy transition. I have also excluded, due to their slightly different genre characteristics, all letters to the editor. In sum, the corpus consists of 98 texts: 16 in *unzensuriert.at*, 73 in *Zur Zeit*, and 9 in *Die Aula*.

Each text was coded by two researchers as (a) accepting the thesis of manmade climate change, as (b) opposing this thesis, or as (c) 'unclear'. Second, all articles were coded using a more elaborate set of variables presented by Van Rensburg (2015: 7) (see Table 7.1). This enabled me to identify the key objects of climate-change scepticism—'objects' that given the discourse-analytical framework I employ can be used as shorthand for topoi.

The framework with which I approached the resultant topoi is that of the DHA in CDS. The DHA, and CDS more broadly, is fundamentally concerned with how social relations of power are exercised through language use, and of how demarcations of *us* from *them* are realized in discourse (see Reisigl & Wodak 2009). The DHA views three elements as constitutive of a discourse: a discourse is macro-topic related (here, the discourse about climate change), pluri-perspective (sceptics and those accepting the view of most scientists concerning climate change) and argumentativity (these different perspectives offering justifications for their stances). This framework is adopted here through an analysis of contributions to the discourse about climate change by far-right actors. To understand the meaning of these contributions, any DHA calls for a comprehensive understanding of context as being four-dimensional: from (*i*) immediate, language or text internal co-text/discourse, to (*ii*) inter-textual/discursive relationships, (*iii*) the context of the particular situation, and, (*iv*) the wider socio-historical context (as briefly discussed above). Against this background, positions are realized through macro-discursive strategies; the main one I will focus on is (*a*) the discursive strategy of argumentation. This concerns arguments employed in the investigated discourse and, in particular, the use of the topoi. Topoi connect a premise (data) with the claim characterizing the argument, and thus serve as conclusion rules ('if-then').[3] In addition to the specific topoi, I will indicate the predominant ways of (*b*) naming actors, phenomena/events, objects and processes, and (*c*) predicating them (attributing characteristics to them) so to better to understand far-right positions.

Analysis

In exploring how climate change is communicated by an influential segment of the Austrian far right, I start with observations on the initial, basic coding of the source material. First, overall, there is a climate-change-sceptic majority: 22 texts accept that climate change is caused by human activity; but almost twice as many, 40, are sceptical when it comes to (manmade) climate change, while in 36 cases the orientation of the article is not clear or no stance is taken.

The *unzensuriert.at* corpus consists of 16 texts, of which none

Figure 7.1. 'After the Ice Age, forest dieback, the ozone hole, mad cow disease, avian flu, and particulates, is global warming now "topical": Threat or media con?' ©Aula-Verlag G.m.b.H. Reproduced by permission of Aula-Verlag G.m.b.H.

accept the thesis of manmade climate change, 7 are sceptical, and 9 'unclear', while for *Die Aula* the figures are 9 texts, of which 0 accept the thesis of manmade climate change, 7 are sceptical, and 2 are 'unclear'. Although the number of articles is low, the topic is at times prominent. For example, at one point (Figure 7.1), the cover page of *Die Aula* raises the question 'Threat or media con?' relatively neutrally (though the cover does flag up 'Climate change [.] The hysteria of the media'), but the answers provided inside are all sceptic or unclear. *Zur Zeit*, too, features climate change prominently as its topic of the week in November 2011, raising a very similar question: 'Climate change—Myth and truth'. And while the situation is much more balanced in *Zur Zeit*, scepticism about the evidence is nevertheless the single most relevant position. Of 73 articles, 22 accept the thesis of manmade climate change, 26 are sceptical, and 25 are unclear.

This may be the broad pattern of the climate change communication, but what of the objects of climate-change scepticism? What relevant topoi are there among the 'sceptic', 'unclear' and 'accepting' communications on climate change? This is best understood in tabular form (Table 7.1). The first number in the various boxes concerns the total number of articles in which the respective object is present. In addition, the numbers in brackets provide the breakdowns (<number of 'sceptic' texts employing the respective object>–<number of 'unclear' texts employing the respective object>–<number of texts accepting the thesis of manmade climate change which employ the respective object>). Unsurprisingly, objects are mostly present in sceptical texts, though there are some in 'unclear' texts and even a few in 'accepting' ones.

Before looking at this pattern in more detail, it is worth mentioning that scientists have, overwhelmingly, identified human activity—for example, the burning of fossil fuels—to be the main cause of rising global temperatures. For example, the Intergovernmental Panel on Climate Change (IPCC 2014: 2) states that 'Human influence on the climate system is clear, and recent anthropogenic emissions of greenhouse gases are the highest in history.' With the results in Table 7.1 in mind, I will first comment on the most fundamental type of climate scepticism, evidence scepticism: scepticism about the very existence of climate change, its human causes, and its impact. The first of these three, trend scepticism, is present, but does not dominate. For example, authors claim, that temperatures are not any longer increasing (globally), that global warming has stopped. In fact, at times texts make this claim based on the data that global temperatures have more recently decreased. This move from data to claim is justified via a topos I refer to as the topos of no more warming ('if temperatures are not increasing

Table 7.1. Objects of climate-change scepticism in *unzensuriert.at*, *Die Aula*, and *Zur Zeit*, based on a revised version of Van Rensburg (2015).

Core objects of scepticism (arguments that define scepticism)				Concomitant objects of scepticism (arguments that strengthen scepticism)		
Evidence			**Processes**		**Response**	
Trend	Cause	Impact	Scientific knowledge generation process	Climate decision-making process	Policy instruments	Policy style
No post-industrial warming 3 (3-0-0)	No CO$_2$ causal mechanism 29 (28-1-0)	Significant positive impacts/ benefits of CO$_2$ foregrounded 8 (6-2-0)	Climate change is a hoax 6 (6-0-0)	Political interference in Intergovernmental Panel on Climate Change 3 (3-0-0)	Carbon pricing will not curb emissions enough 1 (0-1-0)	Economy and jobs should not be harmed 20 (12-8-0)
Data inconclusive 4 (3-1-0)	Entirely 'natural' causes 7 (7-0-0)		A lucrative climate industry now exists 11 (8-3-0)	Socialists and Greens drive the climate agenda 6 (4-2-0)	*Carbon pricing: a money-making scheme* 3 (3-0-0)	*Climate change used to allow migration* 7 (2-3-2)
Warming stopped 6 (5-1-0)	Predominantly 'natural' causes 2 (1-1-0)		Climate activists seek fame and money 2 (2-0-0)	Wealth distribution 4 (1-2-1)		
	Too early to tell 4 (2-2-0)		Scientists manipulate/hide the evidence 13 (10-3-0)	Media sensationalism distort public opinion 13 (9-4-0)		
			Computer model- ling overrated and unreliable 5 (4-1-0)	*Climate change used to curb national sovereignty* 6 (4-0-2)		
				Climate change irrationalism 39 (28-7-4)		

globally, then there is no climate change'). The third form of evidence scepticism, impact scepticism, is present too, but, as in the case of trend scepticism, does not dominate. Here, what I term the topos of benefit warrants a move from the necessity of CO_2 for life on Earth to discarding positions which view (too high levels of) CO_2 as dangerous ('If he or she thinks that CO_2 is not beneficial, then he or she cannot be trusted with deciding about fundamental issues concerning our planet'). For example, Harald Winter argues in *Zur Zeit* that

It is particularly ridiculous if one speaks of CO_2 as 'climate poison' or 'environment poison'. Would this 'poison' not exist in our atmosphere, would life as we know it not be possible. As is generally known, plants, with the help of light and out of water and CO_2, produce longer hydrocarbon molecules and oxygen of which ultimately all animals and plants live. (Winter 2011: 13)

And yet, the topos most important to evidence scepticism concerns the relation between humans, CO_2 and greenhouse gases more generally, and climate change (cause scepticism)—the topos of climate-neutral human CO_2 emissions ('If manmade CO_2 is not causing climate change, then man cannot be held responsible for climate change'). For example, in *Die Aula*'s own response to the question on its cover (Figure 7.1), Gerhoch Reisegger (2007: 30) speaks of 'ridiculously small, but allegedly increasing proportions of CO_2'. Thus, 'besides the fact that there is no reason for the "climate catastrophe" due to increased CO_2 or "greenhouse gases", humans would not nearly be in the position to influence the "climate"' (Reisegger 2007: 30). Doubt that humans are significant enough in our eco-system to have causal powers is also voiced by Wolf-Rüdiger Mölzer, Andreas Mölzer's son who notes in *Zur Zeit* that the 'manmade share of CO_2 in the air thus [amounts to] only a ridiculous 0.00046%, therefore about every 217,391th air molecule—this simple calculation speaks for itself' (2014: 48). Casting doubt on the significance of human activity is sometimes explicitly connected to natural developments as when authors point to the sun as the cause of climate change (for the German case, see, Forchtner et al. 2018: 599), a claim also put forward by Strache (2017), the FPÖ chairman.

It comes as no surprise that the process of manmade climate change is regularly referred to as 'climate change', in scare quotes. Even more often, and a manifest strategy to cast doubt on its existence, it is qualified with 'allegedly' (*angeblich*), thus again casting doubt on what scientists overwhelmingly agree on. Similarly, CO_2 is at times referred to ironically as 'evil' (*böse*).

Another set of objects concerns relevant processes, beginning with the status of climate science and scientists, the process of generating scientific knowledge. In line with existing research on both far-right (Forchtner et al. 2018: 596–7) and conservative climate-change communication (for example, McKewon 2012: 284), scientists are regularly accused of manipulating evidence (for example, referring to the Climatic Research Unit at the University of East Anglia and alleged malpractice there) and of drawing on unreliable simulations to boost belief in this 'scam' and support those depending on climate change policies. In the corpus studied here, this is indeed the single most prominent object in this column (Table 7.1). One headline, for example, reads 'Climate change: undesirable research findings are hushed up' (*unzensuriert.at* 2010) while Reisegger (2007: 29) speaks of 'corrupt "scientists"'. Similarly, Arno Delegesta (2008: 20) mobilizes Fred Singer to describe 'facts' presented by 'scientists' as being based on 'predominantly incorrectly measured, wrongly interpreted or selectively selected data in the interest of desired outcomes' in *Zur Zeit*. In fact, Singer plays a key role in anglophone climate-change-sceptic debates, and is described by Conway & Oreskes (2012) as a key player in the drive by corporate interests to delegitimize the overwhelming scientific consensus on manmade climate change. Furthermore, and also in *Zur Zeit*, Jan Ackermeier (2009: 19) speaks of 'unfair tricks', 'fabricated consensuses', and 'data manipulation' allegedly uncovered through the hacking of the Climatic Research Unit at the University of East Anglia in 2009. The lexis employed here draws on the semantic field of 'deception', feeding into a topos of scientific untrustworthiness ('If established scientists/science working on climate change do not follow proper scientific procedures, then their warnings concerning climate change cannot be trusted').

While all this appears to attack science as such, it is an attack on a particular kind of science (as perceived by these actors)—and in line with the often 'populist' attitude of far-right actors today (populism here being understood as the articulation of an opposition in society between 'the pure people' and 'the corrupt elite'—and populists are supposed to articulate the general will of the former; see Mudde 2007: 23). What is attacked is 'mainstream' or 'establishment' science; science seen as serving the interests of the established order, holding *us* ordinary people down (Forchtner & Kølvraa 2015: 214 for the Danish case). However, this does not imply that the far right does not mobilize science itself, including scientists who allegedly stand up to 'dogma', and who have the courage to speak truth to power. Indeed, at various points the word is given to scientists, be they international ones such as Singer or local ones such as Gerhard Gerlich, and articles try to prove the nonexistence of manmade climate change by providing ostensibly scientific calculations of the relevance of CO_2 and the non-existence of the greenhouse effect (as in Wolf-Rüdiger Mölzer's remarks above). As such, 'elite science' is juxtaposed with 'people science', a dichotomy that resonates with the basic stories told by populist far-right actors.

Second, process scepticism covers the nature of the public sphere in which the status and consequences of climate change are negotiated and decided. Here, the dominant object is again familiar from literature on far-right and conservative contributions to the discourse about climate change. It concerns claims that public debate is distorted by hysteria and apocalyptic viewpoints, ridiculing proponents of the thesis of manmade climate change as being irrational, and, in doing so, often drawing on religious tropes (Forchtner & Kølvraa 2015: 213; Forchtner et al. 2018: 597).[4] For example, in an article on 'Climate hysteria and propaganda' in *Zur Zeit*, Winter (2011: 13) writes of 'apocalyptic horror reports', 'scaremongering', and 'prophets of the climate apocalypse'. Such nominations from the semantic fields of irrationalism and religion are indeed widespread and employ lexis such as 'alarmists', 'climate delusion', 'dogma', 'heretics', 'priests of the climate religion', 'eco-high priests', 'CO_2-believers', 'climate cult', 'climate preachers', climate sinners', and 'sale of indulgences'. As a concomitant form of climate scepticism, this topos of (religious) irrationalism ('If those arguing in favour of climate change are driven by (religious) irrationality, then their agenda should be doubted') does not necessarily doubt climate change, but does delegitimize proponents of the thesis of manmade climate change.

Let me illustrate what we have seen so far—scepticism about manmade climate change coupled with attacks on established science and the ridiculing of those accepting this thesis—by turning to an extreme, and extremely curious, case. Walter Lüftl, a prominent figure on the extreme right, who has repeatedly raised his voice in the climate change debate in Austria and Germany (concerning the investigated corpus, see Lüftl 2007a, b), became (in)famous for his revisionist report entitled *Holocaust: Glaube und Fakten* (1991) (republished in

English as 'Holocaust: Belief and Facts' in the revisionist *Journal of Historical Review* in 1992), a report which, for example, doubts the mass murder in the gas chambers of Auschwitz for technical reasons. Lüftl's take on climate change is arresting because of his move from Holocaust denial to climate change denial. Lüftl (2001) had long argued that the population was made feeling insecure through a series of lies—he lists twelve—including the hole in the ozone layer, (manmade) climate change and the greenhouse effect, mad cow disease, and 'history lies'. Lüftl is an extreme example, but he illustrates how climate-change scepticism can be a consequence of how the extreme right views the world, emerging from conspiracy theories about the manipulation of 'the people'.

Finally, when it comes to response scepticism, the object 'Economy and jobs should not be harmed' is the most central. This, again, is in line with previous research on climate-change scepticism, as well as the wider concern among the far right today (Lockwood 2018; Forchtner et al. 2018). The claim mainly covers a macro-perspective on competition between countries or regions (for example, the US and China are regularly named as *others*, as having an advantage vis-à-vis Austrian or European industry), but I have also included claims about what might be detrimental to the finances of 'the little guy'. In both cases this claim forcefully reproduces a populist outlook. It contains warnings against Europe's deindustrialization (a common way of naming the threat as seen by the far right), which is viewed as being the fault of those in power (be they the national government or the EU). This justification can be conceptualized as the topos of *we* first ('If cutting back emissions causes too much harm, then we should not do so'). For example, it is claimed that 'the so-called "manmade climate change" is not to be accepted as fact and more than merely controversial' before pointing out that only some states have accepted the Paris Agreement (the follow-up to the Kyoto Protocol), and which 'will thus suffer a huge competitive disadvantage' (*Zur Zeit* 2015: 49).

Conclusion

In identifying the major positions and topoi in the predominantly climate-sceptic communication of selected Austrian far-right sources, what does this chapter tell us about the far right? First, and related to my initial observation on the paucity of research on far-right climate change communication, we do now know that key sections of the Austrian far right tend to be climate-change sceptics. As such, this study contributes to the existing body of empirical research on far-right climate change communication and confirms a previous observation that the ideology-driven affinity for nature protection, where relevant, does not necessarily extend into the area of climate.

Why is this? As I have argued above, I do not view this as being due to an outright rejection of environmental concerns. Indeed, four texts explicitly assert the importance of protecting the environment, including a climate-sceptic one. However, when turning to the climate, this concern for the environment does not necessarily result in an acknowledgement of manmade climate change. I would argue that other elements simply take priority over that of nature protection; for example, climate change provides these actors with the opportunity to articulate a gulf between 'pure people' and the 'corrupt elite'. In other words, agendas that for whatever reason are prioritized can 'override' the far right's ideological affinity to environmental protection. An article in *Zur Zeit* (Howanietz 2008) further illustrates the interplay of priorities, for while apparently accepting manmade climate change, it argues that in the medium term, global warming will be far less explosive than, for example, same-sex marriage.[5] In addition, the article also features polemical passages which echo sceptical contributions to the discourse about climate change (for example, CO_2 as a 'climate killer'), rejections of the Kyoto Protocol as 'economic mayhem' and endangering the country's 'security of supply' of energy, and opposition to 'EU constitutional dictates'.

Interestingly, and in contrast to other studies (Forchtner & Kølvraa 2015; Forchtner et al. 2018; Lockwood 2018), fears at the loss of national sovereignty were not strongly present in the material analysed (see Table 7.1). Similarly, 'climate refugees' were discussed in seven articles, but this is hardly an overwhelming number, even though it might signal the advent of such a subject position. Its presence is not limited to climate-change sceptics; rather, both 'believers' (for example, Sailer 2007) and those who do not even consider whether climate change exists or is manmade (for example, *unzensuriert. at* 2017) warn against climate change as a justification for asylum. Another observation is that not only are those who accept the thesis of manmade climate change outnumbered by sceptics, but they also lack the zeal and certainty with which the sceptics make their point. It is not simply a question of 'sharper language', though, for climate-change sceptics they can frame their stance using tropes that are well known from other discourses in which the far right participates (anti-government and anti-EU; in favour of 'the little guy' who must pay increased taxes; and so on).

Second, and concerning my specific interest in whether the Austrian far right is climate-change sceptic or not—in the context of existing findings which claim that the FPÖ accepts the thesis of manmade climate change—the analysis illustrates that the majority of texts in key publications of the Austrian far right, which are related to the party, are climate-change sceptic. Indeed, while I did not analyse materials published by the FPÖ, the investigated corpus cannot be fully separated from the party, whether ideologically or personally. One explanation for this puzzle could be that sources that do not directly speak for the party are able to articulate ideological preferences more clearly than it is possible in, for example, performances in the parliament (though this is not necessarily convincing given the performance by Winter 2015). A more persuasive answer will require more work on this and similar cases—additional work which will benefit our understanding of how far-right ideology operates in an area not commonly associated with far-right politics.

Notes

1 This research was supported by FP7 People: Marie-Curie Actions (grant number 327595). I am thankful to Ruth Wodak and an anonymous reviewer for their comments on an earlier draft of this chapter.

2 I am thankful to members of the Doew, who not only arrived at this circulation number, but also helped with the process of data collection for this chapter.

3 See Wodak 2015: 53 for a list of topoi in 'right-wing populist rhetoric',

and Boukala 2016 for a comprehensive discussion of the discourse history approach to topoi and their relation to Aristotelian dialectic and rhetoric.

4 For religious tropes in climate-change-sceptic Australia, see Jaspal et al. 2016; McKewon 2012; for the UK, see Atanasova et al. 2017.

5 For more on the author of the article and his politics, see Rheindorf & Wodak 2019.

References

Ackermeier, J. (2009), 'Farce um Klimaerwärmung: "Klimagate": Hacker finden umfangreiche Beweise für Datenmanipulation', *Zur Zeit*, 52–3: 19.

Atanasova, D. & Koteyko, N. (2017), 'Metaphors in Guardian Online and Mail Online opinion-page content on climate change: War, religion, and politics', *Environmental Communication*, 11/4: 452–69.

Bailer, B. & W. Neugebauer (1994), 'Die FPÖ: Vom Liberalismus zum Rechtsextremismus, in Dokumentationsarchiv des österreichischen Widerstands', in Dokumentationsarchiv des österreichischen Widerstands (ed.), *Handbuch des österreichischen Rechtsextremismus: Aktualisierte und erweiterte Neuausgabe* (Vienna).

Barcena, I., P. Ibarra & M. Zubiaga (1997), 'The evolution of the relationship between ecologism and nationalism', in M. R. Redclift & G. Woodgate (eds.), *The international handbook of environmental sociology* (Cheltenham).

Boukala, S. (2016), 'Rethinking topos in the discourse historical approach: Endoxon seeking and argumentation in Greek media discourses on "Islamist terrorism"', *Discourse Studies*, 18/3: 249–68.

Campbell, T. & K. Aaron (2014), 'Solution aversion: On the relation between ideology and motivated disbelief', *Journal of Personality & Social Psychology*, 107/5: 809–24.

Carvalho, A. (2007), 'Ideological cultures and media discourses on scientific knowledge: re-reading news on climate change', *Public Understanding of Science*, 16/2: 223–43.

Conway, E. & N. Oreskes (2012), *Merchants of doubt* (New York).

Delegesta, A. (2008), 'Der Klimaschwindel: Erderwärmungs-Irrtümer und CO_2-Lügen: Die "Klimawissenschaft" ist als Wissenschaft einfach noch nicht gefestigt', *Zur Zeit*, 27: 20.

Doew (2017), 'Die Aula 2017: Gegen "Ostküste", "Blutsvermischung" und "parasitäres Großkapital"', *Doew*, www.doew.at/cms/download/q38k/aula_2017.pdf.

Forchtner, B. & C. Kølvraa (2015), 'The nature of nationalism: "Populist radical right parties" on countryside and climate', *Nature & Culture*, 10/2: 199–224.

— A. Kroneder & D. Wetzel (2018), 'Being skeptical? Exploring far-right climate change communication in Germany', *Environmental Communication*, 12/5: 589–604.

— (2019a) (ed.), *The far right and the environment: Politics, discourse and communication* (London).

— (2019b) 'Nation, nature, purity: Extreme-right biodiversity in Germany', in C. Kølvraa & B. Forchtner. (eds.), *Cultural imaginaries of the extreme right* (special issue, *Patterns of Prejudice*, 53/3).

— (2019c), 'Climate change and the far right', *WIREs Climate Change*.

Gärtner, R. (1994), 'Die "Aula" und die Wissenschaft', in W. Purtscheller (ed.), *Die Ordnung, die sie meinen: "Neue Rechte" in Österreich* (Vienna).

Gemenis, K., A. Katsanidou & S. Vasilopoulou (2012), 'The politics of anti-environmentalism: positional issue framing by the European radical right', paper given at the MPSA Annual Conference, Chicago, 12–15 April.

Holzer, W. I. (1994), 'Rechtsextremismus: Konturen, Definitionsmerkmale und Erklärungsansätze', in Dokumentationsarchiv des österreichischen Widerstands (ed.), *Handbuch des österreichischen Rechtsextremismus: Aktualisierte und erweiterte Neuausgabe* (Vienna).

Howanietz, M. (2008), 'Die Klimaschutzbefohlenen', *Zur Zeit*, 22: 16.

IPCC (2014). *Climate change 2014: Synthesis report: Contribution of working groups I, II and III to the Fifth Assessment Report of the Intergovernmental Panel on Climate Change*, ed. R. K. Pachauri & L. A. Meyer (Geneva).

Jaspal, R., B. Nerlich & K. van Vuuren (2016), 'Embracing and resisting climate identities in the Australian press: Sceptics, scientists and politics', *Public Understanding of Science*, 25/7: 807–24.

Kaiser, J. & M. Rhomberg (2016), 'Questioning the doubt: Climate skepticism in German newspaper reporting on COP17', *Environmental Communication*, 10/5: 556–74.

Kedourie, E. (1966), *Nationalism* (London).

Krange, O., B. Kaltenborn & M. Hultman (2018), 'Cool dudes in Norway: Climate change denial among conservative Norwegian men', *Environmental Sociology*, doi: 10.1080/23251042.2018.1488516.

Lockwood, M. (2018), 'Right-wing populism and the climate change agenda: Exploring the linkages', *Environmental Politics*, 27/4: 712–32.

Lüftl, W. (2001), 'Die Lügen unserer Zeit', *Vierteljahreshefte für freie Geschichtsforschung*, 5/3: 325–26.

Lüftl, W. (2007a), 'Dichtung und Wahrheit', *Die Aula*, 6: 31.

Lüftl, W. (2007b), 'Neue Abzocke der Autofahrer?', *Die Aula*, 11: 37.

McCright, A. & R. Dunlap (2011), 'Cool dudes: The denial of climate change among conservative white males in the United States', *Global Environmental Change*, 21: 1163–72.

McKewon, E. (2012), 'Talking points ammo', *Journalism Studies*, 13/2: 277–97.

Mölzer, A. (1994), 'Was heiß schon "grün"?', in Freiheitliches Bildungswerk (ed.), *Mensch und Umwelt: Grüne Fragen—Blaue Antworten* (Vienna).

Mölzer, W.-R. (2014), 'Verrückte Sache—unser Klima: Verrückt ist der Streit, ob sich die Erde nun erwärmt oder nicht', *Zur Zeit*, 22: 49.

Mudde, C. (2007), *Populist radical right parties in Europe* (Cambridge).

Olsen, J. (1999), *Nature and nationalism: Right-wing ecology and the politics of identity in contemporary Germany* (New York).

Painter, J. & N. Gavin (2016), 'Climate skepticism in British newspapers 2007–2011', *Environmental Communication*, 10/4: 432–52.

Rahmstorf, S. (2004), *The Climate Sceptics* (Potsdam).

Reisegger, G. (2007), 'Klimawandel, "Treibhaus"-Effekt, Emissions-"Zertifikate"', *Die Aula*, 6: 28–30.

Reisigl, M. & R. Wodak (2009), 'The discourse-historical approach', in Wodak, R. & M. Meyer (eds.), *Methods of critical discourse analysis* (London).

Rheindorf, M. & R. Wodak (2019), '"Austria First" revisited: A diachronic cross-sectional analysis of the gender and body politics of the extreme right', in C. Kølvraa & B. Forchtner (eds.), *Cultural imaginaries of the extreme right* (special issue, *Patterns of Prejudice*, 53/3).

Sailer, G. (2007), 'Klimawandel und Flüchtlingshorror: Das "Global Warming" wird eine neue Völkerwanderung bringen', *Zur Zeit*, 31: 25.

Schaller, S. & A. Carius (2019), *Convenient truths: Mapping climate agendas of right-wing populist parties in Europe* (Berlin).

Scharsach, H-H. (2017), *Stille Machtergreifung: Hofer, Strache und die Burschenschaften* (Vienna).

Schiedel, H. & W. Neugebauer (2002), 'Jörg Haider, die FPÖ und der Antisemitismus', in A. Pelinka & R. Wodak (eds.), *'Dreck am Stecken': Politik der Ausgrenzung* (Vienna).

Smith, A. (2009), *Ethno-symbolism and nationalism* (London).

Strache, H.-C. (2013), *ORF Wahl 2013 Konfrontation Strache-Spindelegger*, 9 September, www.youtube.com/watch?v=YCyIqDiTQWw.

— (2015), *ORF hosts Strache at Sommergespräche*, 17 August, www.youtube.com/watch?v=I85NzqKXV_o.

— (2017), *Ö1 hosts Strache at Journal zu Gast*, 3 June, www.youtube.com/watch?v=mm_fyo3ksEs.

— (2018), 'Strache: "Wir Österreicher sprechen ja nicht zufällig Deutsch"', *Der Standard*, www.derstandard.at/2000093340857/Strache-Ich-lebe-mit-diesen-Vorwuerfen-sehr-gut.

Turner-Graham, E. (2013), '"An intact environment is our foundation of life": The Junge Nationaldemokraten, the Ring Freiheitlicher Jugend and the cyber-construction of nationalist landscapes', in A. Mammone, E. Godin & B. Jenkins. (eds.), *Varieties of right-wing extremism in Europe* (London).

unzensuriert.at (2010), 'Klimawandel: Unerwünschte Forschungsergebnisse werden totgeschwiegen,' www.*unzensuriert.at*/content/00612-Klimawandel-Unerw-nschte-Forschungsergebnisse-werden-totgeschwiegen.

— (2017), 'EU-Beschluss: Spezieller Schutzstatus für jene, die durch Klimawandel "vertrieben" werden,' www.*unzensuriert.at*/content/0023677-EU-Beschluss-Spezieller-Schutzstatus-fuer-jene-die-durch-Klimawandel-vertrieben.

van Dijk, T. (1991), 'The interdisciplinary study of news as discourse', in K. Bruhn-Jensen & N. Jankowksi (eds.), *Handbook of qualitative methods in mass communication research* (Abingdon).

van Rensburg, W. (2015), 'Climate change scepticism: A conceptual re-evaluation', *SAGE Open*, April-June: 1–13.

Voss, K. (2014), 'Nature and nation in harmony: The ecological component of far right ideology' (PhD diss., Florence).

— (2019), 'The ecological component of the ideology and legislative activity of the Freedom Party of Austria', in Forchtner 2019a.

Winter, H. (2011), 'Veränderliches Klima: Klimaschwankungen sind nichts Neues', *Zur Zeit*, 4: 22.

Winter, S. (2015), *Stenographic protocol: National Assembly of Austria*, 8 July, 85th session.

Wodak, R. & A. Pelinka (2002), *The Haider phenomenon in Austria* (New Jersey).

— (2015), *The politics of fear: What right-wing populist discourses mean* (London).

Zur Zeit (2015), 'Der große "Wurf" in Sachen Klima? Klimakonferenz wird zum "Hemmschuh" der heimischen Wirtschaft', *Zur Zeit*, 51: 49.

— (2017), 'US-Austritt aus Klimaabkommen', *Zur Zeit*, 24: 5.

CHAPTER 8

Gender and body politics of the extreme right in Austria

Party politics meets popular culture

Markus Rheindorf & Sabine Lehner

In discourse-historical research on constructions of national identities, the 'body of the nation' or 'national body' has been an integral analytical category since the 1990s (Wodak et al. 2009). The concept was originally focused on territory, its landscapes and borders, buildings and cultural artefacts of the 'built environment'. It has recently been linked to the previously separate strand of research on 'body politics' (Wodak 2015; Brown & Gershon 2017; Forchtner & Kølvraa, forthcoming) and thus also opens up the 'national body' to an explicitly gendered reading.

The electoral successes of far-right movements across Europe, but particularly of extreme-right parties such as Austria's FPÖ, Germany's AfD, or Hungary's Fidesz indicate an acceptance of far-right positions in mainstream politics and society at large. Prominent examples include the securitization of migration (Vollmer 2019), the ameliorization of 'Fortress Europe' in border policies (Wodak, this volume; Lehner & Rheindorf 2018), the denial of climate change (Forchtner, this volume) or the endorsement of racist and antisemitic conspiracy theories. Among this general trend, the particular combination of nativist, heteronormative, and sexist positions that characterizes the body and gender politics of the extreme right has seen some normalization. Examples such as abortion law in Poland, biologist legitimation for denying asylum to refugees, imposing clothes prohibitions on Muslim women in France, Denmark, and Austria all demonstrate that extreme-right ideology has a keen interest in enforcing its body and gender politics. While in opposition, political parties may attempt to do so through agitation and scandal; when in government, they will attempt to legislate corresponding measures; but in all contexts, such efforts have repercussions on the level of discourse across social fields, for example, the media and popular culture.

In Austria, popular culture has long shown prominent traces of nationalism and conservative gender constructions. In particular, the musical genres of *Schlager* and *Volksmusik* have always relied on a heteronormative and deeply reactionary vision of gender roles, as evidenced by lyrics, artists' performances, and fan culture. Nonetheless, their gender and body politics has not traditionally been that of the extreme right. For roughly a decade, however, the controversial but immensely popular artist Andreas Gabalier has successfully brought to this sector of popular culture a body and gender politics shared with the extreme-right. Apart from his lyrics and performances, Gabalier has used interviews, public occasions, and social media to propagate his outspoken views on gender-related issues such as family life, marriage, homosexuality, and gender roles.

Although Gabalier has always been careful to disavow any affiliation with individuals identified as on the far right, and has also resisted public attempts at appropriation from, for example, FPÖ politicians, our contribution to this volume will show that his stage persona, performances, and other contributions to discourse need to be regarded alongside those of the FPÖ and its members insofar as they share key ideologemes with respect to gender and body politics. After outlining our theoretical framework, i.e. the discourse-historical approach as well as body and gender politics, we discuss the construction of important historical figures informing the Austrian national body. The analysis focuses on the recontextualization of contemporary extreme-right gender and body politics in the FPÖ's programme and in Gabalier's lyrics and public statements. Finally, the chapter concludes by discussing the overlaps between the gender and body politics in party politics and popular culture as represented by the FPÖ and Gabalier.

Theoretical framework

We situate our analysis in the framework of the discourse-historical approach (DHA) as a linguistically informed but strongly interdisciplinary, multi-method research programme in discourse studies. Research within the DHA frequently works with a variety of empirical data but also emphasizes the importance of textual, situational, historical, and cultural context in the interpretation of its results (Reisigl & Wodak 2016). Previous work within the DHA has shown the discursive construction of national identities to be informed by a shared political past, present, and future, a shared culture and language, homogenizing self- and other-representations, and an identificatory national body (Wodak et al. 2009). The latter is commonly conceptualized as the nation's territory, its 'natural' landscape as well as its built environment (for example, architecture, sites, and material art), its institutions (for example, executive, legislative, judiciary), and sometimes also its national 'heroes' (in, for example, politics, the military, sports or the arts). We follow research on the increasing significance of 'embodiment' (for example, Smith & Porter 2004), the representation of particularly prominent, and idealized bodies in the discursive construction of national identities. From this perspective, the performance of individual bodies may be highlighted and indeed appropriated by political actors in the construction of national identities. Such performances, whether by artists or athletes, are invariably gendered, and the discourses they are situated in powerfully regulate and articulate their gender performances.

At this juncture, the link between the national body and gender is crucial since 'All nationalisms are gendered' (McClintock 1995: 352). National figures of identification are role models also on the level of gender identity, and their performance of gender is thus compelled by social sanction and taboo (Butler 1988: 520). Thus, the national body is gendered through the performance and representation of national heroes. One can thus expect contestation of gender identities to leave traces in the performance of such public figures. The body of such a figure of national pride, arguably more publicly than any other, embodies 'possibilities both conditioned and circumscribed by historical convention' (Butler 1988: 521). Because group reproduction—both biological and social—is fundamental to nationalist politics (Peterson 1999: 39), nationalist body politics essentializes and inscribes 'compulsory heterosexuality' onto the national body—reproduced and concealed in the heteronormative matrix 'through the cultivation of bodies into discrete sexes with 'natural' appearance and 'natural' heterosexual dispositions' (Butler 1988: 524). This perspective, also associated with the notion of biopolitics, conceives of national sovereignty and identity through bodies and their gendered interrelations 'across society and everyday life' (Vaughan-Williams 2009: 732). Nationalism, being deeply inscribed with 'masculinized memory, masculinized humiliation and masculinized hope' (Enloe 1990: 44), is vulnerable to any threat to the binary opposition of heteronormativity. To maintain and naturalize the binary order of gender as 'sex', heteronormative biopolitics relies on strategies of exclusion and hierarchy (Butler 1990: 148).

The 'cultural significations' that politicians, athletes, and performing artists who occupy this symbolic space embody are often more stylized and hyperbolic than everyday gender performances. Nevertheless, such staged performances must be able to 'align to produce a culturally meaningful whole' (Bucholtz & Hall 2016: 10–11). In Butler's terms, the gendered body must become 'intelligible' as it enters a discourse, i.e. it must make sense in that discourse's particular terms or provoke censure (Butler 1988: 528). Gender identities, never independent of the complex negotiations of national identity, are continually renegotiated according to sociopolitical and situative contexts. Such developments are often experienced as a 'loss of identity', and consequently trigger a reaction that may well take the form of a counter-conception of identity that is claimed to be 'original', 'authentic', or 'traditional'.

Gendering the Austrian national body

In the historical context of the gendered national body in Austria, we find several leading rulers of the Habsburg Empire, some of whom have been heavily mediatized. In popular culture and educational materials, these are imbued with the nostalgia of a small modern state looking back at its imperial past, metonymically represented by a few ruling figures. Discursively, they have been constructed for the past

70 years as idealized figures of the benevolent if strict mother of the nation (Maria Theresa), of the forever youthful princess (Sisi), and the doting and essentially harmless patriarch (Franz Joseph), while the realities of ruling, including warfare, are downplayed or entirely negated. Austria's imperial rulers represent highly conventionalized types of womanliness and essentially impotent manhood, built around a harmless, peaceful, marrying nation. Notable is the absence of war heroes or military leaders in the popular imaginary, although Prince Eugene of Savoy, Field Marshal Schwarzenberg, and Count Radetzky are represented in statues and street names. Masculinity, especially in its aggressive, belligerent, and empire-building guise, presents something of a conundrum for Austria's imagined national past.

The tumultuous years of the First Republic of Austria (1918–1938) yielded no heroic figures to add to the popular imaginary, but the founding figures of the Second Republic have become enshrined: Theodor Körner, Leopold Figl, Julius Raab, Karl Renner and, more recently, Bruno Kreisky are identificatory figures—remarkably across the entire political spectrum. They are, needless to say, all men, and consistently constructed as statesmen. The discourse of national identity in Austria has avoided idolizing strong leaders since the fall of National Socialism.

Something of an *Ersatz* in the discursive construction of national identities have been sports personalities, especially skiers, and, to a limited degree, soccer and tennis players as well as Formula 1 racers. Such heroes have been predominantly male, and their masculinity has been linked to a traditional, rural identity, thought of as being 'authentic' to the mountainous regions of Austria. Characteristics such as ruggedness, down-to-earth simplicity, and a disregard for the trappings of 'modern, effeminate society' and particularly the 'urban intelligentsia' were traditionally associated with such figures. Correspondingly, prominent scientists, scholars, or intellectuals such as the novelist and Nobel laureate Bertha von Suttner or the founder of psychoanalysis Sigmund Freud are considered important figures of Austria's shared history, but do not draw much popular interest. More popular but also controversial in Austria are musicians. Leaving aside Mozart—although his popularized persona remains a trope of Austrian culture—recent decades have seen the hyper-masculine, macho persona of Falco, the girlish rock artist Christina Stürmer, and rural folk performers such as the skier-turned-singer Hansi Hinterseer.

While all Austrian parties tap into the national body by their use of the tropes of Austrian culture, often also including popular culture, the FPÖ has been particularly successful in appropriating symbols of the national body. A case in point is their 2015 election campaign 'anthem', which visually paraphrased the Austrian national anthem in showing a multitude of Austrian flags being waved, beautiful landscapes and landmarks, craftsmen at work, and white people in traditional family settings (Rheindorf & Wodak, forthcoming).

The recontextualization of extreme-right body politics

The following analysis covers the recent recontextualization and resemiotization of extreme-right body politics in Austria, meaning both the discourses that seek to regulate bodies through institution-alized political power and discourses that seek to embody such body politics. Specifically, we analyse data collected in the fields of politics (publications and performances by a political party, party-affiliated organizations or media) and popular culture (musical performanc-es, lyrics, album covers, interviews etc.). This allows us to identify articulations of body politics across a range of fields, showing how extreme-right positions appear at closed-door meetings (backstage politics, see Wodak 2014) as well as political handbooks and pam-phlets for election campaigns (frontstage politics) and in popular culture. On the one hand, we focus on the Austrian Freedom Party as a longstanding political movement on the far right (Scharsach 2017); on the other hand we focus on the immensely popular musician Andreas Gabalier and the ways in which his performances articulate extreme-right positions in popular culture. The advantage of such a comparative approach is that it reveals the links between party poli-tics and other social fields of action (Reisigl & Wodak 2016). Some of these links can be read as appropriations of popular culture or an individual artist by party politics, but one might also regard it as the penetration of extreme-right ideology into seemingly innocuous entertainment as part of an ongoing process of normalization. From the latter perspective, normalization describes how extreme ideologies are incorporated into the mainstream of politics and popular culture, among other fields.

Programmatic positions in recent FPÖ publications

Although the FPÖ can be categorized as an extreme-right party, and although its leadership under Heinz-Christian Strache since the ousting of the late Jörg Haider has been consolidated by members of duelling fraternities on the far right of the political spectrum, it is not a homogenous movement. Arguably, no public figure in the FPÖ more closely identifies with extreme-right ideology than Johann Gudenus, head of the FPÖ's Vienna chapter and Deputy Mayor of Vienna since 2015. Gudenus, whose father was convicted of Holocaust denial, is one of the authors of the FPÖ's party programme, and is known for his racist, nativist, antisemitic, and homophobic scaremongering by means of conspiracy theories that describe Austria as a doomed nation: 'The powerful European lobby of homosexuals wants absolute equality for homosexuals and lesbians. It is hard to imagine where all this will lead' (Pollak 2015).

Even so, Gudenus's utterances are not extraordinary for the FPÖ, and bear a strong similarity to the party-affiliated publication 'For a Free Austria' ('Für ein freies Österreich'), written by Michael Howanietz, a local FPÖ politician. Written in a sensationalist style, the book closely mirrors the official 'handbook' of FPÖ politics ('Handbuch freiheitlicher Politik'), drafted by the party leadership to serve as an internal guideline for party functionaries regarding key policy areas. We focus on the former publication as it constitutes a less constrained articulation of extreme-right ideologies. 'For a Free Austria' has endorsements written by the FPÖ's chairman, Strache, and vice-chairman, Norbert Hofer as forewords. The text defines itself as a call for 'an autonomous, independent country', meaning independent of transnational organizations, international law, international economy, the exchange of goods, which are described as ways in which Austria is being controlled by foreign powers (Howanietz 2013: 6). The various strands of argument in the book—all ultimately intended to present the FPÖ as Austria's salvation from immanent doom—are linked to the extreme right's constructions of the national body. In other words, the book calls for 'an independent country that depends on its many existent strengths, its Nature, its infrastructure and the productive power of its people' (Howanietz 2013: 7).

The book's arguments relate to the national body as 'state territory' and its 'borders', as 'landscape and Nature', and as 'the core family' and 'procreation'. Indeed, the call for 'liberation' from foreign control is presented as a duty to 'our children', and in particular of men's duty to their families: 'We owe it to those who come after us, our children' (Howanietz 2013: 7). The book is also very clear about the link between individual identity and the nation: 'The nation, once the main carrier of identity, has been replaced by societies and clubs and brands, weak prosthetics for the true belonging of national identity' (Howanietz 2013: 15). Such true belonging or 'Heimat' supposedly still exists in the country and rural areas, manifest in higher birth rates, hardy craftsmen working with their hands as in centuries past, and 'timeless values' (Howanietz 2013: 77). The author even postulates a spiritual and biological link between the Volk, or people and the soil, the 'most sacred property' of the nation (Howanietz 2013: 141). Equating soil and blood, to protect this 'eternal Heimat' is thus to protect one's true self (Howanietz 2013: 137).

This extreme-right worldview casts the modern, urban, and intellectual as weak as opposed to the archaic. Migrants are seen as a threat precisely because they have stronger identities: their 'assault' or 'invasion' to 'demographically displace' the Austrian people makes the latter 'a species on the brink of extinction' (Howanietz 2013: 19–20). To be modern, to include women in the workforce, say, is thus seen as a form of 'self-demotion' and 'self-destruction' (Howanietz 2013: 21), echoing Sarrazin's *Deutschland schafft sich ab* ('Germany is Doing Away with Itself') (Sarrazin 2010). The battlefronts of this struggle are many: 'It starts with a few English terms, inappropriate concessions to culturally foreign (*kulturfremde*) 'neo-Austrians' and years with a low birth-rate. Every unborn potential mother and father of the future accelerates the process of self-annihilation' (Howanietz 2013: 22). This, of course, links directly to attacks on legal abortion, and is a key point in the FPÖ's policy handbook. Here, the argument is presented in the form of statistics: with alleged 'estimates of over 50,000 abortions per year' as opposed to '76,344 births in 2009, that would mean that 4 out of 10 children are killed in their mother's womb. This would make the uterus the place with highest likelihood of death in our country' (FBI 2013: 160). This not only constitutes an attack on women's legal right to seek an abortion—until 3 months after conception and beyond, under grave threat to the physical or mental health of the pregnant woman or a serious risk that the child will be severely handicapped or if the pregnant woman was under the age of 14 at the time of conception (§ 74 of the Austrian Criminal Code, StGB)—it also constructs any such woman as 'killing a child'.

The gravest threat to the nation, however, is identified in decaying national pride: Honour and loyalty to the nation are seen as the foundation for heterosexual relationships (Howanietz 2013: 34).[1] This makes those who would weaken nationalism also conspirators against the family: 'die Familienzerstörer', destroyers of families (Howanietz 2013: 32). This circular argument defines the core of the FPÖ's gender politics as a deeply archaic biopolitics:

> The child needs the safety of the family. Its pillars are father and mother as positive male and female example. Both have been made deeply insecure in this self-understanding by the deliberate demolishing of the nature-given roles. Their disorientation leads to temporary relationships, because the image corresponding to the inner longing of the respective counterpart is not found. The man, who has been cast from the throne of the head of the family, still longs for a female partner who, in spite of the girls-own the-world magazines, is still able to think in homemaking categories, whose brood care drive exceeds the imposed ambitions for personal fulfilment. Woman, re-defined by feminist deconstructivist ambitions as a birth-certificate mother under the obligation to personal fulfilment still longs for a real man, who gives her all the emotional and economic securities that a young mother needs in order to devote herself almost without worries to her offspring. (Howanietz 2013: 32)

The book shamelessly uses hyperbole and straw man fallacies to drive home this point: 'Because we are still permitted, without official permission, to have children and raise them as best we can. Independent of ideological approaches that want to tear away children from their parents immediately after birth' (Howanietz 2013: 34). The purported 'conspiracy to brainwash children and abolish natural genders' is seen as the cause for women wanting a career and financial independence, which in turn is seen as the cause for 'many young women misrepresenting the initially desired impregnation as sexist harassment' (Howanietz 2013: 118) and ignoring their 'motherly brood care instincts' (Howanietz 2013: 119).

The other side of this gender politics is to denounce 'effeminate' and 'feminized' modern man, biologically destined to be 'provider and protector of the family' (Howanietz 2013: 119). Sportsmen are described as the 'last remaining idols' who may still be regarded as 'heroes', since traditional ideals such as 'soldierly virtues' and 'chivalry' have been 'sacrificed to the Zeitgeist' (Howanietz 2013: 35). Blame for this decay of traditional gender roles is placed on the left, feminists, civil society, NGOs, international organizations, corporations and, most of all, the media, which the book describes as 'weapons of mass destruction' when it comes to destroying the Volk. Comparing this inner weakness to the external threat of migrants, the book offers two alternative prognoses for the future: The true Austrian Volk will either slowly degenerate and die off, 'eaten from the inside like wasp larvae eat maggots' (Howanietz 2013: 117) or current developments will lead to a violent 'civil war' (Howanietz 2013: 121). The author clearly prefers the latter, arguing that like any conflict it would be 'productive' and 'awaken potential' (Howanietz 2013: 133). Either way, he concludes, 'Europe will burn' (Howanietz 2013: 134).

Although the FPÖ's public campaigns strike a notably softer tone, the FPÖ's gender politics remain visibly patriarchal, centred on the reproductive obligation of citizens. In several TV debates leading up to the presidential election in 2016, candidate Norbert Hofer maintained that any marriage of gay or lesbian couples as well as related adoption rights would destroy 'natural family structures': 'The life partnership of man and woman becomes a family only through the child'. He also voiced his rejection of gender mainstreaming: 'The aim of "gender mainstreaming" is nothing short of creating the "new human being" that Marxists-Leninists already aspired to.' Similar to many fundamentalist US Tea Party Republicans, Hofer also rejected 'pro-choice' policies for women, i.e. women's right to decide on abortion. Hofer also described 'the womb as the place with the highest mortality rate in our country' (PULS 4 2016). This attempt to regulate and police women's bodies and minds objectifies women in a way that is characteristic of the extreme right. In the gender politics of such ideologies, the 'national family' must preserve the traditional paternalistic order of the sexes and maintain the nation's body as white and pure. This draws on fascist imaginaries as extensively investigated by Musolff (2010) and Richardson (2017) in their research on the concept of the Volk and the 'Volkskörper' across German and British nationalistic writing since the eighteenth century. In summary, the extreme right's construction of the national body shows a constant effort to mobilize feelings of national pride and the need to defend the nation by reasserting gender relations as heteronormative and primarily reproductive.

Gabalier as Mountain Man

Born in 1984, Andreas Gabalier began his musical career in 2008 and quickly became popular with a predominantly young and rural audience in Austria and Germany. His songs are, with small exceptions, written in German and performed in a non-standard version of Austrian German. The musical style is an updated version of Volksmusik or Schlager, for which the translation 'folk music' is woefully inadequate, because it has no claim to an authentic folklorist tradition. His lyrics idealize the beauty of Austrian landscapes, traditional values, family, romance, and love of one's homeland or Heimat, but also incorporate masculine sexual conquest. In interviews and public events, he has called for the protection of traditional gender roles and decried the alleged marginalization of heterosexual men. Gabalier thus positions himself as advocate and representative of traditional masculinity vis-à-vis an equally traditional femininity.

Although Gabalier began his career with songs that idolize the authenticity of his 'mountain home' and the hard work of his grandfather's generation, he later mixed this style with rockabilly and pop, trivializing the pathos of Volksmusik to sexual encounters, male bonding and national pride. Gabalier has sought to embody the rural stereotype of a mountain farmer by amassing characteristics such as mountain peaks, antlers, pitchforks, folk dress, hardy craftsmen and sexualized yet innocent country girls. A recent development, however, is the particular brand of pop music performed by Andreas Gabalier since 2008, which he himself has labelled 'Volks-Rock'n'Roll'. In his music, lyrics, stage performances and interviews Gabalier effects the culturalization of extreme-right ideologies on a grand scale. This has spilled over into legal battles over whether he can be prevented from playing a concert at the Vienna Konzerthaus because of his controversial views.

Gabalier's song 'Mountain Farmer Boys' ('Bergbauernbuam') represents his idealized stage persona during his early career: a hard-working mountain farmer, in close communion with nature, a man carved from the wood of local trees, strong and virile as a bull. He envisions an archaic time in which the man of the house had to leave the homestead and venture into the 'wide world' to provide for his 'little girl'. In Gabalier's songs, there are no women except mothers and grandmothers, and the 'little girl' here remains somewhat ambiguous as a possible lover or daughter.

Among his most controversial positions, we find numerous coded allusions to National Socialism: The song 'Biker' evokes an old bond between Austrians, Italians, Germans and Japanese; 'Mein Bergkamerad' envisages the friendship of male bonding as strong and enduring as the 'iron cross' at the top of a mountain, amidst puzzling allusions to threatening storms, fire, and death. This theme was continued and led to public controversy with his third album, 'Volks-Rock'n'Roller'. The German Volk, while it can be translated as 'people' and is used in the compound Volksmusik, has strong associations with National Socialism, which used it ubiquitously. The album cover showed Gabalier, a mountain range on the horizon, holding an accordion in weirdly contorted posture that, from the angle the picture is taken, imitates a swastika. The album's songs are an exercise in misogynist heteronormativity and banal nationalism: Gabalier imagines himself a stag in pursuit of a 'sweet little doe' ('Sweet Little Rehlein') while also reimagining, yet again, the ideal 'sons of the eternal homeland' as strong, hard, and tied to the landscape 'through blood' ('Heimatsöhne').

In the 2015 song 'Der König der Alpen' he describes himself as the 'Germanic prince', hinting at German nationalist convictions in Austria that both predated and outlived National Socialism as a political movement. Holding that Austria culturally is part of the Germanic nation

Figure 8.1. Cover of Andreas Gabalier's album 'Volks-Rock'n'Roller' (Koch Universal Music).

(de Cillia & Wodak 2006), this view is closely tied to assumptions of cultural and racial supremacy (Reisigl & Wodak 2001).

After 'Home Sweet Home' (2013), which draws on an anachronistic longing for the beautiful and pure homeland, mixed with male bonding, Gabalier seems to have completed the ideal version of his persona in his fifth album, 'Mountain Man' (2015). The eponymous song, like the cover, presents a hyper-masculine version of Gabalier in the tradition of male superheroes like Superman: exaggerated muscles, wearing body armour and supposedly traditional leather pants as well as a red-and-white cape in the colours of the Austrian flag, he is 'Mountain Man'. The cover shows him flying across a vaguely Alpine landscape with a mountain range in the background and foothills extended below that; while the peaks are covered in snow, the hills below are circular and topped with nub-like shapes. Although Gabalier repeatedly denied the association with female breasts, he eventually

Figure 8.2. Cover of Andreas Gabalier's album 'Mountain Man' (Electrola Universal Music).

admitted to having intentionally provoked scandal. Mountain Man's role is established only in the heteronormative relation of saving a girl, scantly dressed and straddling him in a sexualized position. In contrast to his exaggerated proportions, the girl appears diminutive, about half his height. We take the portrayal of physical proportions as indicators of the gender inequality and dominance inscribed into the nationalist heteronormativity that his work expresses.

On stage, he gathers about him a plethora of masculine and nationalist paraphernalia ranging from traditional lederhosen to stag antlers, flags, and dolls. Gabalier's on-stage performances are thus patchwork exercises in trivial shamanism as much as in banal nationalism, treating the objects of male–national pride like totems. In 'Dirndl lieben'

('Loving girls'), Gabalier thus ostracizes progressive, emancipated women. They are referred to as 'Frauen' (women), withholding the apparently affectionate diminutives 'Dirndl' and 'Mäderl' (girls). Notably, he links the lacking femininity of emancipated women to 'being like a man' and takes the fact that this does not sexually arouse him as proof of his own heterosexuality. In another song ('My grandfather said'), Gabalier explicitly derives his view of women from his grandfather, lashing out against feminism and homosexuality. The song's phrasing 'But not all of us are into men | We much prefer to nibble at a real girl' not only reveals anxiety in the face of an (imagined) homosexual majority and defines who can be regarded as a true girl, denying emancipated women that gender identity, but it also incorporates the victim–perpetrator reversal that Gabalier publicly expressed in interviews and at the Amadeus Music Award (as will be seen). The true heterosexual man, he implies, is in the minority today, and he must defend his natural right to not only desire girls, but to demand that girls be desirable for him.

The Austrian national anthem

Gabalier became a controversial public figure when he performed Austria's national anthem at the Spielberg Formula 1 race in 2014. While not an official representative of the state, this linked him to the national body inasmuch as national anthems are an important part of the national body and pride (Billig 1997). The anthem's text was altered in 2012 by law to include 'daughters' alongside 'sons', changing the line 'Heimat bist du großer Söhne' (homeland are you to great sons) to 'Heimat großer Töchter und Söhne' (homeland to great daughters and sons). The change was controversial and many previous attempts to modify the text had been blocked with arguments pertaining to the sanctity of the text and anti-feminist sentiments.

Gabalier sang the old version of the anthem, deliberately omitting 'daughters', reigniting the debate over the word's inclusion in the first place. Amidst the political attention he received, Gabalier gave several interviews and defended his decision. His most notorious appearance was a live confrontation with the former Minister of Women's Affairs, Maria Rauch-Kallat, of the conservative People's Party. The discussion was moderated by the news show's anchor (MO) with Rauch-Kallat (MRK) on her right and Gabalier (AG) on her left. In the following, we analyse key passages of the discussion.

After introducing the topic and guests, the moderator asks Gabalier whether he had been unaware of the legal change to the text or had deliberately ignored it.

> AG: Well, deliberately ignored, well, I just learned it that way back then. The shitstorm, I think, was not directed at me but in the opposite direction. … I simply believe that this is a little piece of Austrian cultural heritage. A little piece of hysterical, um, historical cultural heritage that in my eyes one didn't have to change. That has nothing at all to do, in my eyes, with whether one is misogynist or not. I believe that I am the very last, everyone who knows me even a little knows how much I adore the ladies and the girls at the concerts and everywhere and sing about them in my songs. Um, that is simply the national anthem.

This is followed by an exchange about the musical arrangement before the anchor asked Rauch-Kallat about the struggle to change the anthem.

> MRK: Ah, it took more than twenty years and I had actually hoped that after it became the law, this tiresome debate would be over … But it has become clear that, ah, apparently, changing two words in a text can move an entire nation and, ah, I believe you, Mister Gabalier, that you are not misogynist at all. … but what you are doing or have done with this, is to give ammunition, so to speak, to all those who are really misogynist and really have a problem with women, um, and I believe that you should have considered that, and when you look at, um, the postings on some newspapers, which are really hateful, which are aggressive, which are misogynist, then, um, that is something which we should actually avoid. … I learned it that way when I was eight, I assume that like all children you were still using diapers when you were one and that you no longer do that now, because you learned to control your sphincter. So I also assume that you have learnt to sing texts differently and I consider it disrespectful towards the law, there is a law now, one can argue

about whether one likes it or not ... but majority is majority and the Parliament has decided ...

AG: One really has to say that it was the Parliament that decided that, I don't believe that the and— that the people, that the Austrians were really asked about this, otherwise the waves wouldn't be as high now and even the largest radio station Ö Drei, which is something of an opinion- leader, they have a vote since Monday where more than 95 per cent are in favour of the old version ... there you can see that the majority is actually in favour of it. I have also spent a lot of time these last few days in the car and read the most diverse newspaper, television and radio online websites. On many that are not always entirely in favour of me, because one cannot reach everyone with my music, and even there one can read again and again, um, that people who say they actually never needed that Gabalier person, but that this was great, because this is simply somehow also a little piece of cultural heritage that needs to be safeguarded and maintained.

MO: But when you hear how long the struggle has been for these two words to appear in the national anthem, do you understand then that some suffragettes complain?

AG: Um, on the one hand I do understand it perhaps, because I do indeed understand that women are fighting for their rights, but I don't think that this has to be set down in a hysteri– um historic piece of music in this way, I believe there are many other ways to give women their rights, and I don't think that in the year 2014 one still has to go on about this continuously, that women have to be continuously emphasized somewhere and and that is, I think that is so self-evident.

Gabalier argues, first, that the issue is not one of law but of what he learned in school. He presents this as self-evident ('I just learned it that way') without providing a conclusion rule as to why that would explain his actions. He adds other arguments that have characterized the debate over the anthem's change in very predictable ways: Second, since the anthem is 'historical' or 'a little piece of Austrian cultural heritage'—and thus part and parcel of Austrian national identity—it must not be changed. Third, his twice-repeated slip of the tongue when he means to say 'historical' but mispronounces 'hysterical' presents a case of calculated ambivalence (Klein 1996; Engel & Wodak 2013). He thereby expresses one of the oldest stereotypes used to denigrate suffragettes while maintaining plausible deniability. Thus, his utterances resemble rhetorical strategies used by the extreme-right FPÖ (Wodak 2015). His fourth argument is an ad hominem disclaimer that seeks to present his character as above suspicion. He claims to be well known for 'adoring' ladies and girls. This, too, is a recurrent strategy of the FPÖ: No matter how discriminatory a particular statement may have been, the fact that one has friends of that minority is quoted as evidence for being beyond reproach, or, indeed, incapable of being racist, sexist etc. ('apparent denials', Van Dijk 2004: 15).

Gabalier's fifth argument relates to the alleged damage that changing the anthem's lyrics has done, not to the piece as such on aesthetic grounds—another frequent argument and related to his first—but to the audience's enthusiasm in singing along at sporting events. 'No one sings along anymore', he says, and expresses regret over the loss of national unity in singing the anthem, as if this had somehow weakened Austria's nation-ness to the core.

Rauch-Kallat's counterargument expresses the hope that the struggle should have been over once the change had been made by law and indicates her surprise that 'changing two words ... can move an entire nation'. She then characterizes the public debate, particularly in social media, as hateful, aggressive and misogynist—and blames Gabalier for providing the grounds for that. In her final argument, the former Minister opposes this disrespectful, indeed often criminal outpouring of sexism, to the authority of a legal change made by a majority vote in parliament.

Gabalier does not simply disregard this argument, but uses it in populist terms—again, reminiscent of the FPÖ—to attack the representative parliamentary system as such, questioning both its right to change the anthem and its representativeness of the will of the people. Quoting an unrepresentative survey by a radio station as evidence, he confuses 'the audience' with 'the people', revealing again that his frame is still that of giving his audience what it wants rather than a political process, concluding in an appeal to the audience/people in populist terms as the ultimate arbiter of what is right. Following a quibble over the exact numbers of that survey, Gabalier presents his final argument: there are more important things to change, more important goals in the struggle for women's rights than changing the anthem. This allows him to both present himself as a proponent of women's rights and implies that anyone who focuses on such trivial matters is, in fact, doing the cause a disservice in a misguided attempt to be politically correct. The paternalistic implication, then, is that he has in fact done the women's rights movement a great service by pointing out that there are other, more pressing issues. By claiming that it is self-evident that women have equal rights, even if the anthem only mentions 'sons', he seeks to undermine all arguments for further change in terms of representation.

While Gabalier's argument is flawed on several levels, the most interesting aspect here is the contrast between the significance he attaches to the anthem as integral to national identity, which must be maintained and preserved, and his dismissal of the struggle to change it as trivial compared to other concerns of women's rights. He is thus making a claim on the anthem and, by implication, the construction of national identity on the level of representation, as exclusively male. Women may have the right to vote, have jobs and earn equal wages, but the symbolic integrity of the nation-state must remain a male domain. Apart from the fact the political struggle had taken decades, the fact that many Austrians, male and female, publicly supported his position indicates how widespread and deep-seated this gendered notion of national identity remains. The controversy made Gabalier the public figurehead of the debate about gendered national identity; people from the conservative right and far right rallied around him, decrying the alleged 'gender madness' and the threat of the 'gender conspiracy' of the left. In an absurd continuation of media attention, Gabalier has since been repeatedly interviewed regarding issues of family, children's education, gender roles, marriage and social policies.

Public controversy—defending the nation

In the media, Andreas Gabalier is often opposed to Conchita Wurst, the bearded transgender persona who won the Eurovision Song Contest (ESC) for Austria in 2014. Although both are medially constructed as national heroes, they are diametrically opposed in terms of worldviews and, specifically, the body politics they represent. However, there was no direct personal conflict until the Austrian Music Awards in 2015, where Conchita won three categories and Gabalier only one. Previously, Gabalier had voiced his irritation at the success and public acceptance of Conchita when she was selected as Austria's representative at the ESC 2014. In his acceptance speech at the awards in 2015, Gabalier commented on criticism that had been raised against him, including his performance of the national anthem, and then claimed to be a victim on account of being heterosexual: 'Man hat es nicht leicht auf dieser Welt, wenn man als Manderl noch auf ein Weiberl steht' (You don't have it easy in this world, being a man who still likes girls). The entire passage in his speech is hedged with the generalizing pronoun 'man', thus extending his claims regarding the marginalization and victim-ization of heterosexual men to an unspecified community of men. He thus performs, on stage, the vulnerability of nationalist masculinity and the perceived need to defend heteronormativity as the foundation of his own (very public) identity construction in a way that purports to represent an increasingly repressed majority (Enloe 1990: 44).

In this, but also in the salient use of 'Manderl' and 'Weiberl', Gabalier drew on previous utterances in right-wing political contexts. Most notably, Heinz-Christian Strache had voiced his outrage at Conchita's nomination for the ESC: 'If a guy like Conchita Wurst does not know if she is a man or woman, then she needs a psychotherapist rather than to participate in the Song Contest' (Pollak 2014). Strache here performs two characteristic moves of the conservative right-wing position on transgender identities. He insinuates that transgender people are themselves confused over their gender identity within a binary norm and then qualifies this confusion as a mental disease that should be treated rather than rewarded with public attention. A speech given by Strache at an election rally at much the same time had linked this way of speaking to non-heteronormative gender identities and gay rights as biologically unnatural and a decadent threat to society (Pollak 2014):

> What is the point of the adoption rights for homosexuals? We want to promote children. We want to promote the only form from which children can arise, and that only works between Manderl and Wei-

Figure 8.3. Screenshot of Höbart's Facebook page (Höbart 2015).

berl. That doesn't work between Manderl and Manderl and Weiberl and Weiberl. That's a biological fact. Of course, we don't want to subsidize sexuality. And we don't want to see decadence and hedonism propagated further in our society.

This brief passage exemplifies the ideological pathologization and exclusion of the 'deviant other' based on the simultaneous naturalization of heteronormativity and reproductive sexuality. In the field of politics and policy, in which Strache represents a far-right position, these claims are intrinsically linked to the state's perceived obligation to promote and subsidize reproduction rather than sexuality and, by implication, to enforce the one construction of gender and sexuality that is seen as enabling the reproduction of the nation (Butler 1990: 147–8; Vaughan-Williams 2009: 732).

Beyond the ideological parallels, Gabalier's acceptance speech drew on the salient terms 'Manderl' and 'Weiberl' in his victim-perpetrator reversal, giving expression to the binary gender hierarchy that underlies heteronormativity. Austrian media widely reported on the 'scandal' provoked by his speech, inviting further public statements. Among them were shows of solidarity with Gabalier on the part of Strache's FPÖ, most prominently by Christian Höbart, a member of parliament notorious for hate speech against refugees and Muslims. Twisting the slogan 'Je suis Charlie' created in the wake of the terrorist attack on the French satirical newspaper Charlie Hebdo in January 2015, which was used globally to show solidarity with a victimized group, Höbart superimposed 'Je suis Gabalier' on the Austrian flag.[2]

Gabalier's far-right position appropriated a frame that the FPÖ leader had previously established, and was in turn appropriated by the FPÖ in a show of solidarity with those willing to defend the heteronormative foundation of the nation-state—in this case, by taking a vocal stand against perceived oppression by the liberal mainstream.

Conclusion

Our analysis has revealed similar phrasings, rhetorical strategies, and obvious ideological parallels between the FPÖ's publications and Gabalier's songs and public utterances, particularly in terms of body and gender politics. Both insist on the maintenance of traditional, clear-cut, and dichotomous gender roles, following a heteronormative matrix and sexist constructions of women, purportedly to safeguard the nation. Both similarly insist that alternative gender roles represent a threat to the wellbeing and survival of the nation. Additionally, Gabalier has made various public allusions to National Socialism that indicate sympathy for and proximity to a particular extreme-right ideology, for example, Gabalier's Swastika-shaped body posture or by his songs about 'comrades', soldierly values, and eternal loyalty. The FPÖ has a long and well-documented history of similar proximity, resulting in countless scandals and numerous criminal convictions of its members (for example, MKÖ 2017). The comparison also shows that in a less obvious but still pertinent way, Gabalier applies very similar arguments as the FPÖ, for instance in arguing against the modernized version of the Austrian national anthem's lyrics. Finally, the FPÖ's public endorsement of Gabalier's alleged marginalization as a heterosexual man evidences the political party's very public attempt at appropriation.

Although the gender and body politics in party programmes and popular culture seem separate except for such declarations of solidarity, our study shows that in fact they share much more than just rhetoric. While primarily located in different social fields of action, Gabalier's case shows that the discursive realization of extreme-right gender and body politics is also present in the fields of institutionalized politics and popular culture. Because the two fields have different social structures and orders of discourse, genres, modes of publication etc., the FPÖ's and Gabalier's utterances differ on the semiotic level. Nonetheless, they rely on the same extreme-right ideology. When social actors such as Gabalier are given legitimacy qua public attention in the field of politics, and consequently speak in genres and media associated with that field, these similarities become more evident on the level of linguistic realizations.

Notes

1 'Ehre' and "Treue', the two concepts the book praises in this context, formed the core of the SS motto 'Meine Ehre heißt Treue', which is banned under the Verbotsgesetz 1947. This research was supported by the Austrian Science Fund FWF through the project 'The discursive construction of Austrian identity/ies: follow-up study 2015' (project number 27153). We would like to thank Ruth Wodak and Rudolf de Cillia, who collaborated with us in that project, as well as two anonymous reviewers of an earlier version of this chapter.

2 The blue-and-yellow flag to the right most likely displays the colours of Lower Austria, Höbart's constituency, and not the national flag of Ukraine.

References

Billig, M. (1997), *Banal Nationalism* (London).

Brown, N. & S. A. Gershon (eds.) (2017), 'Body politics', special issue, *Politics, Groups & Identities*, 5/1: 1–3.

Bucholtz, M. & K. Hall (2016), 'Embodied Sociolinguistics', in N. Coupland (ed.), *Sociolinguistics: Theoretical debates* (Cambridge).

Butler, J. (1988), 'Performative acts and gender constitution: An essay in phenomenology and feminist theory', *Theatre Journal*, 40/4: 519–31.

— (1990), *Gender trouble: Feminism and the subversion of identity* (London).

Cillia, R. de & R. Wodak (2006), *Ist Österreich ein 'deutsches' Land: Sprachenpolitik und Identität in der Zweiten Republik* (Innsbruck).

Engel, J. & R. Wodak (2013), "Calculated ambivalence' and Holocaust denial in Austria', in R. Wodak & J. E. Richardson. (eds.), *Analysing fascist discourse: European fascism in talk and text* (London).

Enloe, C. (1990), *Bananas, beaches, and bases: Making feminist sense of international politics* (Berkeley).

FBI (Freiheitliches Bildungsinstitut) (2013), *Handbuch freiheitlicher Politik: Ein Leitfaden für Führungsfunktionäre und Mandatsträger der Freiheitlichen Partei Österreichs* (4th edn, Vienna)

Forchtner, B. & C. L. Kølvraa (eds.) (forthcoming), F. 'Cultural imaginaries of the extreme right', special issue, *Patterns of Prejudice*.

Höbart, C. (2015), *Je suis Gabalier*, de-de.facebook.com/Christian-H%C3%B-6bart-129717993713060/.

Howanietz, M. (2013), *Für ein freies Österreich: Souveränität als Zukunftsmodell* (Vienna).

Klein, J. (1996), 'Insider-Lesarten: Einige Regeln zur latenten Fachkommunikation in Parteiprogrammen', in J. Klein & H. Diekmannshenke (eds.), *Sprachstrategien und Dialogblockaden: Linguistische und politikwissenschaftliche Studien zur politischen Kommunikation* (Berlin).

Lehner, S. & M. Rheindorf (2018), 'Fortress Europe: Representation and Argumentation in Austrian Media And EU Press Releases On Border Policies', in G. Dell'Orto & I. Wetzstein (eds.), *Refugee News, Refugee Politics: Journalism, Public Opinion and Policymaking in Europe* (London).

McClintock, A. (1995), *Imperial leather: Race, gender and sexuality in the colonial contest* (London).

MKÖ (Mauthausen Komitee Österreich) (2017), 'Die FPÖ und der Rechtsextremismus. Lauter Einzelfälle?' *MKÖ*, www.mkoe.at/sites/default/files/files/aktuelles/MKOE-Broschuere-Die-FPOE-und-der-Rechtsextremismus.pdf.

Musolff, A. (2010), *Metaphor, nation, and the Holocaust: The concept of the body politic* (London).

Peterson, S.V. (1999), 'Political identities/nationalism as heterosexism', *International Feminist Journal of Politics*, 1/1: 34–65.

Pollak, A. (2014), 'Strache vs. Conchita: Wurst statt falscher Normen', *Der Standard*, 13 May.

— (2015), *Der Hassprediger: Der aufhaltsame Aufstieg des Johann G* (Vienna).

PULS 4 (2016), Television debate hosted by the Austrian television channel PULS 4, 8 May, https://www.puls4.com/pro-und-contra/videos/wer-wird-prasident/Ganze-Folgen/Wer-wird-Praesident.-Das-Duell-vom-08.05.2016.

Reisigl, M. & R. Wodak (2001), *Discourse and discrimination: Rhetorics of racism and antisemitism* (London).

— — (2016), 'The discourse-historical approach (DHA)', in R. Wodak & M. Meyer (eds.), *Methods of critical discourse studies* (London).

— — (forthcoming), ' Austria first" revisited: A diachronic cross-sectional analysis of the gender and body politics of the extreme right', *Patterns of Prejudice*, special issue, *Cultural imaginaries of the extreme right*.

Richardson, J. E. (2017), 'Fascist discourse', in J. Flowerdew & J. E. Richardson (eds.), *The Routledge handbook of critical discourse studies* (London).

Sarrazin, T. (2010), *Deutschland schafft sich ab: Wie wir unser Land aufs Spiel setzen* (Munich).

Scharsach, H. (2017), *Stille Machtergreifung: Hofer, Strache und die Burschenschaften* (Vienna).

Smith, A. & D. Porter (eds.) (2004), *Sport and national identity in the post-war world* (London).

van Dijk, T. A. (2004), 'From text grammar to critical discourse analysis: A brief academic autobiography', www.discourses.org/From%20text%20grammar%20to%20critical%20discourse%20analysis.html.

Vaughan-Williams, N. (2009), 'The generalised bio-political border? Re-conceptualising the Limits of Sovereign Power', *Review of International Studies*, 35/4: 729–49.

Vollmer, B. M. (2019), 'The paradox of border security: An example from the UK', *Political Geography*, 71: 1–9.

Wodak, R., R. de Cillia, M. Reisigl & K. Liebhart (2009), *The discursive construction of national identities* (Edinburgh).

— (2014), 'Political discourse analysis: Distinguishing frontstage and backstage contexts: A discourse-historical approach', in J. Flowerdew (ed.), *Discourse in Context: Contemporary Applied Linguistics*, iii (London).

— (2015), *The politics of fear: What right-wing populist discourses mean* (London).

CHAPTER 9

Islamophobia without Muslims as a social and political phenomenon

The case of Poland

Adam Balcer

In recent years Europe has been experiencing a rise in support for right-wing populist parties, matched with a clash between antagonistic forms of national identities occurring within European societies. The real or possible immigration of Muslims bringing a change of religious structure became the main issue used by right-wing populists to gain votes. In effect, Islamophobia became the distinctive feature of right-wing populism. The conceptualization of Islamophobia is inspired by Chris Allen, who defined it as an ideology 'that sustains and perpetuates negatively evaluated meaning about Muslims and Islam ... shaping and determining understanding, perceptions and attitudes ... that inform and construct thinking about Muslims and Islam as Other' (2010: 190). Todd Green, author of *The Fear of Islam* (2015), defines Islamophobia in terms of the features that are attributed to Islam and Muslims in the anti-Muslim discourse. Islam is presented as the enemy: aggressive, expansive, monolithic, and static, absolutely separate and different, inferior, and manipulative. The anti-Muslim discourse exaggerates genuine problems existing in many Muslim societies and countries (religious fundamentalism, homophobia, authoritarianism, patriarchy, antisemitism). In Europe such discourse focuses particularly on Muslim immigrants and co-nationals presenting them as a completely alien group impossible to integrate and the fifth column undermining the social cohesion. In consequence, the anti-Muslim discourse, mixed with racial prejudice, is treated as natural (self-defence), and discrimination against Muslims is held to be either justified or fabricated (Green 2015).

Paradoxically, a scholarly analysis of the results of various elections in Europe shows that the right-wing populists that play the anti-Muslim card are mostly popular in regions characterized by very small Muslim communities (see, for example, Fourquet 2016). This social phenomenon may be called 'Islamophobia without Muslims'. Poland constitutes a particularly interesting case in hand. Although Muslims are an extremely small and well-integrated minority in Polish society, Poland has no conflicts with Muslim countries (excluding the most recent tensions with Iran), and it is not faced with a massive inflow of Muslim refugees or illegal immigrants, yet the country has seen a dramatic rise in anti-Muslim feeling in recent years. Islamophobia in Poland distinguishes itself by the sheer scale of the religious and historical references, its strong rejection of the modern, European, secular and liberal paradigm, and its soft Euroscepticism in the name of traditional and conservative values ('a genuine West').

The general rise of xenophobia in Polish society, and with it growing antipathy towards Muslims, started after 2010, but the refugee crisis in 2015 was the watershed. The activities of various nationalist groups, numerous media outlets, and a majority of the political elite overlapped and succeeded in creating a moral panic in Polish society. These actors misused certain features of Polish society, with the result that social support for Islamophobia snowballed, impelled by a combination of grass-roots social action and state or elite action. The Internet, and especially social media, played an unprecedented role in the dissemination of the anti-Muslim discourse, but its pull also came from the ethnic shape of nationalism long so popular in Polish society, and the persistence of the old antisemitic clichés popular among the right-wing electorate. In fact, some prejudices against Jews and Muslims stem from the same source: Orientalism. The rise of Islamophobia did much for the victory of Law and Justice (PiS) in the parliamentary elections in the autumn of 2015, and it continues as the source of its political modus operandi, which may be defined as the politics of fear. Even more important, Islamophobia constitutes one of key elements in the nation-rebuilding process promoted by PiS, which sees Poland as a monolithic state based on ethnicity, and thus rejects a civic national identity. Paradoxically, Islamophobia became one of the few unifying elements in a deeply divided country.[1] In fact, liberal, moderately conservative, and left parties and the Roman Catholic Church did not react decisively to the anti-Muslim identity narrative promoted by PiS; indeed, some representatives of liberal cultural elites and even more clergy—intentionally or not—endorsed or tolerated anti-Muslim prejudices and negative stereotypes in the public sphere.

Against this background, the chapter will examine how Islamophobia has in recent years become the key instrument for right-wing populists in Europe to gain support, how it relates to the ongoing debate about the shaping of national identity, and what kind of sociocultural environment creates the favourable conditions for the rise of Islamophobia. The chapter will address the dominant arguments and topics in the Islamophobic discourse as it is pursued in Poland, and particularly by PiS, and the practical consequences of Islamophobia on social and political life.

Ethnic nationalism and right-wing populism

Cas Mudde, a prominent Dutch political scientist, defines populism as an ideology that assumes that society is divided into two homogeneous, antagonistic groups, 'the pure people' and 'the corrupt elite', and argues that politics should be an expression of the *volonté générale*, the will of the people (Mudde 2007: 23). The populists' emphasis on the silent majority is often elided with an ethnic brand of nationalism, less sophisticated than the civic version, as it imagines the national community as a homogenous group. Indeed, populism invariably defines the world in simple terms, with its Manichean division into good and bad, friend and foe. The latter in these oppositions can most easily be defined using xenophobia and ethnicity-based nationalism, or nativism. It is indicative that most populist parties in the EU are right-wing nationalist rather than far left. Neither does civic nationalism not automatically present itself as a positive antithesis to ethnic nationalism; in the past, the civic version was often an instrument of forcible assimilation of national minorities. In fact, as a prominent theoretician of nationalism, Anthony Smith, has pointed out, 'nationalism is not just Janus-headed, it is protean and elusive, appearing in a kaleidoscopic variety of guises' (Smith 2004: 243). Civic nationalism may often remain only a beautiful idea, and can easily transform into ethnic nationalism. Worse, certain forms of civic nationalism create a positive environment for nationalist populists. Nevertheless, Smith admits that 'the civil nationalist project requires a degree of sophistication and mass political tolerance, and a sufficient degree of political solidarity to hold together various ethnic and regional segments of the society' (Smith 2004: 244).

It was no accident that civic nationalism, constrained by the rule of law to protect individual rights and national minorities, gained the status of official nationalism in Western countries after the Second World War. Currently, the attitude towards new potential members of nations constitutes an important difference between ethnic and civic nationalism. The former assumes that the nation has an organic character, and thus that certain individuals, only because of their ethnic or religious background, can never be integrated. The latter, meanwhile, perceives the concept of nation in a voluntarist way, and does not exclude a priori integration of any individual.

As far as the most apt description of right-wing populism is concerned, it seems that Ruth Wodak's definition is particularly useful because it underlines xenophobia (particularly Islamophobia), the politics of fear, and ethnic nationalism as the main pillars of its worldview:

> Right-wing populist parties focus on a homogenous demos, a populum (community, Volk) which is defined arbitrarily and along nativist (blood-related) criteria, thus endorsing a nativist body politics. Second, and related to the former, right-wing populist parties stress a heartland (or homeland, Heimat) which has to be protected against dangerous outsiders. In this way, threat scenarios are constructed— the homeland or 'We' are threatened by 'Them' (strangers inside the society or from outside: migrants, Turks, Jews, Roma, bankers, Muslims etc.) … necessarily require a hierarchically organized party and authoritarian structures in order to install law and order and to protect the Christian Occident against the Muslim Orient. (Wodak 2015: 66–7)[16]

Polish identity and spectre of Islam

In Europe, the allure of right-wing populist Islamophobia depends strongly on the social circumstances and cultural and historical context in a given country. Compared to most other EU countries, Poland is home to only a very small Muslim community. According to the most recent census, the number of Polish citizens who declared themselves as Muslims only just exceeded 5,000. Additionally, the number of Muslims with permanent residence permit, refugee status, or foreign citizenship living permanently in Poland is estimated to be 15,000–25,000 (Katolicka Agencja Informacyjna 2018), meaning that the Muslim share of the population oscillates around 0.06–0.08 per cent. Not only that, they are well integrated in Polish society. Of course, there were confrontations with Muslims in Polish history, but coexistence, cultural diffusion, and cooperation was the rule rather than the exception. Currently, Muslim countries and people do not represent a serious direct threat to Polish security.

Despite this, Poles in recent years have been overwhelmed by a widespread Islamophobia directed at their own Muslims (see Table 9.1), even accepting the treatment of Muslims as second-rank citizens.[17] As far as the attitude towards Muslims is concerned, Poland differs from many Western European nations, although some countries, Italy for example, can approach similar levels.

The antipathy towards Muslims found a favourable ground in Poland because of certain features of Polish identity and society. First of all, Poland is the most homogenous EU country in ethnic, racial, and religious terms. According to the 2011 census, over 97 per cent of Poland's citizens declared Polish nationality, while only 1.5 per cent had an exclusively non-Polish ethnicity or nationality (Główny Urząd Statystyczny 2011).[18] In consequence, Poles' contact with Muslims is very limited. Moreover, the rare contacts there are cannot avoid being marked by a certain ignorance concerning Muslims. Although, Muslims in Poland constitute around 0.07 per cent of the total population, the 2016 iteration of a regular survey by IPSOS (Perils of Perception) found that Poles believe that 7 per cent of their country is Muslim (around 100 times greater than the reality) (IPSOS 2016). No other EU nation presents an equivalent level of ignorance as to the number of Muslims in their country.

The negative attitude towards Muslims in Poland to a degree correlates with the popularity of ethnic nationalism, which has increased substantially in recent years. This kind of nationalism is deeply rooted in Polish modern history: it emerged as a nation from the idea of unifying the Roman Catholic Polish-speaking ethnic community, which did not possess a state of its own and was divided between three nation-states, engaged in a fierce rivalry with its neighbours for borderlands which mostly were inhabited by non-Poles.[19] In consequence, the national minorities have often been perceived by many Poles as a fifth column, waiting to be exploited by foreign enemies. Currently, this kind of ambivalence is reserved for immigrants.

The Roman Catholic Church played a key role in the Polish nation-building process in the premodern and modern periods. For centuries it has vigorously promoted an oversimplified vision of Poland as the bulwark of West (which of course was synonymous with Roman Catholicism), originally against the Ottoman Empire and the Tatars.[20] This myth contributed to the divergence between the historical reality and Polish historical memory in relation to Muslims. The Battle of Vienna in 1683, said without any historical basis to have been the battle that 'saved' Europe, occupies a key place in the Polish national mythology and is known by the great majority of Poles, while many considerably more important battles against the Russians that truly did seal Poland's fate are often completely unknown to the Poles, who did not have the chance to learn about them at school.

The rise of Islamophobia must also be seen in the wider context of a general increase in xenophobia in Polish society in recent years. Since 1993 the CBOS, a Polish public research centre, has been carrying out regular research into Polish attitudes towards other nations. It has found that between 2010 to 2016, dislike of almost all 27 nations included in the study rose (by a few to as many as 25 points), albeit with the slightest improvement subsequently (CBOS 2018). The general rise of xenophobia has been connected to such structural factors as the Islamist terrorist attacks in Western Europe since 2014; the economic crisis in the Eurozone, undermining trust in the EU; a belligerent Russia's expansionist policy in Ukraine; the strengthening of Ukrainian national identity after Euromaidan; the further integration of the Eurozone under the German leadership; and most recently the refugee crisis of

2015. However, the Smolensk air crash in 2010 marked the starting point, for with the death of a substantial proportion of the political elite the political and social cleavages already present in Polish society were exacerbated. The conspiracy theories about the crash abounded, and there was a widespread conviction that the Polish nation was the innocent victim of domestic and foreign enemies. It was this self-image that was promoted by PiS and the media sympathetic to the party.

Some of the allure of Islamophobia for Polish society is because it draws on the much older Orientalist, antisemitic stereotypes shared by a good many Poles. As Ivan Davidson Kalmar and Derek Penslar convincingly show in *Orientalism and Jews* (2015), Islamophobia and antisemitism are bound together by indirect multidimensional links that have evolved over centuries. The modern hate speech against Muslims propagated by the pro-government media in Poland is reminiscent of the antisemitic discourse of Roman Dmowski, leader of the main nationalist party (National Democrats) in the late nineteenth and early twentieth centuries.[21] The Jews were presented as an Oriental, Asian community, completely divorced from the accepted racial and cultural point of view—a totally alien civilization. In Dmowski's discourse, Judaism was a political ideology, not a religion, and due to its totalitarian nature wholly bound up with communism—the contemporary answer to Judeo-Bolshevism being Islamofascism. Jews were said to be a fifth column engaged in various conspiracies that threatened the survival of the Polish nation (a security threat), even on the biological level (the incessant comparison of Jews to disease and parasites). Jews supposedly undermined morality (with their 'typically Semitic' sexual perversions). In consequence, according to Dmowski, all attempts to integrate or assimilate Jews were a priori doomed to fail, or even amounted to collective suicide (see Michlic 2008).

Polish society is particularly exposed to the Islamophobic propaganda because of broadly uncritical attitudes towards the Internet, which currently serves as a main media outlet for hate speech. According to the research conducted by Katarzyna Górak Sosnkowska (2014), the beginnings of Islamophobia can arguably be dated to the early spring of 2013, and the Polish Internet. According to the European Commission's Eurobarometer of the autumn of 2016, Poles were top in the EU for confidence in social media as a reliable source of information, despite the fact that it is especially vulnerable to trolls and bots producing fake news: more than 50 per cent of Poles agreed, and fewer than 30 per cent disagreed, while unfortunately it was young people who distinguished themselves by particularly high level of credence they gave social media (while the EU's average was exactly the reverse, European Commission 2016: 31). The degree of trust in social media strongly correlates with the low and ever falling number of Poles who read books and newspapers—one of the lowest figures in Europe. It goes without saying that the Polish Internet is not politically neutral. As Robert Gorwa rightly points out in his study of propaganda, 'Facebook has emerged as a central source of political information and news, and is perhaps even more influential in Poland than it is in countries like the United States, at least for younger users.' Meanwhile, 'there appear to be twice as many suspected right-wing bot accounts as there are left-wing accounts. These right-wing accounts are far more prolific than their left-wing counterparts' (Gorwa 2017: 4). It should be added that according to other researchers, Russia is very active in using various trolls and bots and pro-Russian Polish nationalists the Islamophobic discourse on the Polish Internet (see for instance, Kazimierz Wóycicki 2015).

The refugee crisis as a watershed

As has been already stated, the Rubicon was crossed during the refugee crisis when Islamophobia mixed with racism gained a foothold in a Polish mainstream with the support of the majority of the political elite and a considerable part of media. Several mainstream Polish news outlets published front cover images showing Poland 'flooded' by Muslims. At the same time, the presence of Islamophobia on the Polish Internet increased dramatically. According to research by the Centre of Research on Prejudice in 2016 on hate speech against Muslims, the proportion of young people who said they ad recently had contact with it increased between 2014 and 2016 from 55 per cent to 80 per cent (Winiewski et al. 2016).

The banalization of Islamophobic views in the mainstream increased dramatically in 2016 following post-election changes to the state-owned Polish Television (Telewizja Polska, TVP) and Polish Radio

(Polish Radio, PR). Under new management appointed by PiS and its parliamentary allies, TVP's current affairs programming (and to a smaller extent PR's) underwent a profound transformation, opening their studios to far-right and openly Islamophobic opinions. The representatives of the radical right gained a public media presence unprecedented in the modern history of Poland. It was an intentional decision of the ruling party. PiS was courting radical right organizations in order to maintain its base in the most xenophobic part of society and to shift the political centre decisively to the right, making itself the 'new' mainstream.[22] Simultaneously, opposition politicians and intellectuals who supported the idea of relocating refugees became the targets of massive hate campaign by the pro-government private and public media, orchestrated by PiS. The moral panic that dominated the media and Internet led the overwhelming majority of Poles to believe that the large number of refugees fleeing Syria and Iraq represented a grave security threat to Poland (in the form of terrorism, criminality, and sexual assaults).

Under the sheer weight of anti-Muslim propaganda, Poles began to be far more lenient towards hate speech. In the research conducted in 2017 by the Centre of Research on Prejudice, respondents were asked to take a position on the statement 'Let refugees come to Poland. It will give us something to burn in the power stations. And those who are too big to fit into the ovens can be made into a dog food.' Just over 50 per cent of Polish respondents said this statement was unequivocally offensive; some 35 per cent of them admitted to using this kind of hate speech against Muslim refugees (Hansen 2017). The dehumanization of Muslims and refugees was the next step. In the summer of 2017, in order to measure the scale of the dehumanization of Muslim refugees, the Centre for Research on Prejudice used a popular image of the 'Ascent of Man,' with five silhouettes depicting human evolution from the earliest ape-like humans, becoming increasingly upright and with primitive culture (depicted by a spear carried over the shoulder), to 'normal' humans. Respondents were asked to indicate their perception of the 'evolvedness' of refugees, whereupon almost half of them chose non-humans and fewer than 45 per cent picked the fully evolved human (Ambroziak 2017).

The rise of xenophobia translated into skyrocketing hate crimes, varying from hate speech to physical violence, and motivated by racism and religious and ethnic hatred. In 2010, Polish prosecutors had brought around 180 criminal cases concerning hate crimes; in 2016 the number was some nine times greater. It fell slightly in 2017, but because of the new, more lenient approach to such crimes on the part of the prosecution service, which was controlled by PiS.[23] Indeed, after PiS won the general election in the autumn of 2015, the number of discontinuances and acquittals in cases of hate crime increased dramatically. In 2016 more than 75 per cent of criminal proceedings were discontinued, and many hate crimes were either not processed at all or were dropped after a cursory investigation, because the prosecution service considered them of 'low societal harm'. Another serious problem was the considerable underreporting of such crimes in Poland, far higher than in many Western European countries. According to research by the Polish Ombudsman in collaboration with the Office for Democratic Institutions and Human Rights (ODIHR) and Organization for Security and Co-operation in Europe (OSCE), only 5 per cent of such crimes were reported to the police in two Polish regions (Rzecznik Praw Obywatelskich 2018).

According to official statistics, after 2016 there was a significant change in the profile of the most frequent victims in criminal proceedings concerning hate crimes, with a dramatic rise in crimes against Muslims. In 2017, the most common victims were either Muslim or came from mostly Muslim nations—around half of all hate crimes committed against a specific person—and non-Muslim foreigners were attacked because their physical appearance was thought to be Muslim. These cases were registered as concerning race or ethnicity. Given the size of Muslim population, the number of attacks against members of this community in Poland was proportionately far greater than in other Western countries.

Islamophobia à la PiS

The Islamophobic discourse promoted by PiS is based on certain leitmotivs, familiar from other right-wing populist parties, but with their own Polish peculiarities. The key factors are a higher level of religiosity and conservatism in comparison to the rest of Western Europe, and the identification of Roman Catholicism with ethnic nationalism by many Poles. This is seen far more often among present and potential voters for PiS. The result is that in addition to the security and economic arguments in its Islamophobic discourse, PiS puts special emphasis on religious factors and the supposedly fundamental cultural differences between Poland, Western Europe, and Muslims.

The key features of PiS's Islamophobic discourse can be extracted from interviews, speeches, social media posts, tweets, and statements by its leaders. The Minister of National Defence, Mariusz Błaszczak, a former Minister of Internal Affairs, claims that Europe is witnessing a clash of civilizations with aggressive and assertive Islam, a clash between a civilization of freedom (Christian Europe) and a civilization of slavery (Islam). In his opinion, even a small number of Muslim refugees taken in by any European country will always snowball, and they will never integrate because of their cultural background. Muslims 'create closed enclaves which are a natural hotbed of terrorism' (Wirtualna Polska 2017). During an EU summit of interior ministers, Błaszczak—by his own account—said that the best approach to Muslim integration 'was established 2,000 years ago. It is Christianity. This concept refers to human dignity and the position of the human being. In the eighth century, Charles Martel stopped the Muslim onslaught in France' (TVN24 2017).

The Islamophobia promoted by PiS is based on a vision of Poland as the bulwark (antemural) of the Christian West. It was no accident that President Duda decided the Battle of Vienna should occupy a central place in the Strategy of the Polish Politics of Memory (dedicated to an 'assertive' promotion of Poland's history abroad). According to Duda, 'Poland was saving Europe. Saving it not just from a major crisis, but we can say from a disaster, like that time when the Polish army under the command of John III Sobieski stopped the Turkish onslaught on Vienna' (Prezydent RP 2016). A simpler version of this narrative was ventured by Patryk Jaki, the current deputy minister of justice and PiS candidate for mayor of Warsaw in 2018, who during the refugee crisis organized a demonstration against the Islamization of Poland remarking that 'In 1683 John III Sobieski stopped the march of this savage mob towards Europe. He defended our Christian, real roots' (Dąbrowska & Szacki 2017).

PiS's Islamophobia reflects its worldview, based on the merging of Polish exceptionalism and Messianism (traditionally associated with the idea of Christendom's bulwark) and the rejection of 'fake' liberal, secular Western Europe in the name of a genuine Christian Europe or West. In the PiS discourse, feeble Europe—in something of a contradiction—poses a serious challenge to Polish identity and sovereignty. Moreover, it uses Muslims as a weapon against Poland. According to PiS, the European mainstream elite, under German leadership, wants to provoke a massive inflow of Muslims to Poland in order to undermine Polish national homogeneity and by default make Poland easier to control. According to Kaczyński

> Poland today is the subject of pressure regarding the shape of our life, the situation of an average Pole; the shape of our society. We are being proposed to radically change, to create a multicultural society, to create a new identity. … It is a matter of sovereignty. If we maintain it, we will defend ourselves successfully. … The concepts of societies that have no identity, these concepts are convenient for those who have billions, because such a society is extremely easy to manipulate. If there is no strong identity, anything can be done with the society. (WPolityce 2016)

According to PiS, political correctness and multiculturalism, or *multi-kulti*, are responsible for a declining and decaying Europe's submission to aggressive Islam. Immediately after the Islamist terrorist attack in Nice in 2016, Minister of the Interior Błaszczak claimed that 'terrorist attacks are provoked by a crazy ideology of *multi-kulti* and far-left political correctness.' According to Błaszczak, Western Europe's reaction to terrorism is limited to marches in solidarity and 'drawing flowers with coloured pencils in all the colours of the rainbow. For me, there is a clear reference to the LGBT' (Gazeta.pl 2016). PiS openly associates Muslims not only with terrorism, but also with criminality and especially rape. In one of his speeches, Kaczyński asked rhetorically

> Do we want to have in Poland these phenomena which we already know from Western Europe, including the most dangerous of them, terrorism, but also street terror, fear of walking outside, often even

during the day, often in the city centre? Is that what we need? Don't you know about events that took place in Germany, where censorship, which practically existed there, led to the situation that they were not disclosed by the press? I mean attacks on women, harassment, or even rape. Do you really want that? (Kaczyński 2017)

According to PiS, the Western European left and liberal elites alienated from ordinary people should be blamed for this dramatic situation. Joachim Brudziński, current Minister of Internal Affairs and one of Kaczyński's closest associates, said they were witnessing the 'madness of opening doors in France and Germany, and chancellor Angela Merkel welcoming and embracing beefy youngsters allegedly fleeing the war.' In Brudziński's opinion, the refugees in fact rape and harass women, 'and the next day feminists run with flowers to these Arab bullies, saying, It's not your fault, you were just brought up that way. This craziness must be stopped sometime, and Poland will do it' (Gazeta.pl 2017).

PiS's anti-refugee discourse occasionally shifts from cultural to biological and racist arguments. For instance, during the parliamentary campaign in 2015, Kaczyński said 'There are already signs of the emergence of diseases that are highly dangerous and have not been seen in Europe for a long time: cholera on the Greek islands, dysentery in Vienna. There is also talk about other, even more severe diseases. Also there are some differences related to geography, various parasites, protozoa that are common and are not dangerous in the bodies of these people [but] may be dangerous here' (Cieński 2015). There are racist allusions in PiS's Islamophobic discourse too. In 2018 Brudziński, praising the performance of Polish police, said 'Let's walk around the suburbs of Paris, London, Stockholm, Marseille, Rome, Cologne in the evening and you will appreciate our parochial, clean country' (Prończuk 2018). The minister, responding to a question about what he meant by the word 'clean' in the context of security, said that he had in mind the clean streets of Poland's cities.

PiS, in the name of its crusade against political correctness and *multi-kulti*, created an atmosphere that is indulgent towards hate crimes against Muslims and other groups. Kaczyński openly declared that Poland will never accept the laws against hate speech which in his opinion destroyed freedom of speech in Western Europe. In April

2016 the Prime Minister Beata Szydło disbanded the Council for the Fight against Racism and Xenophobia. On several occasions, ministers of the interior have said that repeated xenophobic attacks on foreigners in Poland are 'absolutely marginal'. Government financial support for NGOs responsible for the integration of immigrants was cancelled. PiS also cancelled all training for policemen and officials about xenophobia.

The Roman Catholic Church and Liberals: Polish specificity

One reason Islamophobia can flourish in Poland is the negligence, indulgence, underestimation, and tolerance of it among liberal elites and, following their lead, certain sections of society. In comparison to their Western counterparts, their liberalism is often rather superficial and inconsistent. The mainstream liberal press and television could have guests who voiced radical anti-Muslim opinion, but few were unequivocally rebuffed by the presenters. The xenophobic anti-Muslim articles published in even the 'moderate' conservative media before 2015 often met with only weak condemnation from the liberal media. Such statements, if they had been made about other religious groups (Jews, for example), would meet with a widespread outrage among the liberal elites. Much of the Polish liberal intelligentsia welcomed, or still welcome, Oriana Fallaci's books. As Christopher Hitchens, a British essayist who can hardly be described as an admirer of Islam, called Fallaci's writings 'a sort of primer in how not to write about Islam', being 'replete with an obsessive interest in excrement, disease, sexual mania, and insect-like reproduction, insofar as these apply to Muslims in general and to Muslim immigrants in Europe in particular' (Hitchens 2003). The refugee crisis did not change the situation much. In the autumn of 2018, the Batory Foundation affiliated to the Open Society chose to nominate for the Beata Pawlak Memorial Award a book entitled 'Archipelago Islam', an extended interview with a Polish writer who converted to Islam. The prize is awarded to books that increase knowledge about foreign cultures. The nominee equated Islam with Nazism and communism, and described the European left and Merkel as idiots who did not want to fight Muslim immigration.

The Polish opposition largely succumbed to blackmail and pressure from the PiS regarding Muslim refugees. In the autumn of 2016 the Polish opposition twice voted almost unanimously in parliament for resolutions that supported the negative position of the government on a permanent EU relocation system for refugees. The opposition did not object when the government failed in its obligations concerning voluntary relocation, as endorsed by the EU in September 2015, and regularly uses a hate speech about Muslims. The opposition also supported another government resolution condemning the genocide committed by the so-called Islamic State (ISIS) against Christians. The comparison between this resolution and the resolutions of the European Parliament concerning ISIS shows striking differences between the mainstream of the Western European political elite and the Polish. In the Polish version only Christians and other religious minorities were mentioned as ISIS's victims. The main victims of ISIS, the Sunni and Shia Muslims, were absent from the Polish resolution, while the far greater war crimes committed by Assad's regime have never been condemned by the Polish parliament, which similarly has never paid homage to moderate Muslims fighting ISIS.

The Roman Catholic Church, which is highly respected in Poland, did not counter PiS's openly Islamophobic discourse. Many priests and bishops not only avoided criticizing it, but endorsed the position of the ruling party on refugees and Islam, explicitly or implicitly. In November 2015, as the refugee crisis reached its peak, the episcopate issued an official letter about the persecution of Christians in Iraq and Syria. Muslims were treated implicitly as a monolith. The letter claimed that an average of 100,000 Christians are martyred every year worldwide, in what is an enormous exaggeration. The Polish bishops who marked the centenary of the Armenian Genocide during the First World War greatly overestimated the number of those from Christian nations massacred by the Young Turks of the Ottoman Empire. Genocide arranged by a secular nationalist Turkish elite that admired the West and was allied with the Central Powers was presented as religiously motived hatred of Christianity, and explained by pointing to the traditional Islamic image of Christians as infidels. The Polish bishops ignored the many historical examples of Muslim tolerance towards Christians, the suffering of Muslims at the hand of

Christians, and the positive instances of cooperation and coexistence between representatives of both religions, such as the Kurds heroically fighting ISIS. The official letter was read out at Sunday Mass in all churches in Poland.[24] There is a striking difference between the narrative heard from many representatives of Polish clergy about Muslims and the response of Pope Francis. He has not refrained from justified criticism of the persecution and discrimination of Christian minorities in Muslim countries (their situation is mostly worse than that of Muslims living in Christian countries), but simultaneously acknowledges that Muslim communities are extremely diverse, and should not be blamed collectively for crimes committed by radicals. The Pope also keeps to an unequivocally positive position on refugees.

Islamophobia and the threat
of the de-Europeanization of Poland

Poland is the prime example of Islamophobia without Muslims. The antipathy of Polish society towards Muslims began to be seen in 2010, but accelerated dramatically during the refugee crisis. Islamophobia became one of the central tenets of a politics of fear pursued by PiS, and contributing to its social popularity. PiS peddles a specifically Polish version of Islamophobia that has strong religious overtones. However, the scale of the antipathy towards Muslims is now so great –present also in the electorate of the liberal and left opposition, though to a lesser degree than in the case of the right - that even if Poland were secularized it is highly probable that Islamophobia would remain an important element in Polish nationalism (as in Czechia). Such a hypothesis is based on a predominance of ethnic definitions of Polish national identity among Poles, and the flaws of Polish liberalism and the Roman Catholic Church. The rise of Islamophobia in Poland should be treated as the flip side of de-Europeanization and the authoritarian turn, seen in Poland by several watchdogs (Freedom House, Amnesty International, Human Rights Watch). At first glance, the link between political trends and Islamophobia is not obvious. Islamophobia, after all, became a question of identity. However, changes in the categories of identity in most cases have serious, indirect, and long-term implications for political life. Identity underpins the ethnic and collective definition of national community as a supposedly exclusive and homogenous monolith, defined in simple opposition to the other (the alter ego), or eternal enemy. This kind of monolithic national identity implicitly hinders the entrenchment of the division of powers, the rule of law, and the protection of individual human rights. Further, the rise of Islamophobia is one of the key factors in Poland's identity alienating it from the EU. Most of Poles do not treat European citizens of Islamic faith or Muslim cultural background as their fellow citizens within the EU, but exclude them a priori from the European political community. This feeling of alienation may strengthen in coming decades, because of the continuing increase in number of European Muslims and their representation in the political, business, and cultural elites of Western Europe.

The militant nature of Polish Islamophobia aside, fear of Muslims has also weakened Poles' solidarity with other Europeans in the security sphere. Poles broadly favour the use of force by the EU or NATO in the fight against Islamic terrorism, but their support for the direct engagement of the Polish armed forces in support of European allies who are the victims of terrorism orchestrated by ISIS is very limited. According to a poll by CBOS after the terrorist attacks in Paris in November 2015, as many as 85 per cent of Poles were opposed to their country's military involvement on the side of the Western allies against ISIS, while only 10 per cent supported the action (CBOS 2015: 12). By comparison, a French opinion poll by the Pew Research Center in the spring of 2017 found almost 55 per cent responded positively to the question 'If Russia got into a serious military conflict with one of its neighbouring countries that is our NATO ally, do you think France should use military force to defend that country?' Fewer than 45 per cent were against (Pew Research Center 2017).

The rise of Islamophobia has exposed the fragility of Polish national identity, supposedly so strong and self-confident. The prospect of having to take in 6,000 Muslim refugees under the framework of the EU relocation programme prompted hysteria in Polish society. One opinion poll at the height of the refugee crisis found almost 45 per cent of Poles feared the Islamization of Poland because of Muslim immigrants, while half did not share these fears (IBRIS 2015). Such a society is vulnerable to manipulation. Therefore, between 2015 and 2017

PiS managed easily to establish especially in the right wing electorate the idea of the EU and Islam being linked, which is often presented by the ruling elite and pro-government media as a threat to Polish security, identity, and sovereignty. There were worrying signs of this in opinion polls by IBRIS, a Polish research centre, in the spring of 2016 and the summer of 2017. In the first poll, half of the respondents supported the reintroduction of internal border controls in the EU, and slightly more than 45 per cent were against (Stankiewicz 2016). In 2017 more than half the respondents supported Poland's exit from the EU if membership were to be made conditional on the acceptance of 6,000 refugees under the rules of the relocation programme, while fewer than 40 per cent were ready to accept them in order to remain in the EU. An even higher proportion of Poles were ready to forego EU funding—from which Polish people benefit enormously—if it were conditional on the acceptance of refugees (Dziennik 2017).

Certain factors may help diminish Islamophobia in Polish society. There is near-universal support for membership of the EU (around 85 per cent), and while the escalating conflict between the Polish government and the EU states and institutions about the dismantling of the rule of law in Poland provoked the discussion about the Polexit, or Poland's exit from the EU. The fear of Polexit seems to have had a positive impact on the Polish approach to the refugees from Muslim countries. The opinion poll conducted in the summer of 2018 showed the change in comparison to the aforementioned survey from the summer of 2017. On the later occasion half were ready to accept the refugees if Poland's membership of the EU were conditional upon it (Wirtualna Polska 2018). However, PiS and the small nationalist parties that are playing with Islamophobia and Euroscepticism currently command the support of around half of all Poles with defined political sympathies, which confirms the ambivalence of Polish national identity.

Note

1 Moreover, weak state instiutions were a predominant feature of Polish statehood in the early modern period.

References

Allen, C. (2010), *Islamophobia* (Burlington).

Ambroziak, A. (2017), 'Prawie połowa Polaków i Polek odmawia człowieczeństwa uchodźcom. Nowy sondaż postaw', *Oko.press*, oko.press/prawie-polowa-polakow-polek-odmawia-czlowieczenstwa-uchodzcom-nowy-sondaz-postaw-wobec-uchodzcow/.

CBOS (2013), 'Co łączy Polaków?', www.cbos.pl/SPiSKOM.POL/2013/K_168_13. PDF.

— (2015), 'Zagrożenie terroryzmem po zamachach w Paryżu', www.cbos.pl/SPiSKOM.POL/2015/K_177_15.pdf.

— (2018), 'Stosunek Polaków do innych narodów', www.cbos.pl/SPiSKOM.POL/2018/K_037_18.pdf.

Center for Research on Prejudice (2017), 'Postawy wobec muzułmanów a przywiązanie do grupy własnej w Polsce', cbu.psychologia.pl/uploads/PPS3_raporty/islamofobia_fin_17–8–2017.pdf.

Cieński, J. (2015), 'Migrants carry "parasites and protozoa," warns Polish opposition leader', *Politico*, www.politico.eu/article/migrants-asylum-poland-kaczynski-election/.

Dąbrowska, A. & W. Szacki (2017), 'Minister Patryk Jaki: twarz nowej sprawiedliwości', *Polityka*, 23 May, www.polityka.pl/tygodnikpolityka/kraj/1705686,2,minister-patryk-jaki-twarz-nowej-sprawiedliwosci. read?page=78&moduleId=4677.

Davidson Kalmar, I. & D. J. Penslar (eds.) (2005), *Orientalism and the Jews* (Waltham).

Dziennik (2017), 'Wolimy wyjść z Unii Europejskiej niż przyjąć uchodźców?' wiadomosci.dziennik.pl/wydarzenia/artykuly/553529,sondaz-polacy-uchodzcy-ue-kryzys-migracyjny-ibris.html.

European Commission (2016), 'Media pluralism and democracy', Special Eurobarometer 452.

Fourquet, J. (2016), 'Présidentielle autrichienne: Quand la question des migrants reconfigure le paysage électoral, Ifop', *Chroniques Allemandes*, www.ifop.com/wp-content/uploads/2018/03/910-1-document_file.pdf.

Gazeta.pl (2016), "LGBT, malowane kwiatki'. Tak, Błaszczak naprawdę powiedział TO po zamachu w Nicei', wiadomosci.gazeta.pl/wiadomosci/7,114871,20404131,z-czym-blaszczakowi-kojarzy-sie-reakcja-na-zamachy-bardzo.html.

— (2017), 'Pierwszy duży wiec poparcia dla rządu PiS od dawna: Brudziński popłynął', wiadomosci.gazeta.pl/wiadomosci/7,114884,22348003,brudzinski-grzmi-na-pis-owskim-wiecu-atakuje-gwiazdki-i-celebrytow.html.

Główny Urząd Statystyczny (2011), Narodowy Spis Powszechny 2011, stat.gov. pl/spisy-powszechne/nsp–2011/nsp–2011-wyniki/struktura-narodowo-et-niczna-jezykowa-i-wyznaniowa-ludnosci-polski-nsp–2011,22,1.html.

Gorwa, R. (2017), 'Computational propaganda in Poland: False amplifiers and the digital public sphere', working paper, 4. comprop.oii.ox.ac.uk/wp-content/ uploads/sites/89/2017/06/Comprop-Poland.pdf.

Green, T. H. (2015), *The fear of Islam: An introduction to Islamophobia in the west*. Minneapolis.

Hansen, K. (2017), 'Mowa nienawiści: Raport z Polskiego Sondażu Uprzedzeń 3, Centrum Badań nad Uprzedzeniami UW', cbu.psychologia.pl/uploads/ PPS3_raporty/PPS3_MowaNienawisci_Hansen_fin.pdf.

Hitchens, C. (2003), 'Holy Writ', *The Atlantic*, www.theatlantic.com/magazine/ archive/2003/04/holy-writ/302701/.

IBRIS (2015), 'Obawy przed islamizacją Polski w wyniku napływu imigrantów z Bliskiego Wschodu', www.ibris.pl/Obawy_przed_islamizacja_Polski_w_wyni-ku_naplywu_imigrantow_z_Bliskiego_Wschodu.

IPSOS (2016), 'Perils of perception', www.ipsos.com/sites/default/files/2016–12/ Perils-of-perception–2016.pdf.

Kaczyński, J. (2017), 'Wystąpienie Prezesa PiS w Szczecinie', *YouTube*, www. youtube.com/watch?v=_XPbfOT-B-w.

Katolicka Agencja Informacyjna (2018), 'Muzułmanie w Polsce', ekai.pl/ muzulmanie-w-polsce–2/.

Konferencja Episkopatu Polski (2015), 'Kościół prześladowany w świecie—list pasterski', episkopat.pl/kosciol-przesladowany-w-swiecie-list-pasterski/.

Michlic, J. B. (2008), *Poland's threatening other: The image of the Jew from 1880 to the present*. Lincoln.

Mudde, C. (2007), *Populist radical right parties in Europe*, Cambridge.

Pew Research Center (2016), 'Topline Questionnaire Pew Research Center Spring 2016 Survey', assets.pewresearch.org/wp-content/uploads/sites/2/2016/07/ 14095942/Pew-Research-Center-EU-Refugees-and-National-Identity-Report-FINAL-July–11–2016.pdf

— (2017), 'Topline Questionnaire Spring 2017 Survey', passets.pewresearch.org/ wp-content/uploads/var/www/vhosts/cms.pewresearch.org/htdocs/wp-con-tent/blogs.dir/12/files/2018/07/09101525/FT_18.07.09_NATO_topline.pdf.

Prezydent R. P. (2016), 'Wystąpienie prezydenta na debacie NRR dot. polityki historycznej', www.prezydent.pl/aktualnosci/wypowiedzi-prezydenta-rp/ wystapienia/art,29,wystapienie-prezydenta-na-debacie-nrr-dot-polityki-his-torycznej.html.

Prokuratura Krajowa (2018), 'Statystyki i sprawozdania', pk.gov.pl/dzialalnosc/ sprawozdania-i-statystyki/.

Prończuk, M. (2018), 'Minister Brudziński igra z ogniem: Polska to piękny, "czysty" kraj. A nienawiść rośnie', *Oko.press*, oko.press/min-brudzinski-igra-z-ogni-em-polska-to-piekny-czysty-kraj-a-nienawisc-rosnie/.

Rzecznik Praw Obywatelskich (2018), 'Jedynie 5% przestępstw motywowanych nienawiścią jest zgłaszanych na policję—badania RPO i ODIHR/OBWE', www. rpo.gov.pl/pl/content/jedynie-5-przestepstw-motywowanych-nienawiscia-jest-zglaszanych-na-policje-badania-rpo-i-odihrobwe.

Smith, A. D. (2004), *The Antiquity of Nations* (Cambridge).

Sosnkowska, K. G. (2014), *Deconstructing Islamophobia in Poland: Story of an Internet group* (Warsaw).

Stankiewicz, A. (2016), 'Sondaż: Polacy nie chcą uchodźców, Rzeczpospolita', www.rp.pl/Spoleczenstwo/303299865-Sondaz-Polacy-nie-chca-uchodzcow. html.

TVN24 (2017), 'Błaszczak o uchodźcach: "Karol Młot w VIII wieku zatrzymał nawałę muzułmańską"', www.tvn24.pl/wiadomosci-z-kraju,3/blaszczak-o-uchodz-cach-karol-mlot-zatrzymal-nawale-muzulmanska,748547.html.

Winiewski, M., K. Hansen, M. Bilewicz, W. Soral, A. Świderska & D. Bulska. (2016), 'Mowa nienawiści , mowa pogardy', *Fundacja Batorego*, www.batory. org.pl/upload/files/pdf/mowa_nienawisci_mowa_pogardy internet.pdf.

Wirtualna Polska (2017), '"Niewątpliwie atak terrorystyczny": Błaszczak: Polska jest bezpieczna', wiadomosci.wp.pl/niewatpliwie-atak-terrorystyczny-blaszczak-pol-ska-jest-bezpieczna-6156274194245761a.

— (2018), 'Sondaż, który nie jest po myśli PiS: Nadal nie chcemy uchodźców, ale nastąpiła mocna zmiana', wiadomosci.wp.pl/sondaz-ktory-nie-jest-po-mysli-pis-nadal-nie-chcemy-uchodzcow-ale-nastapila-mocna-zmia-na-6267908552910977a.

Wodak, R. (2015), *The politics of fear: What right-wing populist discourses mean* (London).

Wóycicki, K. (2015), 'Internet and "information warfare" of president Putin', https://kazwoy.wordpress.com/2015/11/21/internet-and-information-war-fare-of-president-putin/.

Wpolityce (2016), 'Jarosław Kaczyński na kongresie PiS: Suwerenność jest wartością samą w sobie, jest sprawą godności narodu. Nie poddamy się kon-cepcjom Sorosa!', wpolityce.pl/polityka/295423-jaroslaw-kaczynski-na-kon-gresie-pis-suwerennosc-jest-wartoscia-sama-w-sobie-jest-sprawa-godnos-ci-narodu-nie-poddamy-sie-koncepcjom-sorosa?strona=3.

Appendix

Table 9.1 Attitudes towards Muslims living in the country

Country	Favourable	Unfavourable	Don't know/Refused to say
Poland	19	66	16
Italy	25	69	6
Germany	65	29	6
France	67	29	4

Source: Pew Research Center 2016.

Table 9.2 The importance of have been born in the country for being truly a member of the nation

Country	Important	Not important	Don't know/Refused to say
Poland	80	19	1
Italy	79	21	0
Germany	34	64	2
France	47	51	1

Source: Pew Research Center 2016.

Table 9.3 The importance of belonging to a dominant denomination for being truly a member of nation.

Country	Important	Not important	Don't know/Refused to say
Poland	71	28	1
Italy	66	31	2
Germany	30	68	2
France	23	75	2

Source: Pew Research Center 2016.

Table 9.4 Perceptions of the threat posed by a large influx of refugees from countries such as Iraq and Syria.

Country	Major threat	Minor threat	Not a threat	Don't know/Refused to say
Poland	73	21	4	2
Italy	65	25	8	1
Germany	31	44	23	2
France	45	20	35	3

Source: Pew Research Center 2016.

CHAPTER 10

The determinants of (right-wing) political engagement among adolescents in Sweden

Beint Bentsen & Pieter Bevelander

Right-wing political parties have found electoral success in many European countries in recent decades and Sweden is no longer an exception. In three consecutive elections, the Sweden Democrats (SD) went from 5.7 per cent of the votes in 2010 and 12.9 per cent in 2014 to 17.5 per cent in 2018; many studies have tried to explain this political condition. However, to what extent does the future potential electorate—adolescents—resemble the current political situation in Sweden? Are adolescents influenced by this trend, or do the young have a different political affinity to adults? In order to answer these questions, we use unique representative information from the 2013 High-School Attitude survey for Swedish individuals aged 15–19. This enabled us to assess the correlation of a wide variation of potential explanatory factors such as individual demographic, family, school, and societal factors and attitudinal determinants on the propensity to have a right-wing populist-party (RWPP) preference. Despite the inclusion of many possible factors, we find that potential voters for the SD, a right-wing political party, are largely boys from lower socio-economic backgrounds, living in the small and medium towns where the SD is an established party. These individuals feel threatened by future immigration, are not satisfied with democracy, and have little interest in politics. Interestingly, these results agree with the results for adults.

Over the past three decades, foreign-born populations have increased both in number and as a share of a host country's population. At the same time, populist radical-right parties with an anti-immigrant policy agenda have gained electoral success in many European countries (see Schain 2018). Compared to other countries, Sweden is a relative latecomer to this trend (Rydgren & Van Der Meiden 2016), as it was only in the 2010 elections that the anti-immigrant party, the SD, first crossed the electoral threshold to enter the Swedish parliament (Statistics Sweden 2011).

Studies of adult attitudes towards immigration, refugees, and multicultural society indicate that there was an electoral basis for such a party. Demker (2014) and Demker and Van Der Meiden (2016) find that about 43 per cent of the population would like to reduce or end immigration, 44 per cent would like to see a reduction or end to asylum-seeking, and 12 per cent believe that immigration is a threat to Swedish culture. This is significant because it is known from earlier studies that, more than any other factor, anti-immigrant sentiment predicts RWPP support (Arzheimer 2018; Mayer & Perrineau 1992; Van Der Brug, Fennema & Tillie 2000). This has also been found to be the case in Sweden and for the SD in particular (Valdez 2014; Widfeldt 2018).

Earlier studies of attitudes towards immigration and ethnic groups among the Swedish adolescent population clearly show more positive attitudes compared to Swedish adults (Bentsen 2017; Lövander 2010; Ring & Morgentau 2003). However, there is little research on the political preferences and party sympathies of adolescents in Sweden, and those that do exist are mostly descriptive. For example, the 'Intolerans' report, which measures intolerant attitudes among young people in Sweden towards minorities, indicates that about 6 per cent had some sympathy for the SD in 2003 (Ring & Morgentau 2003). This was in response to a question asking respondents to indicate up to two parties that they 'liked' from a list, so the result is not directly comparable to those in this study. A similar survey for 2010 showed that 5 per cent preferred the SD (Lövander 2010). As adolescents are the future voters in local, regional and national elections, it is very important to assess current political trends and to understand which factors are correlated with the political engagement of this particular age group.

It is also suggested that this age range is the most important for the development of individual political values and attitudes (Alwin & Krosnick 1991; Krosnick & Alwin 1989; Niemi & Hepburn 1995). Adult civic involvement has already been traced to experiences and engagement in adolescence (Eliasoph et al. 1996) and social influences have been shown to be increasingly important in adolescence rather than at an earlier age (Raabe & Beelmann 2011). In our eyes, this further emphasizes the importance of focusing on adolescence, and particularly on the impact of adolescents' social environment. Given these age-related differences in development and the influences on sociopolitical attitudes and values, we set out to answer the question of whether adolescents are influenced by the same political trends as adults, or whether they have different political affinities. We also look at whether adolescents are influenced by the same factors that have been found to explain right-wing populist-party support among adults.

To study the political engagement of adolescents, we use a unique dataset consisting of a representative sample of the Adolescent Attitude survey of 2013, linked to several individual register sources. Using multivariate analysis, our aim is to study party preference—the complex connection between demographic, family, school, and societal factors as well as the political attitudinal determinants of high-school youth aged 15–19 in Sweden, and how these influences compare with findings in earlier studies of adults. In this chapter we provide an account of the contextual setting, which includes a short description of immigration to Sweden, the development of attitudes towards immigration among adults and adolescents and the populist anti-immigrant party, the SD, in order to discuss the results of our multivariate analysis and to offer some suggestions for future research.

Contextual setting

Immigration to Sweden took off after the Second World War, and included both major waves of labour migration between about 1950 and 1980—mainly from Nordic and European countries—and refugee migration from the 1980s until today, mainly from countries outside Europe. In addition, family reunion migration in Sweden has been very substantial during this entire period due to relatively liberal policies

(Borevi 2018). Moreover, EU migration has gradually increased in importance since Sweden entered the EU in 1995. At time of writing Sweden is a diverse country when it comes to immigrants' country of birth; currently about 1.9 million immigrants have settled in Sweden—close to 18.5 per cent of the population.

Demker (2014) and Demker and Van Der Meiden (2016) argue convincingly that a good indicator for tracking changes in opinions on immigration and multicultural society is the population's general attitude towards the acceptance of refugees. In Sweden, for at least 20 years, this indicator has heavily correlated with a general increase in acceptance of immigrants and immigration. In a European comparison, the 2009 Eurobarometer indicated Sweden as the country the most open to immigration (European Commission 2009). However, Demker (2014) and Demker and Van Der Meiden (2016) also show that individuals who score negatively on attitudes and who dislike immigrants and immigration state that they perceive immigrants as a threat and as a cause of serious social problems. This trend could also be one of the reasons behind the late entrance—in the European context—of an anti-immigrant party in parliament in Sweden.

A small number of neo-Nazi individuals founded the right-wing anti-immigrant party, the Sweden Democrats (SD), in the late 1980s. It is the only Nordic RWPP to have its background in far-right movements and this has arguably delayed their electoral success (Widfeldt 2018). However, in the 1990s the party gradually gained local political success by moving to more mainstream conservative political standpoints on social issues—with the exception of its clearly anti-immigration and anti-'elite' stance. Based on his review of the comparative literature on the topic, Widfeldt (2018) describes the SD as a clear-cut populist radical-right party that fulfils all of the three main identifying criteria of an RWPP party—authoritarianism, nativism, and populism.

In their first term in the Swedish parliament 2010–2014, the SD had no influence on the moving of Swedish migration policy in a more restrictive direction. However, according to Hellström & Edenborg (2016), the party was helped to gain higher political salience among the population in Sweden by actively advancing discourse around national identity and immigration. Moreover, as starting points to make radical political policies, the SD builds on mainstream concerns about the Swedish Muslim population, segregation in the larger cities and problems of integration. Whereas the mainstream media took a critical stance concerning the political standpoint of the SD, it was in social media that the party found an alternative outlet for its political standpoints (Hellström & Edenborg 2016). In the 2014 election, the party gained 12.9 per cent of the votes and doubled its number of seats in the Swedish parliament.

Previous research

Previous studies of RWPP (right-wing populist-party) support in Sweden highlight several different factors to explain how the SD's current success has been possible. On an individual level, Anders Widfeldt finds, in his (2018) analysis, that low trust of politicians, a high level of social capital and a negative attitude towards immigration are the main explanatory factors for SD support. While Oskarson and Demker (2015) focus on the working class, they find that the strongest factors for explaining SD support in this group above all are authoritarian leanings and low political trust. They argue that this combination of political alienation and ideological reasons point to the de-alignment of the working class and the Social Democratic Party. This de-alignment has created an opportunity for a new political party to mobilize along an authoritarian-libertarian dimension; it is this space that the SD now occupies. On a contextual level, Rydgren and Ruth (2013) study a number of explanations for SD support and find that socio-economic factors are very important for understanding their success. Factors that predict SD support were, especially, high unemployment, low incomes and high welfare dependency in the local area. The proportion of immigrants in the local area was also significant but to a lesser degree. What is also important is that they found that living close to, but not within, an area with many immigrants predicted support for the SD.

There have been many attempts to explain political support for populist right-wing parties since they started gaining significant backing from electorates in Europe and North America. A review of the literature shows that there are many factors tested that are disconnected from more established theories (Arzheimer 2018). Among the factors that have been thought to be important we find party identification, the influence of a charismatic leader, the strength of the populist party, party ideology, factors of the party system, levels of crime in society, immigration, unemployment, and media focus. In addition, there are also more-developed theoretical frameworks such as personality theories, social capital, group threat theory and contact theory, all of which we include in this overview (for more detailed reviews, see Mudde 2007; Rydgren 2018).

Socio-economic threat

Socio-economic marginalization is frequently referred to as an explanation for RWPP support. Individuals with a weak position in the labour market, living in segregated areas and with lower levels of education perceive immigrants as a threat to their position. RWPPs often emphasized the belief that immigrants steal jobs from natives or drain the welfare state of resources which should rightly be reserved for natives (Rydgren & Ruth 2013). In the early formulations of group threat theory, different groups in society were seen to have proprietary feelings towards certain goods and positions in society. When these are felt to be threatened, prejudice against the perceived challenger group can arise as a reaction (Blalock 1967; Blumer 1958). Group threat as an explanation for individual behaviour is not new and there is significant research supporting different variations of the classic formulation. Group threat theory helps us to understand voting preferences through its explanation of the variations in prejudice and intolerance that are, again, important predictors of RWPP support. As is also argued by, for example, Lubbers et al. (2002), people who are in a more socio-economically exposed position are likely to perceive immigrants as a threat due to their being in more direct competition over unskilled jobs. These individuals are likely to be susceptible to RWPP messages about competition for social security and jobs, and perhaps more likely to feel that their status is in jeopardy. In more recent research, economic and cultural threat has also been found necessary for nationalist attitudes to translate into RWPP support (Lubbers & Coenders 2017). In studies of Swedish voting patterns, support for a version of group threat has been found. The so-called halo effect, where support for RWPP rises in areas close to immigrant-dense neighbourhoods, is supported by recent research (Rydgren & Ruth 2013; Valdez 2014). A focus on factors associated with an elevated feeling of threat remains important in explaining RWPP support, as does a sensitivity to geographical variations.

Peer effect

There is also a significant field of research investigating the role of transmission from adolescents' social environment—such as their parents and peers—on attitudes and values. In this literature, researchers focus on variations in upbringing, parental attitudes, local culture and socialization in school or the local area. Relevant to our study is the importance this has for intergroup and political attitudes and values. Seminal studies on prejudice and intergroup attitudes have correlated their results with local culture and parental attitudes (Meertens & Pettigrew 1997; Sears & Henry 2003), and Kinder and Sears (1981) find that these developmental and social factors are more important than the influence of threat in explaining prejudice.

More directly, the development of prejudice in children and adolescents has been found, in cross-sectional and longitudinal studies, to be significantly influenced by the parents' level of prejudice (Hjerm et al. 2018; Jugert et al. 2016; Miklikowska 2016). In her longitudinal study of adolescents in Sweden, Miklikowska (2017) found that their level of anti-immigrant attitudes was consistently related to the degree of prejudice of their parents and peers. The parents' education, income and prejudice affected the development of adolescents' level of prejudice over time, as did those of their peers. However, having intergroup friends moderated the effect of parental and peer influence on adolescents. This shows the importance of social contexts for understanding adolescents' level of prejudice and intergroup attitudes—a factor that is also important for understanding levels of support for RWPP parties—and emphasizes their importance for adolescents' general development.

Again, studying the development of political attitudes and behaviour, social context and transmission are seen to be important. Political attitudes and behaviour have been found to be significantly influenced by parents and peers in a number of past studies (Bandura 1977; Dalhouse & Frideres 1996; Degner & Dalege 2013; Jennings & Niemi 1968; Verba et al. 2003). Political party preferences and political attitudes in particular are overwhelmingly influenced by social environmental and contextual factors, though the explained effect is smaller for political behaviour (Hatemi & McDermott 2012).

In 2009, Jennings, Stoker and Bowers carried out a longitudinal study of political socialization over three generations, examining the importance of family, friends, school, and organizational life for the development of political attitudes. They documented that children adopt their parents' political orientations to a significant degree, and that this remains particularly stable for people who acquired similar attitudes to those of their parents before leaving their childhood home. Parents' education and level of income were also found to have an effect. Moreover, the authors found that the political climate in schools and local areas also mattered. Gidengil et al. (2016) recently also found that, although adolescents' political behaviour in the form of voting turnout was significantly affected by their parents' voting practice, it was influenced to a lesser degree by their parents' level of education.

While the most important individual factors affecting transference of attitudes are not completely consistent, there is significant documentation concerning the transfer of attitudes at the meso level. This emphasizes the importance of controlling for factors that relate to parents and the adolescents' immediate social surroundings.

Social capital

Another proposition advanced by researchers is that low levels of social capital among individuals may be a contributing factor in explaining support for RWPPs. In line with Putnam (1993), membership in organizations that are horizontally structured is thought to foster habits of cooperation, trust in others, civic norms, and democratic values, and to build skills that make participation in democratic institutions possible. Rydgren (2009) argues that these norms and values run counter to those—such as intolerance and criticism of the political system—that RWPPs mobilize around; high social capital is therefore predicted to reduce RWPP support. With this general idea of how social capital may contribute to explaining RWPP support, the focus for measuring the concept in the literature has been membership in organizations, and the general social trust that organizational membership is thought to promote. However, the empirical findings in this field have not lived up to the clear expectations from social capital theory. Rydgren (2009 2011) has tested this in several case studies throughout Eastern and Western Europe and finds that membership in organizations does not contribute to explaining support for the radical right. In Widfeldt's examination (2018) of Nordic RWPPs he finds, somewhat perplexingly, that a *higher* level of social capital predicts more support for the Sweden Democrats. This is also in line with the findings of a case study looking at support for the Swiss People's Party (Fitzgerald & Lawrence 2011), while a study of Belgium and support for Vlaams Block found that, in line with the theory, local authorities with a strong organizational life had significantly less RWPP support (Coffé et al. 2007). Widfeldt (2018) again argues that the measure of social capital and the methods that are used in these studies may be a partial explanation for the diverse and unclear findings. However, Rydgren (2009) found that, in Western and Northern Europe, social trust was a better explanatory variable of RWPP support than organizational membership. He also calls for a greater focus on social or generalized trust in explaining support for the radical right, particularly trust defined in a sense that goes beyond the political. While it is clear that past social capital research does not offer a straightforward explanation for RWPP support, it still has some explanatory power, and the possibility to test this further in a large dataset like ours can be a valuable addition to the unclear image that past studies give.

Institutional trust and issue voting

Similar to social trust on the surface, low institutional trust is also considered an important potential explanation for RWPP support. The effect that level of trust has on political behaviour is a longstanding topic of interest among researchers who have gone back to early models of political support and outcomes (for example, Citrin 1974; Gamson 1968; Miller 1974). There has, however, been little agreement on any one definition of trust and researchers have included varying objects of trust into the concept (Bergh 2004). At a minimum, trust is split into at least two levels or objects—trust in political elites, and trust in political institutions (Bergh 2004; Passarelli & Tuorto 2018). Some, like Pippa Norris (2011), have argued for as many as five different levels of trust. However, according to Bergh (2004), there are good reasons for using a simpler model in empirical studies. He argues that political elites and institutions are seen as separate objects when considered by potential voters, but that people tend to simplify things when making political choices—thus researchers limiting themselves to the two levels is advisable in empirical studies.

Studies of the effect of trust find that when belief in political elites' will to represent the electorate in a responsive way is low, voters are left with little reason to give their support to any established party (Bélanger & Nadeau 2005; Passarelli & Tuorto 2018). Low political trust has thus been found to predict abstention from voting (Bélanger & Nadeau 2005), and voting for opposition parties with little possibility of gaining power, like new RWPPs (Bélanger & Nadeau 2005; Bergh 2004). The responsiveness of the party system also seems to be important for the behaviour that low trust predicts. In two-party systems, it is found to be more favourable to the opposition party; however, in party systems where the threshold for entering the political arena is lower—like most multi-party systems—trust seems more likely to promote support for unestablished alternatives on the fringes of the political spectrum (Bélanger & Nadeau 2005).

Lastly, it is important to consider that voters also make evaluations about the political issues that interest them, and about how they perceive the political parties' ability and will to deal with these questions. Based on the party choice models first developed by Morris Fiorina (1981), it is acknowledged that voters also consider parties on the basis of how they associate them with and consider that they deal with specific political issues (Walgrave et al. 2015). When they consider a party to have the best track record or best policy, this significantly motivates their party choice if they see the issue as salient (Bélanger & Meguid 2008). While Sweden is still a country of strong left–right ideological voting (Oscarsson & Holmberg 2015), the importance of individual issues has increased significantly over recent decades (Green-Pedersen 2007). Thus, in addition to the contextual and personal characteristics already mentioned that may influence party choice, it is important that voter interest is also considered in specific political issues.

Research design

The data we use are derived from the third wave of the Forum for Living History Attitude Survey among adolescents in Sweden. The creation of the data includes individual information from the Swedish registry, from which a representative sample was taken of Swedish adolescents in primary school Year 9 and secondary school Years 10 to 12 via cluster sampling, representing the entire country. This sample is linked to registry data on individuals and their parents and schools. The actual survey, with its 7,382 respondents, took place in the classroom and gained a high response rate of 71.7 per cent. The sample used in our analysis consists of the 3,168 adolescents who indicated a party preference on our dependent variable by marking the political party for which they would have voted had they been allowed to vote in an election.

The Appendix shows the number of youth according to party preference, as well as descriptive statistics for both the full and the sub-sample. Our dependent variable, party preference, shows that about 5 per cent of adolescents would have voted for the Left or the Liberal Party. The Social Democrats are preferred by a quarter of the youth and the party with the largest preference being the Moderates (liberal–conservative). The Environmental Party is preferred by 12 per cent of the adolescents, whereas SD, the anti-immigrant (right-wing) party, is preferred by 15 per cent of the Swedish youngsters. Both the Centre Party (the Liberal Green Party) and the Christian Democrats are the least preferred, and only gained 1 per cent of potential votes by Swedish youth. They would not have attained the 4 per cent threshold needed to take a seat in parliament in Sweden.

The independent variables in the analysis are based on the questions asked in the survey and formulated in line with the earlier discussed theoretical propositions at the individual demographic, societal and political attitudinal levels, as well as at family, school and neighbourhood levels. The demographic characteristics are age, gender and country of birth of the individual and his or her parents. In line with earlier results, we expect that males and younger individuals will be more prone to vote for the SD (Oskarson & Demker 2015; Statistics Sweden 2010). The age variation may not be visible within the relatively small age range in our study but, in the 2010 election, first-timers voted about four times as often for the SD compared with older voters. Due to the mobilization against immigration and around questions of national identity, we would also expect that individuals born in Sweden to Sweden-born parents support the SD more than other adolescents.

Family characteristics, in this study, are the socio-economic background of the parents, measured by their educational level and (un)employment status. Based on earlier studies, we expect parents' socio-economic background to have an effect on their children through transmission (Jennings et al. 2009; Verba et al. 2003) and that lower education and labour market attachment are correlated with greater SD support (Hjerm & Nagayoshi 2011; Rydgren & Ruth 2013).

School factors are measured as the type of academic programme the students are studying. To a great extent, this reflects the socio-economic background of the family (Fergusson, Horwood & Boden 2008). In past research, following a vocational as opposed to a university preparatory programme was found to predict attitudes that are associated with higher levels of RWPP support, such as strong anti-immigrant attitudes (Bevelander & Otterbeck 2016).

Societal factors such as the neighbourhood in which the youths are living are also included, and are seen as crude distinctions between individuals who live in either rural Sweden or in small and medium-sized towns or bigger cities and the immediate surrounding area.

The categorical variable for the type of local authority in which adolescents live is based on the classification of local authorities as developed by Swedish county and local-authority interest organizations (Sveriges kommuner och Landsting, SKL). Cities and their surrounding local authorities, with their many commuters, constitute the first category and medium-sized towns and local authorities, with many commuters being a second; small towns and local authorities make up the third category, and the fourth and last represents rural local authorities. This variable for the different local authorities measures differences stemming from the type of area in which the respondents live. There are observed differences between areas in terms of the rural–urban analysis of SD election results (Sundell 2018)—areas that are more densely populated show less SD support. Some of these differences stem from identifiable sources such as education, while others stem from unidentified sources. Studies with more fine-grained geographical distinctions than we have access to in our data have found that support for the SD is greater in areas with few immigrants but which are near to immigrant-dense areas (Rydgren & Ruth 2013). In the same study, local socio-economic conditions were found to be an even stronger predictor of regional differences. In other studies, immigrant-dense areas are found to be more likely to support the SD (Rydgren & Ruth 2011). Due to the grouping of towns with their surrounding area in our analysis, we can probably observe that cities are more likely to support the SD as they contain both the areas that have the highest proportion of immigrants and also the sort of sharp local variations that Rydgren and Ruth (2013) describe. Local economic conditions, on the other hand, may lead to more SD support in rural areas where there are fewer economic resources.

The variable 'SD support in the local authority' is a measurement of the proportion of SD votes in the 2010 municipal election in the local authority in which the young people live. It is included as a general measure of peer influence on SD support. The thought behind this is that influence from the family, friends, or other people with whom adolescents interact in the normal course of events may influence their party choice, as seen in previous research (Jennings et al. 2009). The expectation from this measure is that living in an area with a higher level of support for the SD will mean that the adolescents themselves will also be more likely to support the party.

We measure social capital by the inclusion of whether or not individuals indicate that they are members of a club—such as a sports club—and whether or not they are interested in politics and are satisfied with democracy. We also include a set of indicators that measure social and institutional trust. The measurement 'institutional trust' is based on a broad range of questions concerning trust in various authority figures and institutions in society, such as the police, priests/religious leaders, parliamentary politicians, municipal politicians, and political parties. With this variable, we hope to capture a more general trust than just that towards politicians or political institutions or, more broadly, towards significant societal institutions. Social trust is measured by the question 'To what degree do you think that you can trust other people?'—a standard question used in a number of surveys, including the European Social Survey and previous iterations of the Forum for Living History's Attitude Surveys. As described previously, trust in and engagement with the society in which a person lived and developed civic values is understood to isolate them from the messages around which RWPPs mobilize. Because of this, we would expect that, in line with the general predictions in social capital theory, individuals who have scores that indicate that they are more trusting of, more interested in, and more engaged with society show less support for the SD. However, low trust, in particular, is reported to make voters stick to the fringes of the political spectrum (Bélanger & Nadeau 2005; Bergh 2004). Therefore, it is also possible that the disengagement and dissatisfaction of individuals who have low scores on these variables correlate instead, to some extent, with support for left-wing parties.

Finally, we measure the individual levels of worry over the future through questions about a series of political issues over the next five years—immigration to Sweden, the threat of war or terror, the chance that young people will find work and somewhere to live, increased class difference and, lastly, environmental decline. As in the 2017 edition of the yearly Swedish society and public opinion survey SOM (Andersson et al. 2018), these questions are again combined into a series of four separate dimensions—immigration, the environment, security and economic prospects, respectively. The intention behind the inclusion of these measures is to distinguish how worry about political issues affects adolescents' party preferences. Anti-immigrant sentiment has also been found to be the single most important factor in explaining RWPP support in the past (Arzheimer 2009; Cutts et al. 2011; Mayer & Perrineau 1992; Van Der Brug et al. 2000; Widfeldt 2018), so its inclusion in the analysis is important for this reason alone. In addition, we wish to see how this particular issue vis-à-vis other issues motivates voters' party preferences. In the literature on political parties' issue ownership, building on Morris Fiorina (1981), parties are considered by voters to have ownership of certain political issues based on past performance and stated policy. We would therefore expect in this study that where a respondent is worried about an issue, it would also correspond to support for a party that voters consider to have ownership of the issue (Bélanger & Meguid 2008; Walgrave et al. 2015). From the 2014 Swedish election study (Statistics Sweden 2014), we know that Swedish voters considered the two major parties, the Conservatives and the Social Democrats, to have ownership of economic, employment and security issues—and that the Conservatives score somewhat better, particularly on the first and last of these issues. For immigration issues, they are also seen to rank towards the top, although here they are quasi-tied with the SD. The Green Party is thought to have the best policy, with a good margin, when it comes to environmental issues. Importantly, while the SD are tied for the lead in immigration issues, they have no other issue where voters consider them to be a good choice relative to other parties (Statistics Sweden 2014). Because of this lack of confidence in their other policy areas, and the fact that anti-immigrant attitudes are the strongest predictor of RWPP support in the literature (Arzheimer 2009; Cutts et al. 2011; Mayer & Perrineau 1992; Van Der Brug et al. 2000; Widfeldt 2018), we expect that supporting them can be strongly predicted by worry about immigration.

In the Appendix, Table 10.A1 also provides an overview of our statistical material. We use a sub-sample of all 3,168 individuals who indicated which party they would vote for. Whereas the gender distribution in the full sample is roughly equal, men and boys are slightly over-represented in the sub sample. In both samples, about 70 per cent are youth from secondary schools and 30 per cent from the final year of primary school. This is in accordance with the initial distribution of the survey which, according to data on respondents' backgrounds, shows that about 9 per cent were born outside Sweden, about 20 per cent have roots in a foreign background and 70 per cent are ethnic Swedes in both samples. About 50 per cent in both samples receive university preparatory education and 20 per cent a vocational education, while the other individuals are still at primary school. Slightly over half of both samples are members of organizations. Around two-thirds of the participants have at least one parent with higher education in both samples. Only 7 per cent of the young people surveyed have a parent who is unemployed. Around 80 per cent in both samples live in cities or medium-sized towns, with the other 20 per cent living in small towns or in rural areas. The participants show a lesser interest in politics; in the full sample, about 60 per cent are not very or not at all interested. The sub-sample shows a higher interest in politics, however. This is not surprising since these individuals have also indicated which party they would vote for if there were elections. The complementary question as to whether individuals are satisfied with democracy shows that about 80 per cent of respondents in both samples are quite or very satisfied with it.

For our main analysis we conducted a binary logistic regression in order to study the correlation between the different covariates and those who voted for the right-wing populist and anti-immigrant party, the SD. The second step in our analysis was to conduct a multinomial logistics regression for robustness and to analyse whether the covariates correlating with actual party preference for the SD also correlated with other parties, and to what degree. In our statistical analysis, we converted all scales to z-scores before including them in the models. Converting scales to z-scores on both sides of the equation allows any interpretation to be in units of standard deviation change. This is convenient for our interpretation, particularly when examining the relationship between the different scales.

Multivariate results

In the following analysis we try to establish which factors are important in explaining adolescents' decision to vote for the SD in comparison to the other parties in the Swedish parliament. Table 10.1 thus shows the factors that are correlated to Swedish adolescents' preference for the SD. The regression analysis is binary logistic and the results are, to a significant extent, also confirmed by the results of the multinomial analysis that is provided in the Appendix, Table 10.A2. However, this binary analysis clearly shows the main differences between those who prefer the SD and those who prefer one of the other parties. In line with earlier research for adults, we find a clear and significantly smaller probability of females preferring the SD. Youth who are foreign-born, as well as adolescents born in Sweden to immigrant parents, all have a significantly lower probability of supporting the SD. This is also the case for adolescents who do not live in rural areas or cities. Youth enrolled on a vocational school track also prefer to vote for the SD.

Those who are dissatisfied with democracy or who are worried about future immigration greatly prefer the SD, but not those who worry about the future of the environment. SD supporters also tend to live in local authorities with a higher proportion of SD voters (according to the results of the 2010 election). However, being a member of a club or organization, neither parent having higher education, or both parents being unemployed yields no significant results, and seems not to be correlated with political support. Finally, neither personal nor institutional trust are correlated with support for political parties.

We performed a robustness test, and the Appendix, Table 10.A2, shows the results of the multinomial logistic regression of party preference by adolescents. The reference category is the SD and the coefficients shown are for the other parties relative to them. As expected, females vote to a lesser extent for the SD than for any other party. Age, school type/programme or being a member of one or more organizations make no difference to young people's party preference. Young people born abroad, and those born in Sweden to immigrant parents, clearly prefer to vote for any party except the SD. This also means that, relative to other parties, the Sweden-born offspring of Swedish parents prefer the SD. Scrutinizing the results for type of local authority, less-significant coefficients are measured; however, overall, the results indicate that young people living in rural areas prefer the SD. This is clearly the case for voters for the Left Party and the Social Democrats. The results in Appendix A2 also show that youth with a high interest in politics prefer the Left Party and the Liberal Party much more than they do the SD. Those who prefer the latter are visibly not satisfied with democracy. Nearly all parties show positive significant results for this indicator. Finally, those whose party preference is the SD are worried about future immigration, but not about the future of the environment.

Table 10.1. Binary logistic regression of support for SD over other political parties (Beta coefficients and odds, significance denoted by an asterisk).

		Beta coeff.		Odds
Gender	male	–		–
	female	−0.876	***	0.417
Age		−0.225	**	0.798
Place of birth and parents' place of birth	Swedish parents	–		–
	one immigrant parent	−1.933	***	0.485
	two immigrant parents	−2.360	***	0.094
	foreign-born	−0.724	***	0.145
School type	secondary	–		–
	vocational	0.958	***	2.607
	university preparatory track	0.149		1.161
Parents' education	no higher education	–		–
	higher education	−0.145		0.865
Parents employed	no	–		–
	yes	−0.369		0.691
Worried about future immigration		1.670	***	5.312
Worried about future security		0.007		1.007
Worried about future economy		0.065		1.067
Worried about future environment		−0.520	***	0.594
Satisfaction with democracy	not satisfied	–		–
	low	−0.973	***	0.378
	medium	−1.347	***	0.260
	high	−2.252	***	0.105
Interest in politics	not interested	–		–
	low	−0.446	**	0.640
	medium	−0.402	**	0.669
	high	−0.396		0.673
Organization membership	no	–		–
	yes	−0.057		0.944
Personal trust		−0.069		0.934
Institutional trust		−0.008		0.992
Type of local authority	rural	–		–
	small town	0.652	*	1.920
	medium town	0.581	**	1.787
	city	0.342		1.407
Proportion of SD votes 2010		0.072	***	1.075
Total N		3,153		
Model fit	Cox & Snell R-square	0.340		
	Nagelkerke R-square	0.600		

Discussion

As in many other European countries, right-wing political parties in Sweden were increasingly successful in the last elections. We ask if adolescents today are influenced by this trend or if youth have a different political affinity to adults? Secondly, we investigate whether the factors known to predict RWPP support among adults also hold true for adolescents' party preference.

When looking at the results for party preference among Swedish youth, we find some differences compared to their adult counterparts (Statistics Sweden 2014). Smaller parties such as the Christian Democratic Party, the Centre-Liberal Party, and, to a lesser extent, the Liberal and Left parties, are less popular with young people. This implies that larger parties like the Social Democratic Party, the Conservative Party, and the right-wing populist party, the SD, as well as the Green party, are preferred compared to the adult election results of 2014. This simple descriptive result indicates that, in young people, the SD have a future potential electoral base, and that we can expect this party to be represented in future Swedish elections. We can also see that support for the SD increased slightly more between 2010 and 2014 among adolescents than among adults (Statistics Sweden 2010), and that the Green Party is over-represented among these young future voters. This perhaps indicates that adolescents mobilize along new political divides to a greater extent than do adults. If this is the case, then parties that emphasize these questions are likely to be the winners in future elections.

Considering the analysis of factors that predict support for the SD, many variables point in the same direction for adolescents as for adults. In terms of the theoretical and empirical points of departure for this chapter, we can see that the social capital variables that are the most commonly used have no explanatory power. There is wide variation in the results for social capital in past research on RWPP support (Coffé et al. 2007; Fitzgerald & Lawrence 2011; Rydgren 2009; Widfeldt 2018); in light of this, an insignificant result is not out of order. The descriptive statistics on trust show us that the levels of institutional trust, in particular, as well as social trust, are low among youth who support parties on both the far left and the far right, although those who would vote on the far right have significantly lower levels of trust than those who favour the far left. So, whereas the descriptive results indicate a connection between low trust and voting for the SD, when controlling for other variables, no significant correlation is established. Even when expanding the measure of trust with social and more general institutional trust, just as Rydgren (2009) calls for, it remains a non-significant factor in explaining RWPP support. Thus this broadening of the measure of trust that our data allowed for did not add any significant explanatory power to the analysis.

Furthermore, it is clear from our analysis that those who prefer the SD are neither satisfied with democracy, nor, for the most part, particularly interested in politics. Satisfaction with democracy is significantly lower among SD supporters. This can perhaps be explained by the political constellation in power, as it is quite common for variables such as these to differ according to who holds office (Bergh 2004; Citrin & Green 1986). At the time when the questionnaire survey was conducted, the government consisted of a Centre-Left–Green alliance; moreover, the SD had never held office and been actively excluded from political influence by the other parties. These factors may explain why SD supporters are dissatisfied with democracy. Interest in politics is slightly less clear—SD supporters are found predominantly among those with no or with a great interest in politics.

Structurally, the importance of living in smaller and medium-sized local authorities as well as in those with a larger proportion of SD voters in earlier elections is positive when correlated with SD voting by adolescents. These results indicate that the political environment in which these individuals live affects their political behaviour, as found in earlier studies (Campbell 2006; Jennings et al. 2009). Disentangling the specific factors about the local area that are important, as shown in work by Rydgren and Ruth (2013), could be a valuable addition to such an analysis in future.

We do not find that factors related to parents' socio-economic status affect adolescents directly. However, adolescents enrolled in a vocational school programme and those worried about future immigration have a significant positive correlation with voting for the SD. Educational outcomes have previously been found to be significantly affected by parents' socio-economic status (Fergusson et al. 2008), so we cannot say that there is no indirect parental influence on SD support. Nevertheless, given the importance that worry about future immigration has, we understand this result in line with research by Lubbers et al. (2002) and Lubbers and Coenders (2017), who found that socio-economically vulnerable adolescents who are more likely to be in direct competition for jobs with immigrants and feel threatened by future immigration are more attracted by the RWPPs.

As for the specific policy-related concerns about the future, we can see quite clearly that the worry about immigration and the environment predict the party choice of adolescents. In line with research on issue voting (Bélanger & Meguid 2008; Walgrave et al. 2015) we see that worry about these questions correspond to preference for the SD and the Green Party respectively. Voters also consider these two policy areas to be where these parties have their strongest policies (Statistics Sweden 2014). If anything, this strong association may indicate that the issues are going to increase further in importance in future elections, as these future voters come of age. If this is indeed the case, then other parties may have to adjust their policy positions on these questions if they are to compete effectively for votes in the future. What we cannot say, based on our analysis, is if it is the SD stance on immigration and the environment that has drawn adolescents to supporting them or whether adolescents take this stance because they listen to the SD's message. For studies of political trust it has been found that, once voters start supporting a RWPP, their political trust deteriorates significantly (Hooghe & Dassonneville 2016). One question that researchers should consider in future research is whether a similar interaction is at play with policy stances for adolescents. Currently, though, what we can say is that it is the issues that seem to motivate adolescents' party preference more than anything else—we find no sign of protest voting due to low trust, as is predicted in previous studies (Bélanger & Nadeau 2005; Bergh 2004; Passarelli & Tuorto 2018). There is, however, significant dissatisfaction with democracy among SD supporters.

Last, but not least, we find that the results for young peoples' motivations for supporting the SD are overall in line with those demarcated in earlier studies for adults. In this analysis, we use a unique and larger dataset than earlier research has done and this has allowed us to test for several different explanatory factors. Nevertheless, we see that, even with these added variables, the picture that our analysis paints is largely in line with past research. Individual issues, and particularly worry about immigration, is the biggest explanatory factor. We also find some indication of influence from peers and the local political climate and, to some degree, we note that those in more direct competition with immigration are those who are the most ardent supporters of the SD. This means that adolescents generally seem affected by the same political trends as adults, with similar political preferences.

References

Alwin, D. F. & J. A. Krosnick (1991), 'Aging, cohorts, and the stability of sociopolitical orientations over the life span', *American Journal of Sociology*, 97/1: 169–95.

Andersson, U., A. Carlander, E. Lindgren & M. Oskarson (2018), 'Sprickor i fasaden', in U. Andersson, A. Carlander, E. Lindgren & M. Oskarson (eds.), *Sprickor i fasaden* (Gothenburg).

Arzheimer, K. (2009), 'Contextual factors and the extreme right vote in Western Europe 1980–2002', *American Journal of Political Science*, 53/2: 259–75.

Arzheimer, K. (2018), 'Explaining electoral support for the radical right', in Rydgren 2018.

Bandura, A. (1977), *Social Learning Theory* (Englewood Cliffs)

Bélanger, É. & R. Nadeau (2005), 'Political trust and the vote in multiparty elections: The Canadian case', *European Journal of Political Research*, 44/1: 121–46.

— & B. M. Meguid (2008), 'Issue salience, issue ownership, and issue-based vote choice', *Electoral Studies*, 27/3: 477–91.

Bergh, J. (2004), 'Protest voting in Austria, Denmark, and Norway', *Scandinavian Political Studies*, 27/4: 367–89.

Bentsen, B. (2017), 'Attitudes towards immigrants among youth in Sweden', MiM Working Paper Series, 17/4.

Bevelander, P. & J. Otterbeck (2016), 'Swedish adolescents' attitudes towards immigrants', in J. Jamin (ed.), *L'extrême droite en Europe* (Brussels).

Blalock, H. (1967), *Toward a Theory of Minority-Group Relations* (New York).

Blumer, H. (1958), 'Race prejudice as a sense of group position', *Pacific Sociological Review*, 1/1: 3–7.

Bobo, L. (1983), 'Whites' opposition to busing: Symbolic racism or realistic group conflict?' *Journal of Personality & Social Psychology*, 45/6: 1196–1210.

Borevi, K. (2018), *Familj, medborgarskap, migration* (Stockholm).

Campbell, D. E. (2006), *Why We Vote: How Schools and Communities Shape our Civic Life* (Princeton).

Citrin, J. (1974), 'Comment: The political relevance of trust in government', *American Political Science Review*, 68/3: 973–88.

— & D. P. Green (1986), 'Presidential leadership and the resurgence of trust in government', *British Journal of Political Science*, 16/4: 431–53.

Coffé, H., B. Heyndels & J. Vermeir (2007), 'Fertile grounds for extreme right-wing parties: Explaining the Vlaams Blok's electoral success', *Electoral Studies*, 26/1: 142–55.

Cutts, D., R. Ford & M. J. Goodwin (2011), 'Anti-immigrant, politically disaffected or still racist after all? Examining the attitudinal drivers of extreme right support in Britain in the 2009 European elections', *European Journal of Political Research*, 50/3: 418–40.

Dalhouse, M. & J. S. Frideres (1996), 'Intergenerational congruency: The role of the family in political attitudes of youth', *Journal of Family Issues*, 17/2: 227–48.

Degner, J. & J. Dalege (2013), 'The apple does not fall far from the tree, or does it? A meta-analysis of parent-child similarity in intergroup attitudes', *Psychological Bulletin*, 139/6: 1270–1304.

Demker, M. (2014), *Sverige åt svenskarna: Motstånd och mobilisering mot invandring och invandrare i Sverige* (Stockholm).

Demker, M. & S. Van Der Meiden (2016), 'Allt starkare polarisering och allt lägre flyktingmotstånd', in J. Ohlsson, H. Oscarsson & M. Solevid (eds.), *Ekvilibrium* (Gothenburg).

Eliasoph, N., S. Verba, K. L. Schlozman & H. E. Brady (1996), *Voice and Equality: Civic Voluntarism in American Politics* (Cambridge, MA).

European Commission (2009), 'Eurobarometer 71: Public opinion in the European Union', (Brussels), ec.europa.eu/commfrontoffice/publicopinion/archives/eb/eb71/eb71_std_part1.pdf.

Fergusson, D. M., L. J. Horwood & J. M. Boden (2008), 'The transmission of social inequality: Examination of the linkages between family socioeconomic status in childhood and educational achievement in young adulthood', *Research in Social Stratification & Mobility*, 26/3: 277–95.

Fiorina, M. P. (1981), *Retrospective Voting in American National Elections*. New Haven.

Fitzgerald, J. & D. Lawrence (2011), 'Local cohesion and radical right support: The case of the Swiss people's party', *Electoral Studies*, 30/4: 834–47.

Gamson, W. A. (1968), *Power and Discontent*. Homewood, IL.

Gidengil, E., H. Wass & M. Valaste (2016), 'Political socialization and voting: The parent–child link in turnout', *Political Research Quarterly*, 69/2: 373–83.

Green-Pedersen, C. (2007), 'The growing importance of issue competition: The changing nature of party competition in Western Europe', *Political Studies*, 55/3: 607–28.

Hatemi, P. K. & R. McDermott (2012), 'The genetics of politics: Discovery, challenges, and progress', *Trends in Genetics*, 28/10: 525–33.

Hellström, A. & E. Edenborg (2016), 'Politics of shame: Life stories of the Sweden: Democrats' voters in a counter public sphere', in J. Jérôme (ed.), L'extrême droite en Europe (Brussels).

Hjerm, M., M. A. Eger & R. Danell (2018), 'Peer attitudes and the development of prejudice in adolescence', Socius, 4: 1–11.

Hjerm, M. & K. Nagayoshi (2011), 'The composition of the minority population as a threat: Can real economic and cultural threats explain xenophobia?' International Sociology, 26/6: 815–843.

Hooghe, M. & R. Dassonneville (2016), 'A Spiral of Distrust: A Panel Study on the Relation between Political Distrust and Protest Voting in Belgium', Government & Opposition, 53/1: 1–27.

Jennings, M. K. & R. G. Niemi (1968), 'The transmission of political values from parent to child', American Political Science Review, 62/1: 169–84.

— L. Stoker & J. Bowers (2009), 'Politics across generations: Family transmission reexamined', Journal of Politics, 71/3: 782–99.

Jugert, P., K. Eckstein, A. Beelmann & P. Noack (2016), 'Parents' influence on the development of their children's ethnic intergroup attitudes: A longitudinal analysis from middle childhood to early adolescence', European Journal of Developmental Psychology, 13/2: 213–30.

Kinder, D. R. & D. O. Sears (1981), 'Prejudice and politics: Symbolic racism versus racial threats to the good life', Journal of Personality & Social Psychology, 40/3: 414–31.

Krosnick, J. A. & D. F. Alwin (1989), 'Aging and susceptibility to attitude change', Journal of Personality & Social Psychology, 57/3: 416–25.

Lövander, B. (2010), Den mångtydiga intoleransen (Stockholm).

Lubbers, M., M. Gijsberts & P. Scheepers (2002), 'Extreme right-wing voting in Western Europe', European Journal of Political Research, 41/3: 345–78.

— & M. Coenders (2017), 'Nationalistic attitudes and voting for the radical right in Europe', European Union Politics, 18/1: 98–118.

Mayer, N. & P. Perrineau (1992), 'Why do they vote for Le Pen?' European Journal of Political Research, 22/1: 123–41.

Meertens, R. W. & T. Pettigrew (1997), 'Is subtle prejudice really prejudice?' Public Opinion Quarterly, 61/1: 54–71.

Miklikowska, M. (2016), 'Like parent, like child? Development of prejudice and tolerance towards immigrants', British Journal of Psychology, 107/1: 95–116.

— (2017), 'Development of anti-immigrant attitudes in adolescence: The role of parents, peers, intergroup friendships, and empathy', British Journal of Psychology, 108/3: 626–48.

Miller, A. H. (1974), 'Political issues and trust in government: 1964–1970', American Political Science Review, 68/3: 951–72.

Mudde, C. (2007), Populist Radical Right Parties in Europe (Cambridge).

Niemi, R. G. & M. A. Hepburn (1995), 'The rebirth of political socialization', *Perspectives on Political Science*, 24/1: 7–16.

Norris, P. (2011), *Democratic Deficit: Critical Citizens Revisited* (Cambridge, MA).

Oscarsson, H. & S. Holmberg (2015), 'Issue voting structured by left–right ideology', in J. Pierre (ed.), *The Oxford Handbook of Swedish Politics* (Oxford).

Oskarson, M. & M. Demker (2015), 'Room for realignment: The working-class sympathy for Sweden democrats', *Government & Opposition*, 50/4: 629–51.

Passarelli, G. & D. Tuorto (2018), 'The five star movement: Purely a matter of protest? The rise of a new party between political discontent and reasoned voting', *Party Politics*, 24/2: 129–40.

Putnam, R. D. (1993), *Making Democracy Work: Civil Traditions in Modern Italy* (Princeton).

Quillian, L. (1995), 'Prejudice as a response to perceived group threat: Population composition and anti-immigrant and racial prejudice in Europe', *American Sociological Review*, 60/4: 586–611.

Raabe, T. & A. Beelmann (2011), 'Development of ethnic, racial, and national prejudice in childhood and adolescence: A multinational meta-analysis of age differences', *Child Development*, 82/6: 1715–37.

Ring, J. & S. Morgentau (2003), *Intolerans: Antisemitiska, homofobiska, islamofobiska och invandringsfientliga tendenser bland unga* (Stockholm).

Rydgren, J. (2009), 'Social Isolation? Social capital and radical right-wing voting in Western Europe', *Journal of Civil Society*, 5/2: 129–50.

— (2011), 'A legacy of "uncivicness"? Social capital and radical right-wing populist voting in Eastern Europe', *Acta Politica*, 46/2: 132–57.

— & P. Ruth (2011), 'Voting for the radical right in Swedish municipalities: Social marginality and ethnic competition?' *Scandinavian Political Studies*, 34/3: 202–25.

— & P. Ruth (2013), 'Contextual explanations of radical right-wing support in Sweden: Socioeconomic marginalization, group threat, and the halo effect', *Ethnic & Racial Studies*, 36/4: 711–28.

— & S. Van Der Meiden (2016), 'Sweden, now a country like all the others? The radical right and the end of Swedish exceptionalism', working paper, www.sociology.su.se.

— (2018), *The Oxford Handbook of the Radical Right* (New York).

Schain, M. (2018), *Shifting Tides: Radical-Right Populism and Immigration Policy in Europe and the United States* (Washington, DC).

Schlueter, E., P. Schmidt & U. Wagner (2008), 'Disentangling the causal relations of perceived group threat and outgroup derogation: Cross-national evidence from German and Russian Panel Surveys', *European Sociological Review*, 24/5: 567–81.

Sears, D. O. & P. J. Henry (2003), 'The origins of symbolic racism', *Journal of Personality & Social Psychology*, 85/2: 259–75.

Statistics Sweden (2010), *The Eight Parties Election 2010. General Elections, Election Study* (Stockholm).

— (2011), *General Elections in 2010. Part 1. Election to the Riksdag in 2010* (Stockholm).

— (2014), *The Super Election Year 2014. Democracy Statistics Report No. 20* (Stockholm).

Sundell, A. (2018), 'Sverigedemokraternas stöd i städer och på landsbygden', *Politicologerna*, 15 October.

Valdez, S. (2014), 'Visibility and votes: A spatial analysis of anti-immigrant voting in Sweden', *Migration Studies*, 2/2: 162–88.

Van Der Brug, W., M. Fennema & J. Tillie (2000), 'Anti-immigrant parties in Europe: Ideological or protest vote?' *European Journal of Political Research*, 37/1: 77–102.

Verba, S., N. Burns & K. L. Schlozman (2003), 'Unequal at the starting line: Creating participatory inequalities across generations and among groups', *American Sociologist*, 34/1–2: 45–69.

Walgrave, S., A. Tresch & J. Lefevere (2015), 'The conceptualisation and measurement of issue ownership', *West European Politics*, 38/4: 778–96.

Widfeldt, A. (2018), The radical right in the Nordic countries', in Rydgren 2018.

Appendix

Table 10.A1. Comparison of descriptive statistics for the full sample of respondents and for those who are only part of the ordinal regression.

		Full sample		Regression sample	
		N	%	N	%
Party preference	Left Party			152	4.80
	Social Democrats			819	26.00
	Centre party			38	1.20
	Liberal party			142	4.50
	Conservatives			986	31.30
	Christian Democrats			36	1.10
	Green Party			364	11.50
	Sweden Democrats			465	14.70
	Other Party			151	4.80
Sex	Female	3,631	49.30	1,365	43.30
	Male	3,736	50.70	1,788	56.70
Age	14	45	0.60	18	0.60
	15	2,326	32.00	930	29.50
	16	1,813	24.90	770	24.40
	17	1,469	20.20	666	21.10
	18	1,456	20.00	706	22.40
	19	165	2.30	63	2.00
National background and parents' background	Foreign-born	812	11.00	260	8.20
	Two foreign parents	900	12.20	388	12.30
	One Swedish and one foreign parent	755	10.30	344	10.90
	Two Swedish parents	4,891	66.50	2,161	68.50
Type of school attended	Uni. preparatory	3,272	45.50	1,651	52.40
	Vocational	1,426	19.80	542	17.20
	Secondary school	2,501	34.70	960	30.40
Organization membership	Yes	3,949	54.10	1,830	58.00
	No	3,350	45.90	1,323	42.00
One or more parents with higher education	Higher education	4,503	62.40	2,133	67.60
	No higher education	2,710	37.60	1,020	32.40
Parents' employment	Employed parents	6,829	92.50	2,936	93.10
	Unemployed parents	553	7.50	217	6.90
Political interest	Very interested	577	8.00	379	12.00
	Quite interested	2,057	28.50	1,192	37.80
	Not very interested	2,892	40.00	1,095	34.70
	Not at all interested	1,699	23.50	487	15.40

Table 10.A1. continued.

		Full sample		Regression sample	
		N	%	*N*	%
Satisfaction with democracy	Very satisfied	1,167	16.20	610	19.30
	Quite satisfied	4,626	64.40	1,893	60.00
	Not particularly satisfied	1,110	15.40	512	16.20
	Not at all satisfied	284	4.00	138	4.40
Municipality type	Big city	3,046	41.30	1,349	42.80
	Medium-sized town	3,107	42.10	1,297	41.10
	Small town	683	9.30	292	9.30
	Rural local authority	546	7.40	215	6.80
		Mean	Standard Deviation	Mean	Standard Deviation
Institutional trust 1–5		2.87	0.82	2.50	0.72
Personal trust 0–10		5.89	2.35	5.89	2.36
Worried about immigration 1–5		2.19	1.01	2.25	1.08
Worried about security 1–5		1.97	0.96	1.95	0.95
Worried about the economy 1–5		2.81	0.76	2.84	0.77
Worried about the environment 1–5		2.77	0.90	2.80	0.93
Proportion of SD votes in local authority in 2010		5.85	3.8	5.80	3.81
Total valid *N*		7,382		3,153	
Missing		0		4,229	
Total		7,382		7,382	

Table 10.A2. Multinomial logistic regression of party preference (Beta values and sig. change relative to SD).

Party preference		V		MP		Soc.		FP		M		Other	
Gender	Male	–		–		–		–		–		–	
	Female	0.730	***	1.236		0.974	***	0.741	***	0.878	***	0.514	**
Age		0.328	**	0.239	*	0.339	***	0.357	**	0.177	*	0.095	*
Country background	Swedish parents	–		–		–		–		–		–	
	Mixed-origin parents	0.622	*	0.577	*	0.923	***	0.557		0.698	***	0.515	*
	Immigrant parents	2.042	***	1.889	***	3.303		0.958		1.612	***	1.560	***
	Foreign-born	1.502	***	2.010	***	2.554	***	1.837	***	1.367	***	1.674	***
School type	Secondary	–		–		–		–		–		–	
	Vocational	-0.996	**	-0.898	**	-1.231	***	-1.217	**	-0.903	***	-0.536	
	Uni. prep.	0.046		-0.301		-0.621	**	-0.014		0.039		0.124	
Organizational membership	Yes, ref. No.	-0.33		0.005		-0.094		0.076		0.183		-0.026	
Parents' education	No higher education	–		–		–		–		–		–	
	Higher education	-0.062		0.292		-0.126	**	0.655	**	0.345	**	-0.058	**
Parents' employment	Unemployed	–		–		–		–		–		–	
	Employed	-0.023		0.649	*	0.028		1.127	*	0.710	**	0.871	**
Interest in politics	Not interested	–		–		–		–		–		–	
	Low	0.087		0.085		0.355		1.443	***	0.617	***	0.142	***
	Medium	0.882	**	0.161		0.179		1.810	***	0.486	***	0.268	**
	High	1.729	***	0.158		0.157		1.736	***	0.265	***	0.441	
Satisfaction with democracy	Not satisfied	–		–		–		–		–		–	
	Low	2.166	***	1.955	***	0.762	**	1.46		1.599	***	0.600	***
	Medium	1.478	**	2.074	***	0.952	***	1.554	**	2.537	***	0.361	***
	High	1.679	**	2.796	***	1.467	***	2.348	***	3.555	***	0.888	***
Personal trust		-0.152		0.143		0.021		0.185		0.052		0.163	
Institutional trust		-0.052		0.015		0.005		-0.047		0.105		-0.234	
Worry about future immigration		-2.323	***	-2.031	***	-1.839	***	-1.746	***	-1.457	***	-1.684	***
Worry about future security		-0.071		-0.223	**	0.088		0.019		-0.036		0.011	
Worry about future economy		0.109		-0.114		0.121		-0.044		-0.174	**	0.037	
Worry about future environment		0.588	***	1.283	***	0.547	***	0.482	***	0.399	***	0.386	***
Type of local authority	Rural	–		–		–		–		–		–	
	Small town	-1.635	***	-0.511	***	-0.768	**	-1.690	***	-0.440	***	-0.284	***
	Medium town	-1.435	***	-0.696	*	-0.521	*	-0.888	*	-0.374	*	-0.542	
	City	-1.138	**	-0.380	**	-0.861	**	-0.499	**	0.055		-0.272	***
SD support 2010		-0.067		-0.085	***	-0.059	***	-0.073		-0.082	**	-0.056	**
Total N	3153												
Model fit	Cox & Snell 0.535									Nagelkerke 0.552			

257

CHAPTER 11

The battle over rights in Switzerland

Populist arguments against international law

Gianni D'Amato

> If there is a genuine conflict of laws between federal and international law, Switzerland's obligation under international law takes precedence; this applies even to agreements that do not concern human rights or fundamental freedoms. The precedence set out above also applies in relation to subsequent federal laws, i.e. those which have entered into force in accordance with international law; the lex posterior rule does not apply in the relationship between international law and national law. Switzerland cannot invoke its domestic law to justify the non-fulfilment of a treaty. Accordingly, federal legislation contrary to international law remains regularly inapplicable. (Federal Court Ruling BGE (2012) 139 I 16, p. 28)[1]

In 2013, the European Court of Human Rights took a decision (ECHR 12020/09), one of the few verdicts that became a trigger in Switzerland for the heated battle between the advocates of rule of law and those who argue in favour of the unlimited rule by the people. The case concerned the deportation of a twice-convicted Nigerian national with residence status in Switzerland that would prevent him from seeing his minor children. In 2001, the Nigerian national was sentenced to four months' imprisonment for possession of a small quantity of cocaine. In 2003 he married a Swiss national who had just given birth to their twin daughters. By virtue of his marriage, the Nigerian national was granted a residence permit in Switzerland. In 2006 he was sentenced to forty-two months' imprisonment in Germany for a drug-trafficking offence. The Swiss Office of Migration refused to renew his residence permit, stating that his criminal conviction and his family's dependence on welfare benefits were grounds for his expulsion. An appeal by the Nigerian national, Mr Udeh, was dismissed. In 2009 Mr Udeh was informed that he had to leave Switzerland. In 2011 he was made the subject of a ban prohibiting him from entering Switzerland until 2020. He and his wife had divorced in the meantime. Custody of the children had been awarded to the mother, but the father had been given contact rights.

In its ruling of 16 April 2013, the European Court of Human Rights concluded that the deportation would constitute a violation of Art. 8 of the European Convention on Human Rights. The second section of the court admitted that the second sentence weighed heavily against the claimant. However, his criminal conduct was limited to those two offences, a fact which had not been considered relevant by the Swiss Federal Court, the highest tribunal in Switzerland. It could not therefore be said that the applicant's behaviour indicated that he would reoffend. Moreover, his conduct in prison and the one following his release had been exemplary. These positive developments, particularly the fact that he had been released on licence after serving part of his sentence, should have been taken into account in weighing up the interests at stake, argued the European Court. In that connection the Court considered the argument of the administration purely speculative that the applicant's forty-two month prison sentence was evidence that he represented a threat to public order and safety in the future.

The European Court argued that at the time the judgement was adopted, the total length of the applicant's residence in Switzerland totalled over seven and a half years, which was a considerable length of time in a person's lifetime. In the view of the judges it appeared indisputable that for quite a long time Switzerland had been the centre of his private and family life. Moreover, he endeavoured to maintain regular contact with his children. He had committed the main offence after the children had been conceived; in other words, his wife could not have known about the offence when she entered into a family relationship.

This was a significant factor in the examination of the present case. Furthermore, the twins had Swiss nationality. The enforced removal of Mr Udeh was likely to have the effect of their growing up separated from their father. It was in their best interests that they grow up with two parents and, having regard to the divorce, the only possibility of maintaining contact between the father and the two children was to grant him permission to stay in Switzerland, given that the divorced mother could not be expected to follow him to Nigeria with their two children. Lastly, even if the authorities were to grant a request that the order prohibiting him from entering Switzerland would be lifted, such temporary measures could not in any case be regarded as replacing the applicant's right to live together with his children. Therefore, having regard to the twin daughters and the family relationship between the father and his children, considering that the former had only committed one serious offence and taking into account that his subsequent conduct had been exemplary, the European Court of Human Rights came to the conclusion that Switzerland had exceeded the margin of appreciation and that a deportation would constitute a violation of human rights (see ECHR 12020/09).

The Swiss People's Party, the strongest political faction in the National Assembly sharing radical populist tendencies, took this judgement as a sign that foreign judges (though one member of the Chamber in the European Court of Human Rights is Swiss) are overruling the will of Swiss authorities and courts to deport undeserving criminal immigrants. Moreover, this was a disturbing case since the Swiss population had accepted in 2010 the 'Deportation Initiative for the Expulsion of Foreign Criminals', an initiative proposed and won by the SVP just to expel people like Mr Udeh. His case and that of others like it were used to submit a series of further popular direct democratic votes, all intending to attack the check and balances assured by the Federal Court and in particular the European Convention on Human Rights to citizens and migrants equally. The direct democratic instruments assured by the Swiss political system proved to be an excellent mechanism to mobilize political sentiments against rule of law, specifically when targeting migrants.

The rise of populism in Switzerland

The mobilization of populist anti-immigrant attitudes has played an important role in recent elections and referendums all over the Western world, not only in Switzerland. The decision of the UK to leave the EU 2016, commonly referred to as Brexit, and the election of Donald Trump as President of the US, like the new Cinque Stelle/ Lega government formed in spring 2018 are credited to a large extent to reflect positions against immigration.[2] The 2017 German general elections have further shown that even a country widely considered as the European outlier in resisting populist moods seems to have come into line with the rest of the continent, not to mention the sensitivities to anti-immigrant appeals in France, Austria, the Netherlands, and in many Central European countries. In observing these shifts, news media and some academics have proclaimed a rise of anti-immigrant populism (Lucassen 2017).

In one country in the heart of Western Europe, it appears that anti-immigrant populism has been a winning strategy in the past twenty years: the Swiss People's Party (SVP/UDC) transformed itself within the period of a few elections from a conservative right-wing party with an 11 per cent vote share in 1987 to the strongest party with 29 per cent support at the last parliamentary election in 2015. The Swiss People's Party consistently politicizes immigration with a clear anti-immigrant position (Ruedin 2013; Ruedin & Morales 2017), and defends this issue ownership with continuously mobilizing communication strategies. At the same time, the party has successfully prevented itself from becoming a single-issue party, offering to the electorate a variation of contentious topics.

Observing the electoral success of the Swiss People's Party and its ostensible winning strategy, the question arises to which extent the organization is capable of transferring its formula to other fields. In an historical perspective, the rise of the Swiss People's Party is surely due to anti-immigrant populism—negative politicization of foreigners, appeals to 'the people', attempts to regulate the presence of immigrants— though the intensity of politicization and its geographical reach are unprecedented. Anti-immigrant populism can be a successful strategy, and it needs not be anti-immigrant only, but can among others also be anti-EU. It is particularly the latter aspect, the anchoring of Switzerland in a 'cosmopolitan' setting, which is viewed as a peril by populist strategists. Thematizing the larger divide between cosmopolitanism and communitarianism seems to be the new winning formula.[3] This conceptualization is important to understand why and how the SVP is politicizing migration and international law. Its main target is not anti-immigrant alone; it is above all anti-cosmopolitan. Therefore, in their view there is no basic distinction between immigration and human rights or international law. They are against all of them.

According to Merkel (2018), this new cleavage between cosmopolitanism and communitarianism is accelerating the decline of traditional mass parties and will favour the rise of the populist organizations which have established themselves across Europe. Since the end of the Second World War, the populist right has conquered political space historically dominated by the left, increasingly addressing cosmopolitan preferences. This is a consequence of a larger cultural evolution that occurred in Western societies. New lifestyles, same-sex marriages, equal opportunities, and multicultural realities have become dominant societal discourses. At the same time, social-democratic parties have adopted neo-liberal positions with the so-called 'third way', after they have invested in the expansion of the welfare state after the Second World War. The leadership of the moderate left favoured a restructuring of social policies, in particular the situation of unemployed workers or single mothers to fit globalization. Thus, the 'new left' was to a lesser extent defined by social rather than by societal policies. An effect of the civil rights movement was that all forms of national identification lost universal credibility, whereas the 'old left' still had an affirmative relation to the nation, as a source for claimed solidarity. At the same time, the electorate of the left changed. It is no longer dominated by unionized workers, but by university graduates—professionals and academics of the middle class (Rennwald & Evans 2014). With that, the discourse of the 'new left' has become a transatlantic hegemony, and any critique is often morally disqualified in public space. This control over the suitable discourse has been interpreted and is referred to by the populist right as political correctness. Their indifference towards cultural modernity can be understood as a reaction of a less educated, perhaps predominantly male lower and middle class, as well as of conservatives in general (see also Harteveld & Ivarsflaten

2016). They see themselves as losers of this recent change (Bauman 1998; Kriesi et al. 2006). Anti-immigrant populism can therefore be a reaction towards a cosmopolitanism perceived as too hegemonic and the moralism of the better-off.

In recent times, this resentment has also seen people round on the legal (and constitutional) securities that immigrants and citizens can benefit from: the priority of rule of law with regard to applicants for access to Swiss nationality, confirmed by a decision of the Federal Court in 2003, has been attacked by the Swiss People's Party in 2008 who tried to abolish this rule through a popular initiative (D'Amato 2018). This effort was declined by the Swiss voting population. Although a procedure that followed rule-of-law principles was confirmed regarding candidates who applied for naturalization, the two following initiatives succeeded in limiting human rights protection, since they targeted other groups that seemed to be less deserving of protection than citizenship applicants. Their attempt to ban the construction of minarets on Swiss soil (2009)—so limiting the freedom of worship— and the initiative that intended to deport criminal foreigners (2010) accomplished a severe restriction of fundamental rights. Rule of law, human rights protection by European and UN conventions and the Freedom of Movement Treaty with the EU (successfully torpedoed in 2014) became subsequently the new targets of populist mobilization. The most recent attempt to attack the human rights regime was put in 2018 to a popular vote. Titled 'Swiss Law instead of Foreign Judges (Popular Initiative on Self-Determination)', the SVP addressed with this new constitutional amendment to give priority to domestic law on international law. Moreover, although they finally lost the voting, it reflects the incessant battle of sovereignists to limit fundamental rights of immigrants (and has effects far beyond them), affirming the unlimited power of popular will on the institutional division of powers. It follows the intent to limit judicial review of political decisions in a direct democratic institutional setting. In essence, it is the battle between rule of law and rule of the people. It is to the arguments of the initiators and the reasoning of their opponents that I will first turn.

The initiative for self-determination

As mentioned before, at the heart of this initiative stands a victory in 2010: the SVP's (Swiss People's Party) success in finding popular and cantonal approval regarding the 'deportation initiative for the expulsion of foreign criminals'. The Initiative required the implementation of an automatic removal of criminal foreigners and of foreign nationals who engaged in welfare fraud.[4] The political debate that followed identified several problems regarding the initiative's implementation, quite usual in a direct democratic setting. For the Federal Government it was obvious that the proposal went against international law and basic constitutional rights, but declared it valid in order not to limit popular rights. It further pointed to difficulties Parliament would face creating a list with clearly defined offences, all addressing automatic deportation. As the extra-Parliamentarian Federal Migration Commission affirmed, the abolition of the case-by-case review was judged highly problematic regarding the respect of the rule of law. The commission also emphasized the incompatibility with the Agreement on the Free Movement of Persons (AFMP) (Wichmann et al. 2010: 9).

To avert the initiative's acceptance and implementation, the Federal Government presented a counter-proposal that considered the claim of the popular initiative to implement a more restrictive law regarding the removal of criminal foreigners, but sought to comply with the current legal framework. The draft foresaw the expulsion of foreign nationals convicted of serious crimes while still allowing a review of each case (Cumming Bruce 2010).

After heated debates and a campaign utilizing controversial 'black sheep' posters (Maire & Garufo 2013), Switzerland's radical right-wing party won the voters' support. The final results of the poll showed that 52.3 per cent of voters and a majority of Switzerland's cantons in the vote on 28 November 2010 chose to support the rightist Swiss People's Party popular initiative. The counter-proposal by the government and centre-right parties found only support from 46 per cent of voters and was therefore rejected.

The Swiss constitution demands that the implementation of the initiative had to be realized within five years. To initiate this process, a working group was charged to find a solution that respected the new provisions and addressed the various legal conflicts. In the autumn of

2012, the Federal Court declared that the legal implementation had to respect and preserve the unity of the Constitution and referred in particular to the rule of law as addressed in Art. 5 of the Swiss Constitution. Even if Parliament might have considered adopting the new constitutional amendment according to the letter, the Federal Court affirmed that removing criminal foreigners had still to respond to the principle of proportionality and to the right to judicial review of individual cases, respecting in particular the right to family according to Art. 8 of the European Convention on Human Rights (humanrights.ch 2015).

In June 2013, the Federal Government submitted an implementation provision to the Parliament that kept its distance from the automatic, unconditional deportation of foreign offenders, and was in line with the requirement to respect human rights. In the meantime, the SVP found new leverage on Parliament, submitting a second 'Enforcement Initiative' with the objective to enforce the result of the first deportation initiative. Moreover, and to assure its success, Hans-Ueli Vogt, Economic Law Professor from the University of Zurich and recently elected MP of the SVP, put a third initiative into the pipeline: the initiative 'Swiss Law instead of Foreign Judges (Initiative for Self-Determination)', which would have had domestic law prevail over international law. It would therefore have guaranteed a strict implementation of the constitutional amendment on the 'deportation initiative' and of future initiatives that conflict with the European Convention on Human Rights. This popular initiative was launched in February 2015 after Parliament, and in particular the Council of States (Senate), emphasized the importance of the judiciary and legislative power's division, and decided to object to an absolute automatic expulsion law by introducing a 'hardship case'. As a consequence, the SVP submitted the initiative on self-determination the same month, collected thereafter 116,428 signatures and lodged them in August 2016 with the Federal Chancellor's Office in order to acknowledge the initiative. The Federal Government published its message July 2017, after asserting its validity and putting the initiative to a vote without a counter-project, it advocated rejection of the constitutional amendment (Botschaft 2017).

The promoters of the SVP initiative argued that Switzerland's sovereignty and independence were in danger. This was because of the politicians, civil servants, and university professors who blocked the Swiss people from having the last word, so deliberately restricting the people's rights (SVP 2015). According to the SVP, the above-mentioned actors increasingly took the view that 'foreign law, foreign judges and courts count more than the Swiss law as determined by the people and the cantons' (SVP 2015). They accused the Federal Council (government), other political parties, the Federal Court, and the *classe politique* of rating the provisions of international law as higher than those found in the Constitution. As a consequence, in the view of the SVP, the legal stability of the country was called into question, undermining Switzerland's legal self-determination. Although in their opinion the Swiss people and the cantons had decided in earlier referendums and popular initiatives to steer immigration and deport criminal aliens, the 'political class'—a jibe at the other parties and the non-SVP majority in Parliament—refused to implement the Constitution, referring to the constraints of international law. 'Self-proclaimed elites' were to be held accountable for the presence of criminal foreigners and continued immigration (SVP 2015). These elites wanted Switzerland to adopt European Law unconditionally through a mutual dynamic agreement, and support the EU Court of Justice in Brussels as the future Supreme Court in disputes between Switzerland and the EU.

In order to prevent such a development, the SVP proposed the revision of two existing dispositions in the Swiss Constitution, Art. 5 and 190, and the addition of a new Art. 56a and a new transitory provision, para 12 of art. 197.

Art. 5 of the Swiss Constitution would have been changed in numbers 1 and 4:[5]

1 The basis and barrier of state action is the law. *The Federal Constitution is the supreme source of law for the Swiss Confederation.*

4 The Confederation and the cantons observe the international law. *The Federal Constitution shall prevail and takes precedence over international law, subject to the mandatory provisions of international law.*

Thereafter, a new Art. 56a with the title 'Obligations to International Law' was formulated for Section 1 ('Relations with Abroad') of the Swiss Constitution:

1 *The Confederation and the cantons do not enter into any obligations under international law that contradict the Federal Constitution.*

2 *In the event of an objection, they shall ensure that the obligations under international law are adapted to the requirements of the Federal Constitution, if necessary by terminating the relevant international treaties.*

3 *The mandatory provisions of international law are reserved.*

In Art. 190 dedicated to the chapter on the 'Federal Court and other judicial authorities', following changes would have been applied:

Federal law *and treaties under international law, the approval of which was subject to a referendum,* are applied by Federal Court and other authorities.

Finally, the transitional provision to Art. 5 para. 1 and 4 (Principles of Rule of Law), Art. 56a (Obligations under International Law), and Art. 190 (Applicable Law) would have had the following wording in a new Art. 197:

Upon their acceptance by the people and the cantons, Articles 5(1) and (4), 56a and 190 shall apply to all existing and future provisions of the Federal Constitution and to all existing and future obligations of the Confederation and the cantons under international law.

Power to the people?
Arguments in favour of the initiative

As described by constitutional lawyer Pascal Mahon (2018), the initiative aimed to ensure that the Constitution would have been placed at the very top of the hierarchy of norms, above international law, and subject only to the mandatory rules of international law. In the event of a conflict with international norms, the Constitution would have had to prevail over international law. This was the idea expressed by the proposed new Art. 5 (1) and especially (4). Moreover, it would have been unconstitutional for the Confederation and the cantons if such an obligation under international law had continued to prevail over the Constitution, as expressed in the proposed Art. 56a. In such a case, there would have been a requirement for the authorities to adapt the international law obligation to domestic law, by renegotiating the treaty or by disapproving it. This would have been the rule expressed in paragraph 2 of the suggested new Art. 56a. However, the initiative, which certainly intended to place the Federal Constitution at the very top of the Swiss legal order, largely above international law, proposed an amendment to Art. 190 of the Constitution reducing the immunity that this provision granted to international law. The initiative therefore proposed a distinction between two categories of international treaties: those whose approval order had been subject to or submitted to a referendum, and those whose approval order had not been subject to or submitted to a referendum. According to this proposed new version, only treaties approved by a referendum would have remained immune in the same way as federal laws; all other treaties would no longer have been decisive for the Federal Court and other law enforcement authorities, which should therefore, in the event of a conflict, have given priority to domestic (constitutional) law over these treaties (Mahon 2018: 121).

This apparent, simple distinction between domestic and international law, although it met with bitter resistance, was successful in fuelling a public debate far beyond the launch of the initiative in March 2015, and was an important stimulus in preparing the elections of 2015. In the eyes of its authors, the initiative consequently aimed at a denunciation of the European Convention on Human Rights where there were repeated and fundamental conflicts with the Constitution. Moreover, the SVP disliked the dynamic case law of the European Court of Human Rights. In its view, the Court interprets the ECHR far too extensively. The SVP vice-president and former Federal Council of Justice Christoph Blocher also played the anti-EU card at the launch of the initiative, declaring the proposal a move against a possible institutional Framework Agreement between Switzerland and the EU. He feared that the EU and the European Court of Justice could become the 'new sovereign' of Switzerland, as they could amend the Federal Constitution through international law (*Neue Zürcher Zeitung* 2015a).

The Initiative on Self-Determination should ensure that even if such an agreement were concluded, our Constitution would be above EU law. (Christoph Blocher in *Tages-Anzeiger* 2015a)

In an op-ed, the author of the initiative, Professor Hans-Ueli Vogt, stressed the fact that through his initiative citizens should have the last word. Instead of facing up to the democratic debate in judicial matters and reaching a consensus supported by all citizens, the opponents of the SVP were steadily invoking international law (*Neue Zürcher Zeitung* 2015a). Moreover, he accused EU Law of being a pioneer of socialism:

> Over the past 20 years, EU law has become a key driver of legislation in Switzerland. This law is often hostile to companies and unilaterally protects consumers, investors and employees. Its aim is not the realization of a market economy, but the unconditional participation of all people in the blessings of free enterprise. (Hans-Ueli Vogt, *Neue Zürcher Zeitung* 2015b)

In Vogt's understanding, sovereignty does not mean a *solo run*. On the contrary, a small state like Switzerland should use its advantage by adapting where it is useful, where it does not hurt its interests, or where resistance is pointless. And the country should always have in mind to conclude favourable economic contracts. Moreover, sovereign states may also terminate treaties if the Constitution is subsequently amended, and such a step would be in the interests of the country.

Therefore, in the eyes of its promoter, a victorious initiative could have strengthened free economy and politically weakened the 'constant talk of the compulsion to adapt to international standards' (*Neue Zürcher Zeitung* 2015b).

> The initiative could restore the balance necessary for the survival of the small state between adaptation and contractual ties on the one hand and the pursuit of one's own advantage on the other. The strongest compulsion would then again be to reflect on our constitution—on the order that has brought us prosperity, a healthy state budget, the freedom to the citizens. (Hans-Ueli Vogt in *Neue Zürcher Zeitung* 2015b)

Vogt also took a critical view on recent developments in human rights. In his view, modern human rights are a programme of the political left. Instead of protecting citizens from the state in assuring liberty rights, human rights—for example, the right to work, to housing and to family reunion—are used to justify claims against the state and thus against taxpayers (Weltwoche 2015). In the case of criminal immigrants, it is wrong, he affirmed, that judges may decide to restrict deportation. These questions should be decided by Parliament and the people (Weltwoche 2015).

During the campaign, the SVP was accused of using popular initiatives—the 'Deportation Initiative' and the 'Enforcement Initiative'—to fight a battle against the courts, expressing blatant distrust of judicial powers. Their goal has been to restrict more and more the freedom of the judiciary in shaping laws, reducing the judicial margin of discretion to protect minorities from political majority decisions. To this allegation, the MP Georg Rutz (SVP) argued that it is justified that the legislator must specify the range of decisions to be made by justices. In his view, this should be the most normal thing in modern constitutional states. It is also normal for the legislator to say where judges should no longer have discretionary powers to define the rules of the game (*Neue Zürcher Zeitung* 2015d).

Marcel Niggli, Professor of Criminal Law and Philosophy of Law at Fribourg and author of a collection of anti-racist legislation, supported this opinion. In an essay in the right-wing weekly *Weltwoche*, he underlined the importance of sovereignty and asserted that the initiative in no way would have affected human rights, since fundamental rights continued to be protected under the Swiss Constitution (Weltwoche 2018). He argued that the adoption of the European Convention on Human Rights was neither subject to an obligatory referendum nor was it subject to a facultative or optional referendum, because—according to the justification of the time it was approved—it could be terminated at any time. A dismissal would therefore be no problem.

Eliminating rule of law through democracy?

It is self-evident that such an attack on the European human rights framework, originally thought up to protect human dignity as much as democracy—both essential concepts born with the Enlightenment in the American and French revolutions (Gross 2018)—met with fierce resistance. The only country in Europe to realize liberalism after the revolutions of 1848, Switzerland succeeded in pioneering democratic innovation. But to a certain extent, as Andreas Gross underlines, democracy was never understood as a human right, but as a privilege for (male) Swiss.[6]

Starting the campaign against the initiative, it fell to Andreas Auer, former Professor of Public Law in Zurich and Geneva, to criticize the incomplete understanding of what constitution, rule of law, and democracy mean in Switzerland. In his perception, even the title of the initiative 'Swiss law instead of foreign judges', was not only logically misguided since its first element has nothing to do with the second—at most, Swiss law could be compared with international law, or foreign judges could be compared with Swiss judges—but also did not correspond to the content of the initiative, where neither Swiss law nor foreign judges were mentioned. And the second, the insinuation that 'Self-Determination' would be ruled by foreign judges, has not been linked to the text, and therefore it was hard to understand how the Federal Chancellery could have accepted the validity of such an initiative (*Neue Zürcher Zeitung* 2015c).

Furthermore, the provision 'The Confederation and the cantons shall observe international law' (Art. 5 para. 4 of the Constitution), carefully chosen by the legislature, was also to be supplemented by the sentence 'The Federal Constitution shall prevail over international law and takes precedence over it, subject to the mandatory provisions of international law'. This contained an unsightly pleonasm, for whoever stands above someone is forced to take precedence over him. This, too, was witness to the initiators' rather wobbly understanding of the Constitution and international law. Just because a constitution pretends to take precedence over international law does not mean that the latter will be subordinated to it, since the fundamental primacy of international law necessarily results from its nature as an international body of rules. A constitution cannot change the legal nature of international law, even with the best will in the world (*Neue Zürcher Zeitung* 2015c).

Even if the initiative had been accepted, it would have continued to be a judge who distinguished in individual cases the sense of different norms, deciding if there is a conflict between norms. Andreas Auer reminded us that indeed single Strasbourg decisions may give rise to justified criticism, but this also applies to certain rulings of the Federal Court. The initiators, in turn, can hardly have forgotten cases such as the one of 9 July 2003 ('unconstitutionality of referendums on naturalisations'), a SVP referendum that was overruled by a Federal Court decision.

For Auer the initiative was a serious attack on the Swiss constitutional state, blatantly undertaking to isolate the Swiss legal system from the European area of fundamental rights, to the development and consolidation of which Swiss legal experts had made major contributions. Above all, however, it would have taken a further step towards the abolition of democracy through democracy. According to the initiative's credo, it should not have been up to (foreign) judges, but only the Swiss people to decide what is right for the country. The people as the sole guideline of state power—the people as contracting party, the people as provider of the constitution, the people as legislator, the people as judge—would have pushed aside all other state organs, including all international ones, as well as the distrusted *classe politique*. This ideology revealed a totalitarian notion of democracy that had nothing to do with Swiss tradition, in which the citizens have much to say, but not everything.

Helen Keller, Swiss Justice at the European Court of Human Rights, saw the reliability of Switzerland in upholding international treaties called into question. One would have thought that Switzerland would abide by its treaties, 'but if people and cantons change the constitution, then we have to take a look' (*Tages-Anzeiger* 2015b). One of the criticisms addressed in the initiative is that the ECHR interprets international law differently from when it was ratified. But a dynamic understanding of legal evolution is mostly linked to new problems that interfere with human rights. In the media, cases often have been portrayed as being 'against Switzerland', therefore avoiding an exploration of the individual case and what it means to be deported after having lived

17 years in Switzerland. In her view, the problem is not the application of international law, but the practice of initiatives. A lot of initiatives seem to have a problematic understanding of the fundamental rights enlisted in the Constitution. Many of them should never have reached a vote because of their unconstitutional content, although Parliament often ignores these constraints when giving approval.

Contesting Marcel Niggli's assumption that the acceptance of the initiative would have had no effect since fundamental rights were already protected by the Constitution, the migration lawyers Fanny de Weck and Marc Spescha referred to attempts to deport convicted second-generation migrants or vulnerable people that were only prevented by reference in the courts to the European Convention on Human Rights, arguments that found often final support in rulings of the Federal Court (de Weck & Spescha 2018). There is no other field than migration where minimal standards of human rights are permanently under attack. But the target is not Strasbourg—the real target is the Federal Justices, who have been alternately called the 'ayatollahs of Lausanne' or 'gravediggers of democracy'. The true intention of the initiative was to create a 'people's justice' in the sphere of migration, abolishing the rule of law and procedures that review individual cases by an independent Judiciary.

Analysis and conclusions

The initiative 'Swiss Law instead of Foreign Judges (Initiative for Self-Determination)' was the most recent in a long series of initiatives that followed the strategy to reverse the philosophy of the new Swiss Constitution, approved in 1999 to assure and secure fundamental rights and human rights protection to all residents. This target has been addressed with different political initiatives. It started in 2008 with the 'Initiative for Democratic Naturalizations', intended to abolish constitutional guarantees for citizenship candidates, reinstalling arbitrary procedures at the level of local authorities, which were eliminated by a Federal Court ruling of 2003. The project was turned down by the people with a 63.8 per cent majority, thus declining a limitation on fundamental rights. Yet the SVP succeeded in 2009 with its Minaret Initiative, banning at the level of the Constitution the construction of minarets on Swiss soil. The people (65 per cent) and a large majority of the cantons approved the amendment, being insensitive to the freedom of religion and belief inscribed in the Constitution. This success was repeated 2010 with the 'Initiative on Deportation of Criminal Foreigners': aliens who committed certain offences were to be expulsed from the country regardless of their status. This amendment found a slight majority of 52.3 per cent, but three-quarter of the cantons said yes, thus eroding the constitutional guarantees of proportionality and excluding a case-by-case assessment. The 'Initiative against Mass Immigration' (2014) was also successful, although the people had approved the agreement on the free movement of persons in three votes since 2002; now 50.3 per cent of the people and more than 15 cantons approved an amendment that has since put the Bilateral Agreements with the EU at serious risk. The 'Enforcement Initiative' of 2016 was a reaction to Parliament's decision to allow a hardship clause after the implementation of the 'Deportation Initiative'. After a criminal offence, no judicial assessment should have been applied, imposing a questionable limitation on fundamental rights. This initiative met with fierce last-minute opposition from civil society to stop the elimination of constitutional guarantees, and did not pass (it had only 41.1 per cent approval and 3 cantons) (see Gross et al. 2018). A series of initiatives pursued the objective of prising the check and balances out of the Swiss constitutional framework. Thus, immigrants and relations with the EU were necessary scapegoats in the undermining of its own institutions, addressing a sense of frustration with a world so interlinked as it is in our day.

In these SVP initiatives, the citizens have been continuously promised the last word. Therefore, according to this view the people should reinstall a constitutional system in which they have the first say, establishing the rules, and deciding on the application of these rules. As the constitutional lawyer Pascal Mahon concludes, the main idea of the initiative has been to bypass or at least reduce other powers (Mahon 2018: 161). In brief, the intention was to overcome the separation of powers, so essential for the modern liberal constitutional state, through a direct legitimising appeal to the people as sovereign. This idea reveals a circular understanding of sovereignty, in which self-determination acquires an exclusive, even totalitarian connotation. It was just this connotation of sovereignty that Hannah Arendt criticized in her notion of politics, favouring a political process embedded in a plural, liberal setting, protected by the rule of law ('rights to have rights'). And it is just that notion that Carl Schmitt ridiculed, attacking the modern constitutional state and insisting on the privilege of the sovereign state to overcome restrictions imposed by the rule of positive judicial norms (Raimondi 2014: 21). The protection of minorities—in Carl Schmitt's extremist view—would be able to reverse the essence of majoritarian rule. Such a system, he sneered, would not be democracy; it would be liberalism protecting itself from democracy.

The result at the ballot box was clearer than some observers had predicted. The initiative on Self-Determination was supposed to save direct democracy. But direct democracy itself had now given to the initiators a clear rebuff. On 25 November 2018, about two-thirds of voters rejected the self-determination initiative, and in all cantons the promoters missed out on majorities. At just below 34 per cent, the approval rate was only slightly higher than the SVP's 29 per cent voter turnout in the last Parliamentarian elections in 2015. In contrast to 2014, when the yes to the mass immigration initiative took everyone by surprise, the SVP opponents were well organized. The alliance of opponents comprised around 70 associations from all political camps. It ranged from business-oriented associations such as Economie Suisse and the major trade unions to grassroots movements such as Operation Libero and Protection Factor Human Rights (*Tages-Anzeiger* 2018a). The electorate was neither blinded by false promises nor convinced by radical solutions. Apparently, a large majority of the population continued to trust the institutions and saw no reason to limit without necessity their discretion in resolving conflicts between constitutional and international law. The citizens did not feel the pinch of foreign control either. Rather, they were aware that international law is not only necessary for an internationally networked state like Switzerland, but that the European Court of Human Rights protects the fundamental rights of all—and not just those of criminal foreigners, as the SVP liked to claim (*Neue Zürcher Zeitung* 2018).

The no to the 'Initiative on Self-determination' has removed from the table an unsuitable solution to the relationship between national and international law. But the question of how a direct democratic country like Switzerland should deal in the future with constantly growing international legal regulation will continue to occupy public opinion. The tug-of-war surrounding the EU Framework Agreement and the UN Migration Compact gives a foretaste of the next debates. The desire to have more to say in foreign policy seems to be gaining acceptance, especially among centre-right parliamentarians. Many consider soft law, such as the UN Migration Compact, to be particularly problematic, since it can generate political pressure through supervisory bodies, although it is not legally binding. The discussion about the effects of globalized law has therefore not come to an end. And the SVP has announced that it will continue its campaigning (Christoph Blocher in *Tages-Anzeiger* 2018b).

The permanent mobilization through direct democracy understood as unfiltered majority rule follows the intention to reconfigure and reshape the federal state and its society. The objective is to roll the country back to before the despised '1968', the metaphor for the expansion of rights that is inflicting harm on communitarian beliefs. This is not an easy task, considering the complexities in a plural society like Switzerland. But the agenda is permanently revitalized by a series of proposition of new amendments to limit the division of powers foreseen by the Constitution. As a side effect, it is conditioning other parties to react to the permanent politicization, succeeding in influencing their stance, particularly when it comes to EU and immigrants. Therefore, the SVP has tried to slowly move the political focus to the right. Cultural hegemony is tamed today largely by the categories produced by the populist SVP, influencing other parties in their vectors of political vision and action. Particularly astonishing are the concessions parties have been willing to make. The orientation that supports including rather than excluding SVP argumentation is all the more remarkable since migration, globalization, and their attendant legal consequences cannot be wished out of the world. As a result, migration issues can always be used, if not misused, for the purpose of political mobilization.

However, one should not fall prey to the illusion that one can have a direct democracy that lacks populist aspects. What is decisive is that democrats in a democratic system are equal to the situation, and ready to commit themselves to open debate, as was the case during the campaign for the Initiative for Self-Determination. In future, too, they will have to engage in a political culture of debate, opposition, and conflict, which ultimately comes down to practised liberalism. Those who would abuse democracy by initiatives such as the one on Self-Determination have run into fierce opposition, and suffered defeats at its hands. The victory on the Initiative on Self-Determination shows one strategy that civil society can adopt to oppose such attacks on democracy. This was an important moment, since in good democracies, as we know, the game is never over.

Notes

1 All translations from German are by the author.
2 I wish to acknowledge funding from the European Commission (FP7 project 'Support and Opposition to Migration', grant number 225522), and the Swiss National Science Foundation (NCCR on the move). This section refers to an already published article, co-authored with Didier Ruedin (2019). I am indebted to Dina Bader and Didier Ruedin, and the Migration Working Group at EUI for comments on an earlier version of this chapter.
3 In Merkel's definition, cosmopolitans opt for open borders, the free flow of goods, services, capital, rights, and people. For them the competence of nation-states and their intergovernmental cooperation cannot effectively respond to the challenges posed by globalization. Supranational authorities should receive therefore more sovereign competences. Communitarians see it antagonistically: they reject globalization and tend to be professionally active only in their home country. Their economic and cultural interests are focused in the nation-state, which should strictly control its borders (see Merkel 2018: 281).
4 Even though the initiative uses the term 'expulsion' or 'deportation', the content of the claimed regulations concerns the law on the revocation of residence permits and the issuing of removal orders. The execution of a persons' removal is regulated in additional articles of the Foreign Nationals Act. This includes autonomously leaving the country as other forms of a more controlled or even forced expulsion.
5 The sentences in italic indicate the new provision that would have altered the existing Constitution.
6 Women were excluded until 1971 from federal citizenship.

References

Bauman, Z. (1998), *Globalization: The human consequences* (Cambridge).

Botschaft (2017), 'Schweizer Recht statt fremde Richter (Selbstbestimmungsinitiative)', *Botschaft zur Volksinitiative*, BBl 2017 5355.

Cumming-Bruce, N. (2010), 'Swiss Right Wins Vote on Deportation of Criminals', *New York Times*, 28 November.

D'Amato, G. (2018), 'The migration challenge: The Swiss left in the arena of direct democracy', in M. Bröning & C. P. Mohr (eds.), *The politics of migration and the future of the European left* (Bonn).

— & D. Ruedin (2019), 'Immigration and populist political strategies: The Swiss Case in European Perspective', in G. Fitzi, J. Mackert & B. S. Turner (eds.), *Populism and the crisis of democracy* (London).

de Weck, F. & M. Spescha (2018), 'Attacke gegen Minimalstandards', in Gross et al. 2018.

European Court of Human Rights ECHR 12020/09 Udeh v. Switzerland.

Federal Court Ruling BGE 2012/139 I 16.

Fitzi, G., J. Mackert & B. S. Turner (eds.) (2019), *Populism and the crisis of democracy* (London).

Gross, A. (2018), 'Ein unteilbares Ganzes', in Gross et al. 2018.

— F. Krebs, M. Stohler & C. Wermuth (2018), *Freiheit und Menschenrechte: Nein zur Anti-EMRK-Initiative* (St Ursanne).

Harteveld, E. & E. Ivarsflaten (2016), 'Why women avoid the radical right: Internalized norms and party reputations', *British Journal of Political Science*: 1-16.

humanrights.ch (2015), *Umsetzung der Ausschaffungsinitiative mit Härtefallklausel*, 16 March, www.humanrights.ch/de/menschenrechte-schweiz/inneres/auslaender/politik/umsetzung-ausschaffungsinitiative.

Kriesi, H., E. Grande, R. Lachat, M. Dolezal, S. Bornschier & T. Frey (2006), 'Globalization and the transformation of the national political space: Six European countries compared', *European Journal of Political Research*, 45/6: 921–56.

Lucassen, L. (2017), 'Peeling an onion: The "refugee crisis" from a historical perspective', *Ethnic & Racial Studies*, doi.org/10.1080/01419870.2017.1355975.

Mahon, P. (2018), 'L'initiative "pour l'autodétermination" et le juge', *Revue jurassienne de jurisprudence*: 109–70.

Maire, C. & F. Garufo (2013), *L'étranger à l'affiche: Altérité et identité dans l'affiche politique suisse 1918–2010* (Neuchâtel).

Merkel, W. (2018), 'Cosmopolitanism versus communitarianism: A new conflict', in M. Bröning & C. P. Mohr (eds.), *The politics of migration and the future of the European left* (Bonn).

Neue Zürcher Zeitung (2015a), 'Allein gegen "fremde" Richter', Markus Hoffmann, 11 March 2015.

— (2015b), 'Verteidigung der wirtschaftlichen Freiheitsordnung', Hans-Ueli Vogt, 13 April.

— (2015c), 'Die Abschaffung der Demokratie durch Demokratie', Andreas Auer, 13 April

— (2015d), 'Wer das letzte Wort im Staat hat', 26 June.

— (2018), 'Klare Abfuhr für radikale Scheinlösung der SVP', Kathrin Alder, 26 November.

Raimondi, F. (2014), *Die Zeit der Demokratie: Poltische Freiheit nach Carl Schmitt und Hannah Arendt* (Konstanz).

Rennwald, L. & G. Evans (2014), 'When supply creates demand: Social Democratic Party strategies and the evolution of class voting', *West European Politics*, 37/5: 1108–35.

Ruedin, D. (2013), 'Obtaining party positions on immigration in Switzerland: Comparing different methods', Swiss Political Science Review 19/1: 84–105.

— & L. Morales (2017), 'Estimating party positions on immigration: Assessing the reliability and validity of different methods', *Party Politics*, doi. org/10.1177/1354068817713122.

SVP (2015), 'Argumentarium Volksinitiative Schweizer Recht statt fremde Richter (Selbst-bestimmungsinitiative)', Ja Zur Selbstbestimmungsinitiative, www.selbstbestimmungsinitiative.ch.

Tages-Anzeiger (2015a), 'SVP will Bundesverfassung über Völkerrecht stellen', 11 March.

— (2015b), 'Die Beschwerdeführer werden dämonisiert', interview with Helen Keller, 29 June.

— (2018a), 'SVP-Gegner bereit für den nächsten Kampf, Fabian Renz and Stefan Häne', 26 November.

— (2018b), 'Das Zuwanderungsproblem ist nicht gelöst', interview with Christoph Blocher, 27 November.

Weltwoche (2015), 'Die Schweiz braucht das Völkerrecht, Roger Köppel and Martin Kappeler', 30 April.

— (2018), 'Das letzte Wort', Marcel Niggli, 4 January.

Wichmann, N., C. Achermann & D. Efionayi-Mäder (2010), *Wegweisen: Ausschaffen: Ein Grundlagenbericht zu den ausländerrechtlichen Folgen der Straffälligkeit: Materialien zur Migrationspolitik* (Bern).

About the authors

Adam Balcer is a political scientist, and expert in the area of Central-Eastern Europe, the Black Sea region, and Muslim communities in these regions. He also works as National Researcher at the European Council on Foreign Relations (ECFR) and is lecturer at the Centre of East European Studies (SEW) at the University of Warsaw. He cooperates with the journals *Nowa Europa Wschodnia*, *New Eastern Europe* and *Aspen Review Central Europe*' and website Dialog Forum: Perspektiven aus der mitte Europas. He has published numerous books, articles and reports, including 'Polska na globalnej szachownicy' (Poland on the global chessboard), and 'Turcja, Wielki Step i Europa Środkowa' (Turkey, Great Steppe and Central Europe).

Beint Magnus Aamodt Bentsen is a PhD student at Malmö University. He works on intergroup attitudes among young people in Sweden, the effect of intergroup contact on attitudes and the consequences attitudes have for behaviour. He holds a BA in Political Science from the University of Oslo and an MA in International Migration and Ethnic Relations from Malmö University.

Pieter Bevelander has a PhD in Economic History and is Professor of International Migration and Ethnic Relations (IMER) at MIM, Malmö Institute for Studies of Migration, Diversity and Welfare, Malmö University. His main research field is international migration and aspects of immigrant integration. Currently he is associate editor of *International Migration Review*.

Floris Biskamp is a sociologist and political scientist at the University of Tübingen, working as postdoctoral researcher and as coordinator of the doctoral programme 'Right Wing Populist Social Policies and

Exclusive Solidarity'. His postdoctoral research addresses the political economy of populism in Europe, focusing on what effects the interdependent positions that national economies hold within the European system have on the type and extent of successful populist mobilization in these countries. Among his research interests are political theory, social theory, political economy, populism, the radical right, racism, and the relation of politics and religion.

Salomi Boukala is Assistant Professor at the Department of Social Anthropology at Panteion University of Social & Political Sciences. She has published widely in the field of critical discourse studies. She is the author of the book *European Identity and The Representation of Islam in the Mainstream Press: Argumentation and Media Discourse* (Palgrave, 2018). Her research interests include argumentation, the discursive construction of political and (supra)national identities, political rhetoric, Greek politics, and media discourse.

Gianni D'Amato is Professor at the University of Neuchâtel, Director of the 'NCCR – On the move', and of the Swiss Forum for Migration and Population Studies (SFM). His main foci include citizenship, mobility, populism, and the history of migration.

Maureen Eger is an associate professor at the Department of Sociology, Umeå University, and a senior fellow at the Centre for Analysis of the Radical Right (CARR). Her research areas are political sociology, the welfare state, immigration, and nationalism.

Matthew Feldman is a specialist on fascist ideology and the far-right in Europe and the US. He has written widely on these subjects for both academic and general audiences. An Emeritus Professor of the History of Modern Ideas at Teesside University, he is a Visiting Professor at Richmond, the American University in London, since 2018. He has a distinguished record of public engagement and policy-based impact. This has included expert witness testimony in several high-profile terrorist trials relating to radical right extremism. He is the author or editor of more than 20 books, including 3 monographs, and more than 40 articles or academic book chapters.

Bernhard Forchtner is a Lecturer at the School of Media, Communication and Sociology, University of Leicester (UK), and has previously worked as a Marie Curie Fellow at the Institute of Social Sciences, Humboldt University of Berlin, where he conducted a project on far-right discourses on the environment (project number 327595). Recent publications include 'Nation, Nature, Purity: Extreme-right Biodiversity' (in *Patterns of Prejudice*, 2019), 'Being Skeptical? Exploring Far-Right Climate-Change Communication in Germany' (with A. Kroneder and D. Wetzel in *Environmental Communication*, 2018) and *The Routledge Handbook of Language and Politics* (with R. Wodak, 2017).

Heather Grabbe is the director of the Open Society European Policy Institute in Brussels. From 2004 to 2009 she was senior advisor to then European Commissioner for Enlargement Olli Rehn. She was previously Deputy Director of the Centre for European Reform and a Research Fellow at Chatham House. Her academic career includes teaching at the London School of Economics, and research at the European University Institute as well as Oxford and Birmingham universities. Her publications include *The EU's Transformative Power: Europeanisation through Conditionality in Central and Eastern Europe* (2006).

Stefan Lehne is a Visiting Scholar at Carnegie Europe conducting research on EU institutional reforms and EU foreign policy. He also teaches at the Diplomatic Academy in Vienna. Previously he worked as a senior EU and Austrian diplomat.

Sabine Lehner is a PhD student in applied linguistics at the University of Vienna, and is writing her thesis on representations of space and borders in public discourses and in narratives of displaced persons. Her research interests are discourse studies, language and space, ethnography, and multilingualism.

Markus Rheindorf is a Senior Researcher and Lecturer at the Department of Linguistics, University of Vienna. His research interests include critical discourse studies, migration studies, media discourse, and populism.

Sarah Valdez is a senior lecturer at the Institute for Analytical Sociology, Linköping University. Previously, she was a research fellow at the Carlos III-Juan March Institute in Madrid. Her research focuses on anti-immigrant politics and segregation.

Ruth Wodak is an Emeritus Distinguished Professor at Lancaster University, UK, and the University Vienna, Austria. She has published widely on populism, identity politics and politics of the past, migration and xenophobia, racism, and antisemitism. Recent books in English include *The Routledge Handbook on Language and Politics* (with Bernhard Forchtner, 2018) and *The Politics of Fear: What Right-wing Populist Discourses Mean* (2015).